THE GENDER TRAP

The
Gender Trap

Parents and the Pitfalls
of Raising Boys
and Girls

Emily W. Kane

NEW YORK UNIVERSITY PRESS
New York and London

NEW YORK UNIVERSITY PRESS
New York and London
www.nyupress.org

References to Internet websites (URLs) were accurate at the time of writing.
Neither the author nor New York University Press is responsible for URLs
that may have expired or changed since the manuscript was prepared.

Library of Congress Cataloging-in-Publication Data
Kane, Emily W.
The gender trap : parents and the pitfalls of raising boys and girls / Emily W. Kane.
p. cm.
Includes bibliographical references and index.
ISBN 978-0-8147-4882-4 (cl : alk. paper)
ISBN 978-0-8147-3783-5 (pb : alk. paper)
ISBN 978-0-8147-3878-8 (ebook)
ISBN 978-0-8147-7144-0 (ebook)
1. Parenthood. 2. Child rearing. 3. Sex differences. 4. Boys--Psychology. 5. Girls--Psychology. I. Title.
HQ755.8.K346 2012
306.874--dc23
2012010688

New York University Press books are printed on acid-free paper,
and their binding materials are chosen for strength and durability.
We strive to use environmentally responsible suppliers and materials
to the greatest extent possible in publishing our books.

Manufactured in the United States of America

c 10 9 8 7 6 5 4 3 2 1
p 10 9 8 7 6 5 4 3 2 1

CONTENTS

ACKNOWLEDGMENTS

This book is about how parents navigate the complex task of managing their children's gender, and so the first round of thanks goes to the mothers and fathers who shared their experiences with me. Some participants may agree with my analysis more than others, but I hope they all recognize the respect I feel for the hard work and loving care they invest in raising their children. Like them, I know firsthand the complexity involved in finding the right balance as we prepare our children for the opportunities we hope their futures hold but also for the risks they will face in the social world.

Many others helped me down the long road of writing this book. Bates College student and staff research assistants helped me gather and review scholarly literature, transcribe interviews, and manage the data analysis software. My thanks go to Jena Caruso, Gretchen DeHart, Bridget Harr, Emma Posner, David Weliver, and Kim Whipkey for outstanding research assistance over the years, and to Lorelei Purrington and Amanda Ouellette for excellent staff support in transcriptions and data entry, respectively. Deborah Cohan was a particularly insightful research assistant midway through the process, and she has continued to offer sage advice and supportive friendship that I appreciate deeply. Especially crucial was Karen Bilodeau, a remarkable sociology major who assisted in my research for several years, during the book's earliest stages. The gifts of her intelligence, organization, academic knowledge, sense of humor, and life experience all contributed immeasurably to the foundation for this project.

Also essential to the book were those who helped to recruit interviewees. To the many people at Bates who passed along information about this book to friends and family members, to the organizations that allowed me to post flyers or distribute information, and to the participants who told their friends about the book, I am thankful for your help in spreading the word. Financial support came from several entities at Bates College: the Faculty Development Fund, administered by the Dean of the Faculty's Office and the Faculty Scholarship Committee; the Department of Sociology; the Summer Research Apprenticeship Program; and the Whitehouse Professorship Fund. For the latter funding, I acknowledge the generous support of David Whitehouse, Bates College Class of 1936, and his wife Constance Whitehouse. I am particularly grateful for the efforts of Dean Jill Reich and Associate Dean Margaret Maurer-Fazio, who helped make possible the full-year sabbatical that allowed me to finish the data analysis and first draft manuscript for this book. An especially important resource is the remarkably collegial, good-humored, smart, and supportive department of which I am fortunate to be a member; I am ever thankful to my fellow sociologists at Bates: Sawyer Sylvester, Francesco Duina, and Heidi Taylor.

Comments and suggestions about the ideas I was developing came from many people, in many venues, over many years. Even the briefest exchanges with discussants at sociological conferences, where I presented papers with preliminary analyses, shaped the trajectory of the work in important ways over the subsequent years. I extend my appreciation to several individuals who probably do not even remember their comments but whose contributions helped shape the direction I took: Barbara Katz Rothman, Sharon Preves, and Shawn McGuffey were discussants or co-panelists who provided especially valuable suggestions at presentations at the annual meetings of the American Sociological Association and the Society for the Study of Social Problems. Prior to writing this book, I published several articles reporting on more limited analyses of the same data, and the journal/edited collection editors involved in those pieces provided deeply thoughtful and informative critiques: Christine Williams, Carol Rambo, Peggy Nelson, and Anita Garey. Anonymous reviewers for the two scholarly journals that published articles also refined and extended my thinking, and I am grateful for their help. Other feedback on ideas, suggestions for literature to consult, and advice about the publication process, both brief and lengthy, was generously offered over the years by Teresa Arendell, Susan Bell, Deborah Cohan, Elisabeth Daley, Francesco Duina, Bridget Harr, Angela Hattery, Rebecca Herzig, Laura Juraska, Kevin Kumashiro, Sheri Kunovich, Cheryl Laz, Kennie Lyman, Georgia Nigro, Jan Phillips, Kimberly Simmons, Stacy Smith, Heidi Taylor, and Christine Tronnier. As we toiled together on a major administrative project over eighteen months during which I was revising, Matt Côté generously supported my efforts to find time for the revision work and kept me laughing when that was just what I needed. I also owe a special thanks to Kirk Read; a year ahead of me in revising and publishing a gender-related book after a sabbatical, his dazzling wit, wisdom, and moral support were invaluable as I navigated the process.

My work on this book followed two decades of publishing articles in scholarly journals, and, though many people helped me navigate the shift in terrain, three deserve particular mention. I am grateful to Katherine Mooney for editing the early stages of the book. Ilene Kalish, my editor at New York University Press, encouraged me to write the best book I could, and the high bar she set for balancing scholarship and accessibility was a challenge that sharpened my work. Thank you, Ilene, for your expertise and attention, for pushing me to clarify what I was trying to argue and make it as engaging and readable as possible. And, for many years, a special friend and colleague, Jan Phillips, helped propel me forward as I worked on this book and in life more generally. In a monthly two-person writing support group, we dined on endless Thai meals, and encouraged each other in the writing and thinking that so often fell behind other obligations for us both. I think of Jan as the midwife of this book, helping me to understand that a book was the right format for what I wanted to say, and traveling beside me throughout its gestation and eventual birth. Thanks so much, my friend.

To my parents, Janet and Jim Wright, my eternal gratitude for the time, energy, and financial resources you invested in my education, and for the decades of supportive interest you have shown ever since. It is difficult to find the right words to convey my appreciation for my partner, David. You have supported my career in countless ways, for more than a quarter of a century, and contributed to the writing of this book with a patient willingness to help me puzzle through a host of dilemmas. Thank you for listening, for cheering me on, for your thoughtful advice and problem solving, and for everything else that would take far too much space to detail. To Samuel and Aaron, my now nearly grown children, thank you for inspiring my interest in this important topic. Over the years you have always been willing to pitch in with keen insight when I needed help: from generating pseudonyms for my participants and their children to crafting labels for concepts and categories to questions of wording, style, and tone. Aaron, those after-school walks during my sabbatical year were a special and joyous time. Your comments and suggestions that year, as well as during the revision process, always helped me move ahead, and what a treat to have shared the thought process with you. Samuel, no matter how busy you were with schoolwork and extracurricular activities, the care with which you always asked about my day, about what I was working on and how it was going, brightened my mood and energized me to forge ahead, as did your advice in response to anything I was mulling over. To you both, thanks for listening to me talk about this book for years and, most of all, for graciously tolerating my fumbling attempts to strike the right balance as a parent. Having the opportunity to know you and share the parenting journey with your father is the greatest gift life has given me, and the greatest gift I could ever want.

INTRODUCTION

"Glamour Babies" and "Little Toughies"

Slogans emblazoned on baby bibs marketed by a leading retailer tell a striking tale about the gender expectations parents face as they outfit their daughters and sons. "Glamour Baby," "Daddy's Princess," "Born to Shop," "Diva," "Hot Babe," and "Pretty Girl" adorn the girls' bibs versus "Wild One," "Little Toughie," "All Star," "Rebel," "The Boss," and "Trouble Maker" for the boys. An equally gender-marked array of shirts is produced by major companies. One store features tees for sizes six months and up announcing, for girls, "Little Angel" and "I'd Rather Be Shopping with Mommy" and, for boys, "Little Bruiser" and "Play All Day, Rock All Night." Another store offers apparel sending similar gendered signals, this time in summer styles for preschoolers: "Poolside Princess" and "Beach Beauty" as opposed to "Shark Attack" and "Danger Zone." Almost always the styles for girls are in shades of pink and the boys' the requisite blue. When my twin sons were born, and throughout their early childhood, I avoided stamping them with these gender labels, selecting clothes and toys I considered neutral. Why be trapped by other people's expectations and assumptions, I reasoned, when one can follow one's own path?

That turned out to be much easier said than done, as eventually I faced a dilemma perhaps familiar to many readers. One day my spouse, having picked up our children at their kindergarten after-school program, reported that he had arrived at the school to find one of our sons sitting alone on the floor quietly crying. When his father asked what was wrong, he choked out that no one wanted to play with *his kind* of trading cards. Five years old, my son and his twin brother had been asking for combat-oriented trading cards wildly popular with young boys at the time. I had objected to the cards' emphasis on fighting, typical of boys' peer cultures in the contemporary United States. My son replied that *all* the boys had these cards. I thought I had found a clever compromise when I told him he could bring some other kind of cards to play with at his after-school program, and sent him off with a brand-new deck of standard playing cards. He immediately discovered that these cards held no interest for his peers, leaving him alone to wonder why. Before this incident, I was pleased about my efforts to discourage gender-typed activities for my sons and gratified that they had wide-ranging interests unconstrained by traditional gender expectations. On that day, however, I thought hard about the price they would pay if they could not participate in the peer culture of their fellow boys.[1] I soon relented, buying each the trading cards they wanted. This was but one in a long line of careful calculations I had made about their expression of gender in relation to the class- and race-specific gendered culture of their white, middle- to upper-middle-class environment. As a parent I had significant power in making those calculations, but my actions were inseparable from my children's own desires and the social world around them.

Parents do not act alone in shaping their young children's gender. The children themselves, plus a host of other factors including schools, peers, television shows, teachers, and video games, influence the process and do so in ways inextricably linked to the construction—and constraints—of race, class, and sexuality. This book focuses on the role of parents in constructing their children's gender, exploring their thoughts, the attributes, interests, and behaviors they accept or discourage for their sons and daughters, their motivations for engaging in actions that reproduce or resist gendered outcomes, and their awareness of their own role in these processes. Although focused on parents, my analysis also emphasizes the context in which parents act. Many other studies have documented that parents of young children often behave in ways that encourage gendered patterns, reproducing gender as a social category in their selection of toys, clothes, and activities as well as their styles of play and emotional expression. Most of these studies rely on check-box survey questions or observations of what parents do in experimental situations, treating parents in isolation from the broader social context and assuming that the motivations for their actions are either unconscious or based on their acceptance of the gendered status quo. Such methods can document the outlines of these practices but tell us little about the nuances of the process or the motivations and barriers shaping parental actions. Those nuances are crucial to understanding what I call the "gender trap," a set of expectations and structures that inhibit social change and stall many parents' best intentions for loosening the limits that gender can impose upon us. To more fully reveal the tensions many parents balance as they navigate that gender trap with and for their children, I draw on in-depth interviews I conducted with more than forty parents of preschoolers, children poised at the age when gender is particularly salient to their sense of themselves. The interviews include the voices of both mothers and fathers from a variety of class backgrounds, racial/ethnic groups, sexual orientations, and family types.

As I listened to these parents in their living rooms, at their kitchen tables, on my college campus, or at their workplaces, it became clear that they are neither passive conduits for social rules dictated by structures beyond their control nor completely free agents who can design the social worlds their children inhabit. Instead, they find themselves in the middle of a dynamic process of reproducing and resisting gendered patterns. Parents engage in this process in dialogue with powerful social institutions, in everyday interactions with those around them, and carrying the baggage of their own beliefs about gender. They re-create gendered structures, enthusiastically and hesitantly, directly and indirectly. They provide opportunities, reinforce or discourage outcomes, and model behavior in ways that shape gendered paths for their children. But many of these parents also creatively tweak and even revise those structures, making it up as they go along and responding to the feedback they receive along the way. The tweaking and revision is especially notable for daughters. I document a range of interests and attributes that parents consider unusual for girls, and that they actively seek to encourage, from sports participation to aspirations toward traditionally male occupations. They want these opportunities for their daughters, and most view their greater availability as a sign of positive social change. At the same time many parents see attributes such as nurturance and empathy for others, as well as interests in, for example, fash-

3

ion and appearance, as natural or inevitable in their young daughters. The combination of typical and atypical patterns these parents craft often leads them back into the gender trap, thwarting the very opportunities they seek to build. Undermining some gendered blueprints at the same time they reinforce others, they unwittingly solidify gendered divisions of labor and power in the workforce, the family, and civil society. For most parents, tweaking and revision are evident also in relation to sons but to a more limited extent. They teach their young sons some basic domestic skills and encourage empathy, even as they prepare those boys to compete in typical male domains and avoid expressing vulnerability. Beliefs about biology and fears about social costs pave the way toward the gender trap, narrowing the range of options many consider acceptable for boys. That narrower range also solidifies gendered divisions of labor and power in ways that advantage boys and men but also constrain them. For both sons and daughters, many parental actions and beliefs construct boys and girls as separate groups with different needs, interests, and capacities, reinforcing a binary approach to gender that may actually create what it purports only to reflect. Weaving these patterns together, I reveal the important role parents play in reproducing gendered power structures. But I also uncover the possibilities for sidestepping the gender trap and creating social change that are implicit in parents' resistance, their ambivalence, and the complexities, tensions, and contradictions inherent in their beliefs and actions.

The Continuing Relevance of Gender

Why even think about gender as a trap? Some would claim that gender inequality is a thing of the past, and gendered childhoods more innocent fun than a foundation for inequality and constraint. In fact, a substantial body of scholarship documents the continuing relevance of gender as a social structure that limits opportunity, restricts individual potential, and distributes social resources unequally. Women remain disproportionately responsible for household labor and child care, even as their labor market hours have risen over recent decades.[2] Their income for that time in the labor market continues to lag behind men's, with women who are employed full-time and year-round earning about seventy-seven cents annually for every dollar a man earns.[3] Inequalities in domestic responsibility and the gendered wage gap are connected as well, with even larger wage gaps evident among parents. This latter pattern is what sociologists Michelle Budig and Paula England call a "motherhood penalty," as parenthood is associated with higher earnings among men but lower earnings among women.[4] In a related pattern, experimental researchers have found that raters evaluate mothers less highly than women without children when asked to review resumes and make hypothetical hiring and salary decisions. For men, parenthood status does not affect ratings significantly.[5] Both the gender wage gap and the motherhood penalty foster women's economic dependence on men, and shape a particularly harsh economic reality for single mothers and their children, who make up an increasingly large share of households with children in the contemporary United States.[6] The wage gap and motherhood penalty also shape the negative impact of divorce on the economic security of women and children. Regardless of parenthood status, men and women continue to be segregated into different occupations, with female-dominated occupations generally earning less.[7] Currently women, on average, hold less authority in the workplace and fewer positions of power in formal politics than men in the United States, and people still tend to perceive women as less effective at leadership.[8] Women are disproportionately affected by sexual harassment, sexual assault, and domestic violence.[9] They are also more likely to suffer from eating disorders and a negative body image, complex phenomena with many contributing factors but outcomes that some scholars have linked to objectified and nearly unattainable media representations of the ideal female body.[10] Media images continue to frame girls and women as more passive, whereas boys and men are represented as more active, authoritative, and in control.[11] All these gendered patterns vary in important ways by other intersecting dimensions of inequality such as race and class, a critical topic to which I return later. But this broad overview documents persistent gender inequalities in the family, workplace, politics, media, and daily life, even while much has shifted in the social expectations for men and women.

This partial list of the constraints and limitations imposed on girls and women is one piece of the continuing relevance of the gender trap, but, as scholars increasingly emphasize, gendered patterns also place significant constraints on boys and men. The benefits that flow from these various inequalities come at great costs. Social expectations for masculinity that emphasize power, toughness, aggression, and emotional reserve all lead men toward a narrow ideal that discourages emotional expression, nurturance, productive conflict resolution, human intimacy, and personal well-being, and even results in shorter life spans for men than women.[12] Some have argued that these social expectations also make it more difficult for boys and young men to succeed in educational settings.[13] Emphasis on male economic achievement pressures men to select particular occupations and to suffer disproportionately if they are unable to fulfill expectations for supporting families.[14] Media representations of the powerful male body increasingly mold how boys and young men view themselves, in some cases leading to a negative body image and troubling outcomes such as steroid abuse.[15] These costs of masculinity are spread unevenly across subgroups of boys and men based on intersecting forms of inequality that I consider throughout my analysis of how parents navigate the gender trap.

Some readers may be surprised that in a book about parents with preschool-aged children, my examination of gender includes frequent attention to sexuality and sexual orientation. Here, too, decades of scholarship on gender leads to a clear conclusion: social expectations for gender are deeply intertwined with pressures toward heterosexual orientation, and social judgments about how well people meet gender expectations are linked to social assumptions about sexuality. This connection is especially marked for boys and men, who are often judged harshly for any deviation from socially sanctioned masculinity. As sociologist David Aveline concludes, "in Western cultural history . . . the link between feminine behavior and male homosexuality has long been ingrained in the cultural script."[16] Given continuing discrimination and prejudice against lesbian, gay, bisexual, and transgendered people, this link figures centrally in the gender trap, reinforcing the constraints that gender expectations create for all people and multiplying the social obstacles faced, in particular, by those with non-heterosexual or non–gender-normative orientations.[17]

It may be tempting to take gender categories for granted, to view them as preexisting facts around which we adjust our lives. But these categories and the expectations we hold for those who occupy them are better understood as the products of a complex social process. Much of that process, the foundation upon which later gender differentiation and gender inequality are built, begins in childhood, with the capacities, attributes, activities, interests, and directions encouraged for boys and girls, and the interpretations that cast shadows or light on the social actions reproducing gendered childhoods. It is the continuing relevance of gender that motivates my interest in how parents participate in that complicated social process, how they reproduce but also resist the gender trap with and for their young children.

Rooted in Nature

Christine is a thirty-one-year-old, stay-at-home mother who identifies as working class. In a small house littered with toys and racks of drying laundry, and bustling with the cheerful thundering of her three children, this white, heterosexually partnered mother describes the contrast she sees between her son and daughter.

> I didn't want to track him one way, but I thought, "Well, he should have a truck." . . . And we got the truck and he just sort of knew how to drive it around. . . . We put it down in front of him and he just instinctively knew what to do with it. . . . He definitely likes the blocks, the trains, the trucks, the building. . . . He loves building. He's practically built a house in his head. I know he's got all these plans for all these things he wants to build. . . . I think it was just inside him. Then there's my daughter, she's in dance class and she loves that. And she loves dressing up. Being mother, you know, being sister. She's very in tune with being a girl. . . . I wanted to make sure that she had a mix of toys too, that she didn't have only dolls. But I also feel like if they show an interest in something then I want to encourage that. She showed interest in dancing and dolls, so we kept going with it.

Christine's words echoed those I expected to hear from many parents I interviewed, a trap baited by beliefs about the innate foundations of gender and reinforced by relatively unconscious parental actions that reproduce traditional assumptions. It turned out that this approach was evident for about one-fifth of my interviewees. For these parents, most gendered interests and attributes of children seem rooted in nature, essentially biological expressions.

Bruce, a middle-class accountant, offers a similar sentiment. Talking in the kitchen of his brick ranch home on a large corner lot, this forty-one-year-old heterosexually partnered Asian American father of two views his son's lack of interest in his older sister's toys as evidence of innate gender differences.

> I think that is a lot of the hard-wired stuff. To even see it and for it to be quite prevalent and to not be interested in it, . . . I think that in a large way is innate. Certainly if there were any toys in his life first, it was the stuff that she was into because except for the generic, neutral baby toys, well, it was either that neutral stuff or the dolls and princess stuff geared towards her. So, he'd be looking at just those two things, and he was still able to not develop an interest in her stuff and instead developed an interest in trucks and trains and dinosaurs.

Both Bruce and Christine framed their analyses by comparing a son and a daughter, but other parents of only sons or only daughters also believed that nature dictates important aspects of gendered outcomes in childhood.

Crafted by Parents

Despite my expectation that most parents would view childhood gender patterns as natural, many parents saw gender-typed outcomes as socially produced by outside forces such as media, schools, peer pressure, and society in general. Others, whether reluctantly or routinely, reported that they themselves were a source of childhood gendering. For example, from the elegant leather sofa in his beautifully appointed home, Jerome, a thirty-two-year-old lawyer, spoke of his role in his son's life. This white, upper-middle-class, heterosexually partnered father of one daughter and one son noted throughout the interview that his son shows some attributes he considers feminine. In a comment that echoes the scholarly literature on perceptions of femininity and male sexual orientation, Jerome mentioned that he sometimes wondered if his five-year-old son might grow up to be gay. He explained his reaction to that possibility by saying, "If Jack were to be gay, it would not make me happy at all. I would probably see that as a failure as a dad, . . . as a failure because I'm raising him to be a boy, a man."

To Jerome, his son's masculinity does not unfold naturally; instead, Jerome feels responsible for crafting it. He wants his son "to be a boy, a man," and considers heterosexuality one of the elements of successfully achieving that outcome. For some parents, such molding of their children carried less negative emotion and was more a matter of routinely steering them toward typical interests. Elaine, a briskly efficient, white, middle-class school administrator who asked to be interviewed over her lunch hour, talked about her nearly three-year-old daughter's strong interest in baby dolls. Thirty-eight years old and a heterosexually partnered mother of two, Elaine saw herself and other family members as the source of that interest.

> I cultivated it and her father cultivated it, and you know, her grandmother too. Yeah, we all have been socializing her that way. You know, we buy her pink and we buy her dolls and little purses, earrings and jewelry and pretty clothes and we go shopping, she loves to go shopping with mommy.

Although expressing some belief in a biological basis for gendered outcomes in childhood, Elaine recognized a social basis as well, including her own actions. This pattern was evident in about one-fourth of the parents I interviewed, who tended to view traditional gender patterns as socially produced, and saw that production as a routine and positive part of parenting

Judged by Society

Parents' role in crafting children's gender felt more routine, even invisible, to parents whose children closely fit traditional gender expectations. But some parents reported feeling judged by others if they, or their children, did not seem to fit social expectations. Walt, an energetic sports enthusiast and father of twins, described his openness to field hockey and tap dancing as activities for his sons. This thirty-three-year-old African American shop floor supervisor, who is heterosexually partnered and identifies as working class, noted casually, "People think I'm crazy," indicating his realization of the judgment that surrounds him. But he also made it clear that reaction does not bother him at all. On the other hand, Belinda, a thirty-eight-year-old, heterosexually partnered, white, middle-class, stay-at-home mother of a son and daughter, recounted feeling insulted by how friends and family reacted to the way she decorated her daughter's room.

> In fact, we have been accused of wanting a son because my husband and I were both military pilots and we didn't know what we were having, a boy or a girl, with Elizabeth, she was first, and we decorated her room in primary colors. I heard they are more stimulating, so we wanted the idea of primary colors to be very stimulating and we did airplanes and helicopters because that was my husband's and my love. And we were accused by several people of obviously wanting a boy and being terribly disappointed we got a girl. And, to me that's kind of insulting because I am a girl and I was a pilot. Why should a girl not have an interest in airplanes and helicopters?

Belinda's use of terms such as "accused" and "insulting" clearly conveys her belief that people are judging her for how well her parenting matches their gender-based expectations.

Another stay-at-home mother of two boys, Tanya, a white, upper-middle-class, thirty-four-year-old in a lesbian partnership, described how people reacted to her infant son's clothing.

> My partner bought Graham this pink sleeper, and I was furious about it. . . . It was like for when he was eight or nine months old. . . . People would see him in that, they'd think he was a girl. . . . And sure enough, there we were at my parents', he had on his pink sleeper, and I came into the house and one of my [teenage] brother's friends was over. He said, "Who is that girl your sister is carrying into the house?" and my brother freaked out, . . . and he just said, "That's my cousin Sarah." . . .

He wasn't going to go into some long summation about how his crazy psycho lesbian sister-in-law bought his nephew that pink thing.

While expressing a deep desire to allow her sons a broader range of interests and attributes than stereotypically associated with boys and men, Tanya is also concerned about going "too far" and attracting painful judgments about herself and her sons. Along with about an eighth of parents I interviewed, she resists many gender-based expectations for her children but feels trapped into balancing that resistance with what she considers just enough gender typing to avoid social repercussions.

Tensions and Practices

These interviewees highlight some of the key ideas framing my analysis of how parents negotiate their children's gender. Two tensions that rang through clearly were between biological and social explanations for childhood gender patterns, and between actions that reproduced versus those that resisted gendered expectations. These tensions were evident not just among the parents I interviewed but often within a specific parent's reported beliefs and actions. The potential or reality of being judged by others was also a salient concern for a significant number of parents. As parents balanced these tensions and concerns, five configurations of parenting practice emerged that help to distill the range of approaches they took.

- "Naturalizers" interpret gendered childhoods as biological in origin and, though occasionally acting to adjust gendered structures, primarily reproduce them. Their concern about others' judgment partly depends on whether their children display any gender nonconformity that makes the parents uncomfortable. Christine, the mother who saw her son's interest in trucks and building, and her daughter's preference for dolls and dance, as natural, is such a parent.
- "Cultivators" act in a way that promotes gendered childhoods for their sons and daughters. They interpret the origins of gender patterns as largely social and express little concern about the judgments of others. For them, reproducing gender is a routine part of parenting, not some-

11

thing that evokes anxiety or concern. Elaine, the mother who reported crafting her daughter's interest in baby dolls, is a good example.

- "Refiners" highlight both biological and social forces in explaining gendered outcomes and act with roughly equal measures of resistance and conformity, always attentive to the actual and potential judgments of others. Belinda, who was criticized for decorating her daughter's room in primary colors and a military theme, is a parent in this group.

- "Innovators" resist gendered structures for their children and are unconcerned about the judgment of others. Walt, who dismissed the claim that he was crazy for considering tap dancing and field hockey as activities for his twin sons, is one of the parents I profile as an Innovator.

- "Resisters," while even more opposed to gendered patterns for their children, display significant concern about being judged by others. Tanya, the mother who was worried about her son wearing a pink sleeper, is a good illustration.

The parents I interviewed engage in a balancing act as they navigate the gender trap, juggling beliefs, actions, and motivations to improvise an approach to gendering their young children. Along the way they reproduce structures that constrain us all, but they also resist them; even parents I categorize as Naturalizers or Cultivators make some effort to revise gender expectations and question essentialist interpretations of gender. These parents, in talking about their experiences and outlooks, voiced neither a passive or inevitable reproduction of tradition nor spontaneous and unconstrained free agency, but instead portrayed a complex and dynamic process fraught with tension but also possibilities. These possibilities, however, were often stalled or narrowed by contradictions sometimes evident to parents but frequently not.

The Social Construction of Gender

My approach to thinking about gender is founded on the view that gender is socially constructed rather than biologically determined, and that gender relations are organized around power and the unequal distribution of social resources. This process of social construction is woven through individual, interactional, and institutional levels, and gender, as a socially constructed source of inequality, is inseparable from other forms of social inequality, including race, class, and sexuality. Most fundamentally, my approach follows other scholarly work which has demonstrated that gender is a social structure central to the organization of societies and a source not only of difference but of power. In the words of sociologist Judith Lorber, gender is "a binary system of social organization that creates inequality."[18] She elaborates:

> As a building block of social orders, gender gets built into organizational structures, floods interactions and relationships, and is a major social status for individuals. Gendered norms and expectations pattern the practices of people in workplaces, in families, groups, and intimate relationships, and in creating individual identities and self-assessments. People's gender conformity supports gendered practices and gender as a social institution; people's gender diversity and deviance challenge it.[19]

Gender is not a straightforward amplification of underlying biological differences between males and females; rather, gender is constructed through social processes and enforced through social mechanisms. As Lorber observes,

> Genes, hormones, physiology, and bodies (what are constructed as "sex differences") are socially constructed as gendered in Western society; they are not the source of gender as a social status. The understanding of male and female bodies as intrinsically and consistently different and as the main marker of social status is not universal.[20]

Certainly a number of fundamental biological variations are linked to physiology and reproductive capacities, but the extent and manner of their importance to the social understanding of gender have varied over time and place in ways that are inconsistent with the claim that biology completely determines gendered outcomes. Against a range of natural variation among individuals, social discourse constructs only two distinct and inter-

13

nally homogeneous categories. Sociologist Michael Kimmel views the biologically determinist account of gender as a "just-so story," a "convenient,
pleasant, and ultimately useful, fiction" that relies on a limited amount of
selective evidence to reason backward and construct an elaborate justification for contemporary arrangements.[21] In a classic synthesis of decades of
scholarship, *Deceptive Distinctions*, sociologist Cynthia Fuchs Epstein argues persuasively that "social factors can account for most of the variation
seen between men and women."[22]

> Men probably will never be able to have babies, but they may be able
> to mother or teach young children as well as women do. Women may
> never win a weight lifting contest competing with men matched
> for weight and training, but they are fast catching up in marathon
> running and solving mathematics problems. It seems clear that in-
> tellectual capacity and emotional qualities are distributed through
> humanity without restrictions of sex any more than race or national-
> ity. Believing, however, that men or women cannot develop certain
> mental or psychological attributes merely because of their sex can re-
> sult in the patterns that people uncritically observe and believe to be
> inevitable.[23]

This means, in exploring gendered childhoods, that it is not inevitable
for girls to prefer pink and boys blue, or for boys to prefer baseball and girls
ballet. Nor is it inevitable for girls to be quieter and more polite, and boys
more rambunctious and assertive. Different male or female preferences and
attributes are shaped and enforced by the social expectations surrounding
children and their parents, and they seem inevitable only after they are
socially constructed through the kind of reverse engineering that Kimmel
identifies.

Gender and Power

From this perspective, gender is not just a source of difference but, more
important, a source of power and inequality. As feminist legal scholar
Catharine MacKinnon articulated more than twenty years ago, men are as

different from women as women are from men, a framing she argues obscures the more important distinction that men, as a group, are dominant over women.[24] Though refined by later scholars to incorporate greater attention to variations among men and women, MacKinnon's approach captures the fundamental assumptions of a power-oriented analysis of gender. Social scientists and activists have thoroughly documented gendered power and its associated inequalities in their myriad daily manifestations. The list of examples includes, at least, domestic violence, wage gaps, glass ceilings, occupational gender segregation and political power imbalances, divisions of household labor, constraints of body image and gendered patterns of self-esteem, sexual assault and violence against gay, lesbian, bisexual and transgendered people, the feminization of poverty, eating disorders, steroid abuse, and gay youth suicide. These examples, which highlight power differences and inequalities, favor boys and men. Jerome, elsewhere in his interview, expands on his desire to raise Jack "to be a boy, a man." He spoke candidly about moments when he was disappointed to see Jack cry or take a passive stance in conflicts with other children. Jerome emphasized the importance of seeing his son as powerful, "standing up and fighting" for what he wants and protecting his younger sister, Louisa, and other female peers. He actively encourages such behavior and discourages Jack from crying or accepting compromises in negotiations with other boys. These are the kinds of behavior that Douglas Schrock and Michael Schwalbe, sociologists of masculinity, refer to as "manhood acts."[25] Through these daily actions, boys and men are constructed as powerful enough to merit positions of control and influence in the workplace, families, and politics, whereas girls and women are constructed as more nurturing, fragile, and in need of protection. As Schrock and Schwalbe put it, "regardless of what individual males consciously intend, manhood acts have the effect of reproducing an unequal gender order," one in which "women as a group are subordinated to men as a group, and some men are subordinated to others."[26] But along with the benefits that boys and men derive from gendered inequality, especially if they are also advantaged by inequalities of race, class, and sexuality, they face constraints from gendered structures as well. Boys and men are often discouraged from expressing the full range of human emotions, as they are channeled away from intimacy with children and one another, and limited to a narrowly defined path. Most of the parents I interviewed seek to avoid that trap, hoping for at least a somewhat broader set of attributes and interests for their young sons. Many, however, prepare their boys to embrace some elements of masculine social power as well, whether because of the direct benefits of power for someone like Jerome or through fear of the judgments boys face if they fail to measure up to the expectations of others for a person like Tanya. It is my concern about power, inequality, and constraint that animates my interest in childhood gendering; my analysis of how parents navigate, reproduce, and resist the gender trap offers critical insight into the maintenance and revision of those structures.

Self and Society

Researchers often identify three levels at which the social construction of gender takes place: individual, interactional, and institutional. Sociologist Barbara Risman notes that "gender is, of course, socialized into our (individual) personalities, but it also sets the parameters for interactional expectations and is built into our social institutions."[27] Risman properly cautions us to recognize that "gendered selves"—meaning the individual internalization of gendered social expectations—are inextricably connected to interactional- and institutional-level processes.

> Far too much explanatory power is presumed to rest in the motivation of gendered selves. . . . Even when individual men and women do *not* desire to live gendered lives or support male dominance, they often find themselves compelled to do so by the logic of gendered choices. That is, interactional pressures and institutional design create gender and the resultant inequality, even in the absence of individual desires.[28]

All three levels figure prominently in my analysis of how parents navigate the gender trap. Individual-level preferences can be crafted by the kinds of things Elaine reports cultivating for her daughter—the pink, the dolls, pocket books and purses, jewelry and pretty clothes and shopping—

16

all of which become part of toddler Gabrielle's gendered self. I offer many examples of institutional forces that also nudge parents toward the gender trap. Some involve parents consciously responding to such forces, as when Pamela—a thirty-six-year-old, white, middle-class, heterosexually part-nered mother of two sons—discourages her four-year-old Evan's interest in growing up to be a day care worker because "he could never support a fam-ily doing that." Such practices, discussed more fully later on, are responses to institutional structures including occupational gender segregation, gen-dered wage gaps, and women's economic dependence on men. Even if these structures do not shape Evan's gendered self, and even if he continues to prefer a nurturing occupation such as day care work, they may well shape his sense of what is possible given the gendered structural expectations surrounding him in the adult world. My analysis also extends to parents who are not consciously thinking about institutional forces, yet such forces still play a role. For the young daughter who might be encouraged to follow her interest in child care, the low wages associated with that work may limit her ability to support herself, thus leaving her financially dependent on a man's higher wages, even if her parents were not consciously intending to point her in that direction. Institutional forces intersect with the lessons parents offer in a variety of ways, often unintended.

The interactional level illuminates the importance of the social judg-ments many parents report feeling, underlining a dynamic social process through which the gender trap is reproduced and, equally important, po-tentially resisted and revised. Sociologists Candace West and Don Zimmer-man stress this level of analysis, arguing that gender is a set of actions, an accomplishment forged in social situations as people interact. In their in-fluential article "Doing Gender," they present an approach that has gener-ated debate and analysis ever since its publication.

When we view gender as an accomplishment, an achieved property of situated conduct, our attention shifts from matters internal to the in-dividual and focuses on the interactional, and ultimately the institu-tional, arenas. In one sense, of course, it is individuals who do gender. But it is a situated doing, carried out in the virtual or real presence of others who are presumed to be oriented to its production. Rather than a property of individuals, we conceive of gender as an emergent feature of social situations: both as an outcome of and a rationale for various social arrangements and as a means of legitimating one of the most fundamental divisions of society.[29]

Our actions are potentially shaped not only by actual interactions but also by our ability to adjust our conduct in anticipation of how others may react. In the terminology of West and Zimmerman, echoed throughout the literature that applies and expands their framework, we are *accountable* to others in our routine everyday interactions. "Accountable" is a term I use often as I explore the way my interviewees talk about social judgments. As Fenstermaker, West, and Zimmerman put it:

> Insofar as societal members know that their conduct is accountable, they will frame their actions in relation to how they might be construed by others. . . . An individual involved in virtually any course of action may be held accountable for her/his execution of that action as a woman or as a man.[30]

Accountability, they argue, is relevant not only when people are crafting gender in accordance with the expectations of others but also when people resist or stray from such expectations. This claim, present in West and Zimmerman's earlier formulation, is one that West and fellow sociologist Sarah Fenstermaker return to defend against criticism that it downplays resistance and social change. They argue that their focus on the *process* by which gender is *accomplished* places activity, agency, and the possibility of resistance in the foreground. As they point out, "within the dynamic nature of the accomplishment of categorical difference reside the seeds of inevitable change."[31] But any such change occurs within the context and constraints of accountability to gendered assessment. Just as Belinda feels accountable to her friends' and relatives' judgments about airplane mobiles in her daughter's nursery, and Tanya feels accountable to her brother and his friends in relation to her son's pink sleeper, gendered assessments surround parents daily, setting potential traps requiring careful navigation.

Intersectionality

A final foundational idea that shapes my approach is intersectionality, the argument that gender, as a social construct, is inseparable from other social categories, including race, class, and sexuality. The various dimensions of social inequality that are built upon the categories and distribution of resources based on gender, race, class, and sexual orientation operate simultaneously in people's lived experience. Gendered expectations may vary across social groups, as intersecting dimensions of inequality often create different opportunities and constraints for gendered selves and gendered interactions across social locations. A leading theorist of intersectionality, sociologist Patricia Hill Collins, notes that structures of inequality intersect and interact as "mutually constructing systems of power . . . that permeate all social relations."[32] For this reason I interviewed parents from a variety of social locations in relation to these structures of inequality, and I tried to be specific about the instances where gendered patterns were evident across social locations versus cases where they developed differently for different groups.

For example, Grace, a white, low-income, part-time custodian and single mother of four, said that she plans to warn her children that some jobs are better suited to men than women, based on her own experience of feeling exhausted by construction jobs for which she considered her body ill suited. As Grace teaches her children to shape their occupational aspirations around biological differences, she is clearly speaking from her class location as someone who has supported herself doing physical work—a specific intersection of class and gender. Meanwhile Tanya, the lesbian mother who "freaked out" about her son wearing pink, did so largely because of the scrutiny she feels her family faces regarding gender. In intersections involving less valorized social locations, such as those of lower income individuals, people of color, and gay and lesbian parents, there is a tendency to view gender as only one factor in the complex of class, race, and sexuality, whereas it is seen as the primary factor among white, middle- to upper-middle-class heterosexual people. These other dimensions of inequality, however, are relevant for all the interviewees. Just as a gay or lesbian parent may be uniquely constrained by homophobic attitudes and heterosexist structures, a heterosexual parent is advantaged by those same social factors. Gender-studies scholar and activist Peggy McIntosh has captured this idea vividly: the advantages of being in socially valued categories fill an invisible knapsack of privilege that those of us in those valued categories carry along and benefit from daily.[33] She also points out, however, that many of us simultaneously carry privilege and disadvantage based on our social locations. Although the lesbian mother I mentioned is constrained by her sexual orientation, she is also at an advantage through her status as a white, upper-middle class parent, secure financially, and free of the additional burdens of racism. Thus, even as my analysis emphasizes the ways in which parents reproduce and resist gendered outcomes with and for their young children, I imbue that focus with attention to intersecting inequalities and systems of power.[34]

Parents, Children, and Gender

More than thirty-five years ago the literature on gender and parenting indicated that new parents often perceive male and female newborns differently, even when there are no actual differences in their appearance or behavior.[35] More recent literature documents practices by which parents, from this first impression on, construct and reproduce gender as a social category through interaction with their children.[36] Some researchers have highlighted subgroups of parents who actively seek to disrupt traditional gendered expectations for their children.[37] Overall, however, the literature documents definite parental tendencies toward differential treatment of sons and daughters, which in some ways are especially pronounced among fathers.[38] By observing parental behavior in experimental or everyday settings, scholars have established certain patterns. Parents tend to select gender-typical toys and activities for their young children, dress them in gendered clothing, and pick out gender-typed décor for their rooms.[39] Parents also treat sons and daughters differently in their degree of vocalization to infants and toddlers, speaking more conversationally to girls and making comments or offering instructions to boys.[40] In relating family stories, parents emphasize emotions with girls

and autonomy with boys. They also engage in more aggressive and challenging styles of play with their sons than with their daughters.[41] Their
expectations for their children's household chores also differ by gender.[42]
Thus, even as they attempt to broaden the range of possibilities for their
sons and daughters beyond what once was considered socially acceptable, parents still shape the gendered interests, attributes, and artifacts
in their children's lives through these various practices. Recent research
also suggests that parenting advice books, although progressing somewhat with the times, still include gender stereotypical advice and limitations on the amount of gender nonconformity they recommend parents
encourage or even tolerate.[43]

Parents do not act alone, however. Their gendering actions must be
understood in the broader context of interactional and institutional
forces from media to schools to relatives, day care providers, even strangers. And along with this powerful array of social forces, children themselves play a key role in the gendering process.[44] For well over a decade,
researchers who study gender and childhood have focused on the power
of peer cultures and have encouraged adults to recognize children as active agents rather than passive recipients of adult influence.[45] As pointed
out more than twenty years ago by Spencer Cahill, a pioneer of childhood
studies, "by the end of the preschool age years . . . children are self-reg-
ulating participants in the interactional achievement of their own normally sexed identities."[46] As they attempt to understand their daily experiences, young children are alert to the interactional and institutional
processes that reproduce gender structures, and most come to see their
own ability to successfully achieve a "normally sexed identity" as part of
navigating their peer cultures and the wider social world. While scholars
continue, of course, to recognize parents' influence in the gendering of
their children—and this book explores that process from parents' perspective—it is essential to keep in mind the agency of children as well
as the myriad constraints surrounding parents. Like Christine, who reported following her daughter's lead when she showed interest in dolls
and dancing, the power parents have to channel opportunities for their
children is limited by social factors and shaped by their children's understandings.[47]

Purpose of the Book

My goal in this book is not to treat parents in isolation nor to blame or judge them for their gendering actions. Rather, I hope to clarify the beliefs and motivations that shape their actions in the broader context of the social obstacles they are forced to negotiate daily, and thus to reveal gendered traps but also opportunities for social change. To this end, I created an open-ended opportunity for parents to talk about their children's gender, building on previous research to consider parents as potentially able both to reproduce and reshape gendered childhoods, and to do so with explicit attention to the social forces constraining them. I interviewed forty-two parents about their beliefs, actions, hopes, and experiences in raising their sons and daughters, with interviews lasting from one to two hours and some more than three hours. A more detailed consideration of my research methods is given in the appendix to this book.

Because scholars widely agree that the preschool years are pivotal for children's emerging gender identity and increasingly gender-typed behaviors, I interviewed parents who had at least one child between the ages of three and five. Given the important role children play in the process of gendering within families, I interviewed parents who were actively negotiating the age range in which their children were increasingly aware of gender expectations. Regardless of the number of children an interviewee had, the questions focused particularly on one child in that preschool age range. I interviewed about an equal number of mothers and fathers from an array of social locations, taking care not to rely on people I knew personally or networks too closely clustered around my college. An advantage of qualitative interviewing is the opportunity to adjust questions as one proceeds, framing new follow-up questions and seeking new interviewees to fill in gaps. I strove to gather an adequately diverse group of parents in terms of gender, race, class, sexual orientation, household configuration, and parental employment status. A chart summarizing the social locations and background information for all participants is included in the appendix.

Qualitative interviews offer depth rather than breadth, as they involve a limited number of people talking at length rather than a large number of people providing limited information. Although an invaluable method, it is important to recognize its limitations. The data accumulated from a small sample may not necessarily be generalized to all parents, and it is important to be cautious in comparing across subgroups. It was essential, however, to talk to parents from a broad range of backgrounds so that the picture I paint is not based on one limited group of parents.

I began each interview by asking parents to recall a time before they were planning to have children and whether they preferred having a daughter or a son. Questions then explored the interests and activities of their children, as well as their thoughts about gender typing in childhood, described more fully in the appendix. Pseudonyms are used throughout, for parents as well as children, to ensure confidentiality. Small details have also been altered to further protect my interviewees' identities; for example, job titles have been replaced with similar but distinct occupations. Specific names of organizations have also been changed.

Organization of the Book

After delineating the conceptual foundations for my analysis by tracing general distinctions in parents' beliefs and actions in relation to gendered childhoods, chapter 1 focuses on parents' recollected preferences for having a son versus a daughter. These recollections are laced with gendered expectations about their children, which I refer to as "gendered anticipation." Biological and social explanations for childhood gender patterns are also discussed, including narratives about hormones, physiology, brain wiring, and other natural processes that parents relied on to explain gendered outcomes, as well as the myriad social processes contributing to gender. Chapter 1 also looks at parents' actions in raising their children, outlining ways in which parents shape gender conventionally as well as their efforts to shift traditional gender expectations, avoid the gender trap, and loosen constraints on children. Five types of parenting practice that emerge from these tensions and motivations are presented. Here I detail the experiences of a specific group of parents, using the analytic distinctions I drew from the larger group to reveal configurations of practice.

Chapter 2 discusses the group I term "Naturalizers," for whom gendered childhoods are biologically based and relatively unproblematic. Although such parents see themselves as bystanders to a naturally unfolding process, they also report actions that produce the outcomes they believe are biologically determined. Within that overall tendency, these parents also attempt to smooth the sharp edges of gendered constraints, aiming to offer their sons and daughters a wider range of opportunities and to respect their children's agency. The parents I refer to as "Cultivators" are the subject of chapter 3. This group views society, which includes themselves, as a key actor in shaping their children's gender but also considers the process and outcome as relatively unproblematic. This group, too, while tending to reproduce gendered patterns, tries to adjust gendered constraints and broaden their children's options. The "Refiners" are discussed in chapter 4. These parents invoke both nature and society, work to reproduce and resist gender expectations and do so while carefully considering people's judgments of themselves and their children. "Innovators," introduced in chapter 5, resist gender structures but ultimately are resigned to the inevitability of some gendering in childhood. "Resisters," the final group and the topic of chapter 6, are even more resistant than Innovators but are more guarded, even anxious and fearful, about the social costs of straying too far from the gendered path.

My concluding chapter summarizes the patterns and themes detailed throughout the book, and highlights how my analysis contributes to understanding the role of parents in shaping gendered childhoods. By emphasizing both stability and the potential for change in gender structures, I hope to illuminate the limits and possibilities of parental agency in a way that proves useful to students and scholars, as well as parents and family advocates. Parents who wish to loosen the gendered constraints imposed on their children, and contribute to relaxing the broader structures of inequality interwoven with those constraints, can and do make a difference. But they do so within the confines of interactional and institutional forces. The potential role that parents can play, and the support they need both interactionally and institutionally in order to execute that potential, is highlighted in this book. Like the balancing act I attempted to craft in response to my son's desire for combat-oriented trading cards, many of the parents I spent time with are improvising, juggling their own beliefs about gender, the judgments of others in everyday interactions, and the power of gendered social structures. As they seek to avoid at least some aspects of the gender trap for their children, they also wander into and sometimes re-produce, wittingly or unwittingly, that very trap, stalling their own efforts. The barriers and pitfalls, as well as the possibilities for avoiding them, are illuminated by the nuanced analysis my interviews allow, as this group of parents offers critical insights into the continuing power of the gender trap but also the potential paths toward social change.

ONE

Wanting a Girl,
Wanting a Boy

Conceptual Building Blocks

From the earliest moment potential parents contemplate raising a child, they wander into a social landscape filled with gendered images, a key feature of the backdrop against which they eventually raise children. For that reason I began my interviews by asking the parents of preschoolers whether they had ever preferred having a son or a daughter, either before they had planned to have children or while awaiting the arrival of the child who would be the focus of our interview. For the many parents who did express a preference, we talked about what a son or daughter meant to them and how they anticipated that parenting would be a different experience depending on their child's gender. The heart of my analysis is the exploration of five configurations of parenting that emerged among the parents I interviewed and their implications for the gender trap. First, however, I establish the analytic building blocks that later define parents' varying approaches to parenting: gendered anticipation; beliefs about the origins of gendered childhoods; actions that reproduce or resist gendered outcomes for children; and the motivations parents report for taking those actions. A preliminary glance at these categories and how each links to the scholarly literature on gender provides a crucial foundation for understanding how I use the tensions between these categories to differentiate the five types of parenting practice explored in detail.

"I Wanted a Soul Mate:" Gendered Anticipation

When asked about their pre-parenthood preferences for sons or daughters, these parents echoed the results of decades of surveys in the United States: if surveyed adults could only have one child, men with a preference have favored sons by more than a two-to-one margin, whereas about half of women preferred a daughter and the other half a son.[1] Among the parents I interviewed, most recalled having a preference, and most men preferred a son, with the women split fifty-fifty.[2]

In the explanations parents offered for their preferences, gendered images came to life. Across different races, classes, and sexual orientations, parents seemed to base their preferences on traditional gendered assumptions about their future children. Although issues arose concerning race and sexual orientation, they did not arise in a manner that appeared to predict preference. For example, two Asian American mothers reported cultural pressure to want a son, but only one of these women actually had that preference herself. One gay father reported that, in awaiting adoption, he thought others might consider it more acceptable for him to adopt a daughter, but he expressed only a tentative preference himself. At this early stage, on the relatively frictionless plane of imagination, parents from all backgrounds expressed a strikingly consistent narrative of traditionally gendered offspring. They recounted envisioning iconic scenes of mothers shopping and talking with daughters and fathers playing catch and watching football with sons. They spoke about sons carrying on the family name and protecting female siblings, and daughters staying close emotionally long after childhood. These parents assumed that their children's interests and tendencies would be determined by whether they were male or female, indicating that they anticipated a highly gendered child. For parents who ended up having a child whose gender they preferred, these anticipations are potentially self-fulfilling prophecies, as they began constructing their child's gender even before the child was born. Even those who did not have a child with the preferred gender may well have laid the foundation for assumptions about what their eventual child would *not* enjoy, given their gendered assumptions about the preferred child.

Future chapters include specific examples of the kinds of images that fleshed out parents' preferences. My purpose here is to introduce and outline the concept of gendered anticipation. For example, in explaining the preference for sons, fathers tended to stress three themes, the most common of which was patriarchal tradition, particularly the continuation of the family name. Almost equally frequent were references to traditionally masculine activities that men look forward to sharing with a son such as sports, roughhousing, hunting, fishing, and camping. The third common theme was the belief that the preference for a son expresses something essential to manhood. As one father noted, "Well, sort of you want to have your own kind, to have experiences with him as a man, I guess." In all three themes, the preference for a son is shaped by gender-linked assumptions about the future child's attributes, interests, and behaviors, as well as by gender-linked images of the relationship between fathers and sons.[3] In effect, even before the child is present in their everyday lives these fathers are constructing a gendered person, falling into the gender trap as they begin to build the foundation of gendered interests and tendencies they expect their child to have.

The two most common reasons for mothers preferring a son mirrored those offered by men: patriarchal tradition and references to sports and other stereotypically masculine activities. Heterosexual women usually imagined a son sharing masculine activities with his father, though some talked about their own involvement in these imagined activities based on their "tomboy" status as children. Mothers who preferred daughters most often mentioned one or more of three themes: the anticipated close emotional relationships; shopping and talking with daughters; and objects such as dolls, clothes, and accessories associated with female children. One mother referred, poignantly, to a daughter as a soul mate, "I always wanted a daughter. . . . I wanted a soul mate, someone who would grow up with me over the years and do things with me." Although the particular themes differ from those that men invoked in relation to sons, these women's same-gender preferences also reveal the anticipatory construction of gender based on the activities and kind of relationship they expect to have with their daughter.

The near uniformity with which parents drew on a limited and traditional set of assumptions suggests the degree to which their individually held images are interactionally and institutionally shaped within the context of the contemporary United States. But as they draw on those socially enforced images, they also reproduce and reinforce them, expecting strongly gendered children and revealing the potential gender trap awaiting those children. These parents also envision themselves engaged in traditionally gendered interactions with their children: mothers and daughters shopping and talking, fathers and sons playing ball or roughhousing. West and Zimmerman's "doing gender" approach, discussed in the introduction, highlights the importance of interactions as an arena in which gender is produced and reproduced.[4] They argue that "gender is not simply an aspect of what one is, but more fundamentally, what one *does*, and does recurrently, in interaction with others." The repeated "doing" constructs and reinforces the presumed essential nature of gender. As Fenstermaker, West, and Zimmerman assert, "social arrangements daily provide for the reproduction of a framework of accountability that casts gender as an essential feature of the individual's very being."[5] In other words, as we engage in daily interactions determined in part by institutional forces, including gender structures, we legitimate and reinforce the assumption that our actions are dictated by an essential part of our "very being." We are held accountable to the assumption that we will conduct ourselves in conventionally gendered ways, and this assumption often *produces* the very outcome it appears only to reflect.

Pre-birth or pre-adoption gendered anticipation contributes to parents' motivation to reinforce gender for newly arrived children, whether in the assumptions they make about the desired son or daughter, or the implied inverse assumptions they might make about a child of the other gender. A wide variety of parents expressed a strong investment in gendered children, imagining that male children would be very different from female children. Though such expectations will not always be realized, there is clearly potential for this gendered anticipation to become a trap that parents may not even realize they are falling into.[6] The ubiquity of these traditional images may nudge parents to unintentionally reproduce them. Given the range of both subtle and overt parental gendering practices that have been documented in the literature and were discussed in the introduction, gendered anticipation provides a firm foundation for the social construction of gender.

30

This construction process has broad implications. Through their gendered anticipation, parents reproduce a framework of accountability to gendered expectations that casts its net beyond their individual children and households. Even if they eventually go on to resist gender-typical patterns, their gendered anticipation contributes to the context for the judgments, or accountability, that were pointed out in the introductory chapter, that is, the expectations about boys, girls, mothers, and fathers that constrain and even trap not just their own families but people in general. For example, in the simple assumption that a son is "just a normal thing for a guy to want," fathers reinforce other men's accountability to an essentialized masculinity, just as the assumption that their sons will enjoy sports reinforces the normativity of a particular kind of boyhood masculinity. For the boys who do not enjoy sports or a "natural" masculine relationship with their fathers, and the girls who do not enjoy shopping, talking, and a close emotional relationship with their mothers, it is easy to imagine judgments that are reinforced through the reproduction of the presumed essential nature of various gendered tendencies. Although gendered anticipation does not strictly determine the interactions parents eventually have with their children, nor do those interactions strictly determine the gendered outcomes for those children, such anticipation contributes to a framework of accountability that shapes the context for these parents, their children, and society more broadly, strengthening the childhood gender trap even before children arrive.

Hardwiring and Social Influence: Beliefs about the Origins of Gendered Childhoods

Interpretations of the origins of gendered childhoods are another key building block in my analysis. My original expectation was that many parents would believe that gendered outcomes were determined mainly by biology. Most did offer biologically based explanations, but significant support was expressed for the interpretation that social forces are, at least, partially responsible. Overall, the more my interviewees endorsed one type of explanation, the less they endorsed the other, but the majority, in any case, held some belief in both simultaneously.

"He Just Instinctively Knew What to Do": Biological Determinism

Over time, although the specifics have shifted, biological justifications for gender inequality have remained evident.[7] Traditional theories about women's delicacy and emotional nature have been used to justify their limited access to politics and the formal economy, but these biologically based notions left huge loopholes for women subordinated by racial and class inequality to perform physically arduous labor, whereas their white, middle- and upper-class peers were cast as domestic creatures unable to withstand the burdens of higher education, paid employment, or political participation. Brain size, the effects of menstruation on the ability to reason effectively, and nurturing instincts were also argued to disadvantage women relative to men in endeavors requiring intellect, rational calculation, and competitive energy. More recently, however, research on gender differences has focused on the brain and hormones, with studies documenting enormous variation *among* males and females and revealing only modest differences between the sexes.

Presumed biological differences between the sexes mask the tremendous individual variation among people, constrain our options, render gendered patterns inevitable, and legitimate the use of gender to allocate opportunities and resources—all of which help reproduce the gender trap and bolster unequal gender structures. A review of debates over the influence of biological differences is beyond the scope of this book, but, as noted in the introduction, many scholars have shown that these influences have been greatly exaggerated in terms of their size, scope, and, especially, their social implications. The more significant issue, then, is how beliefs about sex differences that permeate the daily lives of parents and children affect parents as they attempt to guide their children's behavior. Given the long history of biological determinism in justifying gender inequality and discouraging social change, it is important to consider how parents invoke nature or biology and the implications those invocations might have for reinforcing the gender trap.

Scant empirical literature directly addresses parental explanations for the origin of gender variations among children. One noteworthy study, more than two decades old, is psychologist John Antill's quantitative analysis of parental beliefs about gender differences.[8] About one-third of the nearly two hundred Australian parents in this study considered biological factors the main cause of differences between boys and girls, and about 70 percent considered biological factors at least somewhat important. A decade later, legal scholar Deborah Rhode argued that many parents and other adults find it easier to view gendered childhoods as a natural phenomenon. Commenting on the gender-typed identities and behaviors often seen among young children, Rhode claimed,

> Most adults deny they are responsible. Frustrated parents, beleaguered teachers, and defensive media representatives are sure that the basic causes of sex stereotyping are beyond their control. This perception is part of what makes biological explanations so attractive, however wobbly their foundations. If there is, after all, some "doll gene" that explains toy preferences, this would let folks off the hook.[9]

My interview data, however, provide a different, more focused approach to explore whether and how parents read their children's interests, tendencies, and preferences as biologically determined. For example, Lori, a twenty-nine-year-old homemaker and parent of two children, is a white, middle-class, heterosexually partnered mother who described her three-year-old daughter's interests as natural: "Dolls, that's just what she gravitated towards, you know, and I think it's kind of built into her, you know, a predisposition to play with dolls and stuff like that." On the other side of the coin, Maurice, a thirty-eight-year-old father of three in a gay partnership, contrasted his four-year-old son's energy and messy outdoor play to his two daughters' more sedate behavior. This white, upper-middle-class hospital administrator noted that his son was surrounded by his sisters' "lipstick, dresses, shoes, necklaces. . . . My girls would just love that stuff, but he was quite the contrary, his drive was more on the boyish side. And where that comes from, I really think it's hard-wired. If there's a puddle in the driveway, he's in it." About three-fourths of the interviewed parents offered at least one similar claim that gendered interests are "built in," a proportion close to that noted by Antill.

When parents invoked the biology explanation in relation to girls, most commonly mentioned was the tendency to be quiet, calm, pleasant, nurturing, or maternal. The most commonly noted activity seen as natural for girls was playing with dolls, often linked explicitly to maternal nurturance. Biologically inflected responses about boys were more frequent and expansive, including comments such as "he came out knowing he was a boy" or "he has seemed to have been a boy right from the start." Boys were associated with a broader set of attributes, activities, and interests compared to girls, frequently including aggression, a higher activity level, and strength. The activities or interests brought up most often as natural inclinations for boys were sports and outdoor play, vehicles, building, and construction toys.[10]

Variations also were evident in the way parents *articulated* biological explanations. Each articulation is discussed more fully later on but only briefly noted here. The most common were references to gendered patterns as "built in," "biologically programmed," or "part of what is in us." Sometimes parents added more detail, including factors such as anatomy, hormones, or brain physiology. In some cases, these descriptive articulations were expanded further to specify that the parents perceived a *broader intention or purpose* in the biological differences in terms of nature, evolution, or God. Another articulation of biological determinism that arose with some frequency could be called "biology as fallback." About half the parents who offered any biological explanation explicitly noted that they wanted to discourage gender-typed attributes and interests, but then read the eventual emergence of gender-typing as evidence that biology must be responsible. An example is Bruce, who, in the introduction, described his son's lack of interest in his older sister's toys: "To even see it and for it to be quite prevalent and to not be interested in it, . . . I think that in a large way is innate." In an analysis of his own children's preschool soccer program, sociologist Michael Messner vividly describes the parade floats and chants devised by single-gender teams who dubbed themselves the "Barbie Girls" and the "Sea Monsters."[11] He observes that many parents he heard chatting on the sidelines interpreted the gendered patterns exhibited by these young children as natural and inevitable. He goes on to argue that, "lacking an analysis of structural and cultural context, performances of gender can all too easily be interpreted as free agents acting out the inevitable surface manifestations of a natural inner essence of sex differences."[12] Messner believes that these parents fail to notice the range of social forces shaping their children's behavior, and so they fall back on innate differences as the only remaining explanation for such markedly gendered patterns. This same analysis comes to mind immediately when considering the responses I coded into this fallback category.

All three of these articulations of biological determinism imply inevitability, as they are based on the general belief that at least some gender differences are innate or the more elaborated belief that such natural differences exist for a divine or evolutionary purpose. When parents believe that a nurturing, quiet, and calm demeanor is natural for girls, whereas boys are naturally aggressive, highly active, and stronger, the gender trap is reinforced and reproduced by bolstering biologically determinist ideologies that have historically legitimized gender inequality. Reducing gendered constraints on children requires us to question the notion that gender differences are natural and inevitable, and to recognize their complex social origins.

"A Lot of It's Shoved Down Their Throats": Social Constructionism

A considerable literature has addressed the social determinants of gendered childhoods, but only scant attention has been paid to whether parents endorse social determinism as they seek to explain gender variations among children. Antill's quantitative analysis, documenting that 70 percent of parents consider biological factors at least somewhat important, also indicated that nearly 90 percent felt that upbringing was also, at least, somewhat important, with 30 percent viewing upbringing as the primary explanation.[13] Among Antill's study participants social factors were considered especially relevant for explaining children's gendered interests and activities. But little research has addressed either the basis of parental views of how gendered behavior develops or Messner's observation that many parents "lack a social and cultural context," thus underscoring the importance of exploring how and why parents recognize social influences.[14] Consistent with Antill's results, but delving deeper with qualitative interview evidence, the vast majority of my interviewees expressed at least a limited degree of support for social explanations. Far from a chorus of biological determinism drowning out other interpretations, parents exhibited considerable recognition that social forces played some role in shaping gendered childhoods. Sometimes this was a relatively forceful and expansive claim, as illustrated by the case of Eric, a thirty-nine-year-old, white construction worker who identifies as working class and is a heterosexually partnered father of a five-year-old son and an infant daughter. After describing his son's traditionally boyish interests, he was emphatic in responding to my follow-up question about the origins of those tendencies: "A lot of it's shoved down their throats, you know, from the get-go. . . . We shouldn't jump down their throat and say, 'Hey, that's girl stuff or boy stuff,' whatever, but as a society we really do." Others invoked social sources for gendered patterns more casually, with less concern or criticism, as with Jennifer, a forty-one-year-old electrical engineer. She is Asian American, upper middle class, and heterosexually partnered, the mother of three daughters ranging in age from four to twelve. When asked to speculate why her four-year-old was interested in Barbie dolls, clothes, and makeup, she cited older siblings, peers, and media.[15] She noted, "Well, she watches those shows on Disney, those movies about girls and stuff. And since the older girls, her sisters, play with Barbies, she plays with Barbies. . . . I think it's what they see on TV, too, and what their friends have."

To varying degrees, and with varying intensity, Jennifer and Eric typify the range of parental responses invoking social forces as shaping gendered outcomes. They turn not to nature but to social processes to explain gendered interests. All but two of the interviewed parents offered at least one such response, with equal frequency for both boys and girls, while biological explanations were heard more often for boys. Among the socially determinist responses, the most frequently mentioned characteristic for girls involved different degrees of passivity, including adjectives such as "quiet" but also more negatively tinged words including "passive," "docile," and even "submissive." Biological invocations of quiet and calm were often complimentary, referring to girls as focused and cooperative, but the social explanations tended to suggest that society imposed problematic limitations on girls. Perhaps on the borderline between an attribute and an interest, the second most common comment was the social expectation that girls had to be pretty. Women were more likely than men to mention this expectation. The characteristic of prettiness is the end product of many interrelated activities that were, along with doll play, the interests most often mentioned as socially encouraged in girls: clothing, jewelry, and makeup, as well as shopping for all these items. When social determinism emerged to explain interests that parents considered typical of boys, it was most often associated with sports and vehicles, two of the same interests noted as having biological origins, as well as playing with weapons. For girls, references to activities and interests outnumbered the references to attributes or characteristics among the socially determinist responses; two frequently mentioned characteristics about boys clustered around aggression or toughness and activity or noise. These attributes and interests among boys closely parallel those that were linked to biology, although, like quiet and passivity in girls, parents more often pitched the references as negative attributes when associating them with social causes.

The articulations of biological determinism indicate a range of potential contributors to the gender trap, in that such explanations treat gendered outcomes as somewhat inevitable. In contrast, socially determinist beliefs imply possibilities for change, as these approaches view gendered outcomes as socially constructed and thus potentially avoidable. The social sources parents identified tended to be either "interactional" or "institutional." The most commonly cited were interactional sources, specific individuals or groups with whom children interact directly. This included children's friends, day care or school peers, child care providers, siblings, parents, grandparents, and other relatives. Along with these proximate interactional influences, some parents spoke about wider networks of institutional-level social forces including mass media, advertising, television, books, and movies. The other major institutional category was general references to society, where parents did not specify individual social actors, even strangers, but identified a broad social aggregate. If one wanted to shift gendered patterns, the task would be different if the target, say, was just a grandfather or an aunt rather than society as a whole.

37

Interactional sources often came up in a neutral way, such as, for example, the mother who explained her daughter's interest in dolls by casually noting, "I think that came a lot from her friends that she met at school." Institutional sources, however, were more often described critically, as in Eric's concern that "as a society" we tend to "shove" traditionally gendered patterns "down [children's] throats." Moreover, although interviewees usually simply described interactional or institutional forces, others stated or implied *why* they thought this social construction occurs. Explanations linked to interactional sources focused most often on tradition or history, whereas those linked to institutional forces centered largely on power. As discussed in the introduction, many sociologists of gender view gendered structures not just as socially constructed but as sources of power. Instead of emphasizing differences between males and females, a focus on power draws attention a step further to inequalities between the sexes, or the ways in which gender categories are used as a justification for the uneven distribution of power and social resources.

Just as inevitability is implicit in biological narratives about gender, socially determinist beliefs allow us to sidestep the gender trap by helping us recognize that gendered patterns are not immutable. This foundational sketch of parental beliefs documents that neither nature nor nurture dominates how the parents interviewed for this book understand the gendered patterns they notice among their children. While individual parents vary in the extent to which they lean toward biology or society as explanations, most parents engage in a balancing act encompassing both.

Doing and Undoing Gender: Parents' Actions in Relation to Children's Gender

The parents interviewed reported a range of actions that reproduced or resisted gendered outcomes for their children, and these comprise another building block for defining the five configurations that I discuss beginning in the next chapter. Most parents reported at least some actions reproducing and some resisting the gender trap, and the balance between these opposing actions is the focus of the remainder of this book.

"Yeah, We've Been Socializing Them That Way": Parents Doing Gender

Gwen began shopping for her five-year-old daughter before the child was born. A forty-two-year-old, white, upper-middle-class executive and hetero-sexually partnered mother of one, she learned she would have a daughter from a routine amniocentesis. Well before the birth, she reported, "I bought her some cute little outfits, girl outfits, like dresses and little pretty bonnets. And her Daddy went and bought a really cute pink outfit with roses and lacey ruffles." Although all the interviewees reported at least one example of acting to reproduce traditionally gendered outcomes in their children, for some, like Gwen, those direct actions began during pregnancy or an adoption or foster care waiting period.[16] Routine gendering activity carried on into early infancy as well, with many parents dressing their baby with an eye to gender and enjoying the process. Others talked about dressing their infant in response to the expectations of others. "People were like, 'Oh, you've got a cute little boy there," noted one father who had not dressed his infant daughter in a pointedly feminine way. He went on to say, "Then we made a conscious ef-fort to dress her in a certain way, so they knew she was a girl, we definitely picked up on that fact." Such comments were usually made with reference to daughters, conveying a sense that the default interpretation of strangers was that a baby was a boy unless clearly marked as a girl. This pattern is consis-tent with the general argument in feminist scholarship that the default hu-man being is often conceptualized as male.[17] In the less frequent instances where a parent told a similar story about a son, the parents' response was more distressed, suggesting the asymmetry in the social costs of crossing gender lines that arose often throughout my interviews. Tanya's recounting in the introduction of the pink sleeper incident was infused with this kind of anxiety, as she described being "furious" with her partner for dressing their son in pink in front of her teenage brother and his friends. These perhaps seemingly harmless decisions about infant clothing are directly linked to the gender trap. They are the first steps in a long and complex process of crafting a child's gender, a process that magnifies differences between boys and girls, and reinforces attributes, interests, and tendencies that reproduce structures of gendered power in families, education, the workplace, politics, and other social arenas.

Parental actions that reproduce gendered outcomes can be classified basically as those that encourage or allow traditionally gendered tendencies and those that discourage or even attempt to forbid gender-atypical tendencies. When parents reported accomplishing or "doing" gender with and for their young daughters, the vast majority of their actions encouraged or allowed gender-typical outcomes. This probably reflects the high social value of masculinity, for even though many parents accept some typically feminine outcomes, they do not discourage their daughters from also exploring typically masculine activities and attributes. When parents spoke about actions which I coded as gendering their daughters, some reference was made to actions encouraging attributes considered typical for girls: kindness, nurturance, neatness, and a calm demeanor. But many more parents reported actions linked to clothing, toys, and activities rather than personal characteristics. The attributes, interests, and tendencies parents reported cultivating in boys differed from those for girls in that more gendering actions were reported for boys, especially by fathers. Relative to girls, about three times as many of these actions involved discouraging gender nonconformity rather than only encouraging conformity. In addition, personal attributes comprised a more substantial portion of parental reports, with parents of sons encouraging traits they considered gender typical such as independence, toughness, and chivalrous orientation toward girls and women, as well as discouraging excessive emotional expression (especially frequent crying) and passivity. Clothing, toys, and interests came up frequently as well, with almost all parents who have at least one son mentioning some action to encourage or allow gender-typical outcomes in this domain. Many parents also expressed negative responses to parallel items or activities more commonly associated with girls. Parents, therefore, not only fall into the gender trap by nudging their sons toward traditionally masculine tendencies but also by turning them away from traditionally feminine ones. This negative variation of doing gender coalesced around what I term "icons of femininity" such as dolls, makeup, and the color pink. About two of every three parents who have sons mentioned at least one negative action in relation to such an icon.[18]

Another gender-related outcome that emerged in the interviews was that, through various routine, daily actions, many parents reproduced what social scientists call "heteronormativity": the deeply entrenched assumption that people should and can be divided into two distinct sex categories on which basis they are, or in the case of small children eventually will be, attracted to members of the other sex as heterosexuals. Psychologist Cecilia Kitzinger, who studied how heteronormativity is fortified through everyday conversation, concluded that "the persistent and untroubled reproduction of a taken-for-granted heteronormative world both reflects heterosexual privilege and (by extrapolation) perpetuates the oppression of non-heterosexual people."[19] The significance of heteronormativity has been the subject of decades of feminist scholarship, demonstrating that heteronormativity not only reinforces the power of heterosexuals but also reproduces gender categories and gendered power. Heteronormativity is not just about sexual orientation, it also very much concerns dichotomous and traditionally defined gender categories. Anthropologist Gayle Rubin, in her classic 1975 essay "The Traffic in Women," argued that enforced heterosexuality was a pivotal part of the "sex/gender system," reproducing and reinforcing the socially constructed categories of men and women and the power of men over women.[20] Poet and essayist Adrienne Rich's 1980 article, "Compulsory Heterosexuality and Lesbian Existence," was another particularly influential early exposition further establishing that compulsory heterosexuality is a central practice in the construction and maintenance of gender inequality. Rich contended that an array of social forces, from routine to violent, compel women into heterosexuality, which ties them to male partners and discourages resistance to gender inequality, thereby reproducing gendered power.[21] More recent analysts have elaborated on these founding claims, exploring with an explicitly intersectional approach how heteronormativity is intertwined with various systems of power but also further reinforcing its role in the routine reproduction of gendered structures of power.[22]

Scholars of gender and sexuality who study parenting have documented that parental presumptions of their children's heterosexuality is one way in which parents bolster heteronormativity.[23] More than half the parents interviewed for this book, all of them heterosexual, offered casual comments reinforcing heteronormativity by assuming their child's eventual heterosexual orientation. Parents spoke of their preschool daughter's "boyfriends" or son's "girlfriends," noting "little crushes" on children of the other gender, commenting on their hopes and concerns for the heterosexual dating and marriage they assumed would be in their child's future. These casual comments were made equally often about daughters and sons but, for sons, the positive reinforcement of heterosexuality was coupled with negative references to homosexuality, with about one in four heterosexual parents of sons expressing some negative observation about the potential for their son to be, or be perceived as, gay. My interview schedule did not include questioning about sexual orientation, so these observations were spontaneous rather than prompted. The assumed normality of strict gender divisions and heterosexuality plays a central role in the social construction of gender. So, too, does homophobia. It is telling, however, and consistent with the scholarly literature, that homophobia was evident only in conversations about sons, whereas heteronormativity was equally prevalent whether parents spoke about sons or daughters.

In pioneering and widely influential scholarship on masculinity, sociologist R. W. Connell has argued persuasively that "the explanation for Western culture's homophobia is complex, but part of it must be the degree to which the fact of homosexuality threatens the credibility of a naturalized ideology of gender and a dichotomized sexual world."[24] Like many scholars who have demonstrated that gender nonconformity is linked with presumed sexual orientation more for males than females, parents who expressed concern about homosexuality generally did so for sons.[25] The behavior that parents encouraged or discouraged in their sons fits well with what Connell dubs "hegemonic masculinity": "at any given time, one form of masculinity rather than others is culturally exalted."[26] This specific form of culturally exalted masculinity varies somewhat from place to place. Messner applies this general claim to the example of class- and race-based masculinities in the contemporary United States. He contends that class-advantaged white men's masculinity has, in the last two decades, become increasingly "sensitive and compassionate," but only to the extent that it still encompasses "toughness, decisiveness, and hardness."[27] Emphasizing historic and local variability, Connell's approach and Messner's specific application resonate with West and Zimmerman's description of the normative conceptions of gender to which people are held accountable in their interactions.[28] West and Zimmerman are not claiming that normative conceptions are static or universal but that, in any given time and place, they powerfully shape interactional accountability. The kind of hegemonic masculinity Connell and others articulate exemplifies the locally specific conception of gender that West and Zimmerman write about and against which people's everyday actions are judged.

Connell identified several features of hegemonic masculinity in contemporary Western society including aggression, limited emotionality, and heterosexuality.[29] Messner's work also explored the central role of athletic prowess in this dominant definition of masculinity.[30] Connell and other scholars interested in the social construction of masculinity emphasized its relational meaning: "'masculinity' does not exist except in contrast with 'femininity.'"[31] As Kimmel notes, the "notion of anti-femininity lies at the heart of contemporary and historical constructions of manhood, so that masculinity is defined more by what one is not rather than who one is."[32] Passivity and excessive emotionality, as well as iconically feminine material adornments, are precisely the kinds of features shunned in this hegemonic version of masculinity. Connell and Kimmel also view homophobia as central to this rejection of femininity. Connell states this bluntly: "The most important feature of contemporary hegemonic masculinity is that it is heterosexual. . . . Contempt for homosexuality and homosexual men . . . is part of the ideological package of hegemonic masculinity."[33] Even though no individual fully achieves the standard defined by hegemonic masculinity, it becomes a yardstick by which masculine gender performance is evaluated, a measure that was clearly familiar to many parents I interviewed. As they sought to craft toughness, athleticism, and distance from anything feminine for their sons, and reinforced heteronormativity along the way, such parents were responding to a standard remarkably consistent with Connell's formulation of hegemonic masculinity.

Besides the positive crafting of gender conformity and negative crafting in response to gender nonconformity, another key distinction arising from the interviews was the indirect actions parents take by tolerating or allowing gendered patterns originating outside their actions versus direct actions originated by parents themselves. Indirect gendering basically involves following the lead of the child or others who are encouraging the child, and it was more often reported in relation to daughters, especially by mothers. Like Jennifer, who mentioned the role of older sisters and friends in shaping her preschool daughter's desire for Barbies, these parents are allowing, rather than actively originating, gendered outcomes. Most parents also reported that they originated direct actions to reproduce gendered patterns for their children, more often in relation to sons, primarily because fathers were more likely to make such reports. When fathers reported direct action discouraging behavior they consider atypical in a son, they also tended to do so in a more emphatic manner compared to mothers. Half the fathers of sons, but only about one in ten mothers of sons, reported, categorically, that they answered no to requests from their sons for items such as Barbie dolls, tea sets, nail polish, or ballet lessons.

When asked why they engage in gender-crafting actions, many parents said that they were motivated by personal preference. Both mothers and fathers had certain preferences for sons and daughters, but mothers were especially likely to have such preferences for their daughters and fathers especially likely to have them for their sons. The positive version of these links between personal preference and gender-typical outcomes remind me of anticipatory gendering, creating opportunities for gendered interactions that parents had envisioned with pleasure. But personal preference also shaped action in the opposite direction, particularly regarding sons, most often when heterosexual fathers emphasized personal discomfort, including homophobia, to explain why they encourage their sons to avoid icons of femininity or any hint of non-heterosexual orientation.

"Following the child's lead" was another commonly noted rationale for indirectly crafting gender. At times it was combined with the recognition that outside forces shape the child's preference, and at times parents simply noted that they like to allow their child to choose his or her own activities and interests. Some parents felt neutral or positive about acting in accordance with their child's gender-typical desire, and others offered more frustrated versions of the "following the lead" motivation. Miriam, a thirty-four-year-old, upper-middle-class, stay-at-home parent of four commented that she did not want to buy her daughter "girl stuff." But this white, heterosexually partnered mother concluded that "all the little girls had that kind of stuff, . . .

so [my daughter] wanted it, and how could I avoid it even if I tried, and how could they either?" This version of indirect gendering action was driven more by social forces external to the parent, child, and household that parents saw as problematic but too strong to completely resist. In this example, Miriam invokes her daughter's agency in the desire for "girl stuff." But she also flags the social pressures that shape both her child's desires and the options available for her response as a parent, highlighting a tension between agency and social constraint for both mother and daughter, a tension that at least in this instance leads directly into the gender trap.

Moving on from personal preference or following the child's lead, the final major category of parental motivation is accountability to others, including peers, family members, and others in general. About two out of three parents mentioned accountability to others as the motivation for at least one gendering action. Fenstermaker, West, and Zimmerman argue that gender is something that people "do" in everyday interaction, and this doing is subject to the judgment of others. As West and Zimmerman put it, in introducing their "doing gender" approach, "If we do gender appropriately, we simultaneously sustain, reproduce, and render legitimate institutional arrangements. . . . If we fail to do gender appropriately, we as individuals—not the institutional arrangements—may be called to account."[34] Many parents recognized the risk of being "called to account." When the interviewed parents brought up accountability as a motivation for reproducing typically gendered outcomes, their stories varied according to the child's gender. Regarding daughters, they spoke primarily about clothing, usually without strong concern but with clear awareness of the judgments of others. Regarding sons, actual or potential accountability was mentioned twice as frequently and carried notably more emotional intensity and most often concerned behavior, attributes, or activities. Many used dramatic language to express their fear or anxiety, citing the risk that a son would be "picked on," "roughed up," "ostracized," or become "an outcast" if he did not conform to social expectations for boys.

The Implications of Parents Doing Gender

The range of actions previewed here illustrates how parents can play a role in magnifying differences between boys and girls, and become caught in as well as reinforce the gender trap by contributing to the construction of two categories of people, more distinct and internally homogeneous than they would otherwise be. The specific attributes, interests, and tendencies that differentiate those categories have broad consequences. Regarding boys, actions that craft greater physical activity, competitive orientation, independence, and facility with toys relevant to science and engineering potentially reproduce gendered power in the workplace and politics; for girls, encouraging nurturance, domesticity, and interpersonal skills potentially reinforces gendered divisions of labor in the family and workplace, directing girls toward what scholars of gender, work, and family call "carework," which influences women's options in the labor market and their power and responsibilities in the home.[35] The devaluation of femininity, evidenced by the greater negative response to atypical behavior from sons than from daughters, also facilitates the reproduction of gendered power by reinforcing the lower prestige of pursuits socially marked as feminine.[36] Feminist critics, moreover, have long argued that the excessive focus on women's appearance presents obstacles to self-esteem and achievement in other arenas, making women more vulnerable in various ways.[37] The routine reinforcement of heteronormativity also has important implications for gendered power, given the role that heterosexuality as a social structure plays in differentiating and stratifying men and women.

These potential consequences are visible through the lens of gender, but consideration also should be given to intersectionality. As Connell articulates, hegemonic masculinity subordinates not just femininities but other masculinities as well, marginalizing boys and men who fail to approximate hegemonic masculinity in ways that bolster not just gendered power but intersecting dimensions of power based on race, class, and sexual orientation.[38] At the same time, theorists of masculinity explain that certain costs are associated with the benefits that men, especially those advantaged by inequalities of race, class, and sexual orientation, derive from these intersecting inequalities. Adherence to hegemonic masculinity requires boys and men to suppress their emotions, minimize the depth of their social support and connection, and limit their interests and characteristics, thus restricting the free range of human capacities.

"We're Trying to Let It Be Open": Parents Undoing Gender

In her 2007 article "Undoing Gender," psychologist Francine Deutsch urges more attention to the potential for deconstructing gender through everyday interaction. She argues that scholars working with the "doing gender" approach too often focus on how gender is reproduced, although the approach is equally relevant to considering resistance: "My plea is that we shift our inquiry about ongoing social interactions to focus on change."[39] Risman builds on this argument, and her own previous work, to remind us that "gender structure is not static," and therefore exclusive focus on gender reproduction "leads us to a blind intellectual alley."[40] These recent rallying cries resonate well with what parents told me. Nearly all interviewees mentioned one or more actions they have taken that resist or challenge what they consider traditional gender expectations for children. The specific practices parents used to balance reproduction and resistance are discussed in the upcoming chapters, but here I sketch the outlines of the broad array of those resistant actions.

In some instances, resistant action took the form of "gender neutrality," a purposeful focus on treating sons and daughters in the same way.[41] Miriam offers an example in her approach to toys: "I only ever bought the kids unisex toys: alphabet toys, animal toys, there are virtually no dolls and no trucks." In other instances, parents focused on counteracting a more specific gendered constraint from which they hoped to free their child. Anthony, a white, working-class, heterosexually partnered father of three, for example, talked about his efforts to discourage gendered patterns for his five-year-old son. "Actually, we went out and we bought . . . Nathaniel a little doll. . . . My grandmother had a hissy-fit that we bought my son that doll for Christmas and put it in his stocking." Whether couched in terms of treating all children in the same way or of encouraging them to cross gender boundaries in their activities, mothers and fathers reported actions to undo gender with similar frequency for both sons and daughters. Differences were also evident, however, depending on parent and child genders. Parents, especially mothers, expressed greater enthusiasm for undoing gender in daughters, and fathers, in particular, expressed greater caution and more caveats regarding sons.

Some parents allowed their sons to experiment with, or participate in, iconically feminine activities such as trying on makeup or nail polish, wearing pink, or having a Barbie doll. But these were generally expressions of muted tolerance of their sons' interest in feminine icons, whereas other pursuits considered unusual for boys garnered more encouragement. Two-thirds of the parents with at least one son reported actions that crafted domestic skills, nurturance, or empathy. They allowed or more actively promoted traditionally feminine toys such as baby dolls, doll houses, and kitchen centers to encourage domestic competence, nurturance, emotional openness, concern for others, and nonviolence. Those attributes are consistent with Messner's claim that sensitivity and compassion are increasingly acceptable within hegemonic masculinity.[42]

The specifics of parents' resistance varied for sons and daughters. For instance, about twice as many parents spoke of girls' clothes, often in relation to concern that typical girl clothing could restrict their daughter's activity level. Occupations or careers were mentioned three times as often in relation to daughters, with parents specifically discussing activities to help their girls develop aspirations that include traditionally male-dominated jobs.[43] Some parents linked this broad horizon for daughters with emphasis on independence, including the desire for their daughters to be able to support themselves financially. Parents spoke of dressing daughters in sports-themed clothing, as well as buying them toy cars, trucks, trains, and science or building toys. Some described their efforts to promote, and their pleased reactions to, what they considered traditionally male activities such as t-ball, football, basketball, fishing, outdoor play, martial arts, and learning to use tools. Several commented favorably on their daughters as "tomboyish," "rough and tumble," and "competitive athletically."

Similar to the parental actions that reproduce gender more traditionally, the resistance that parents described included both indirect and direct actions. Some let their children "do whatever they want," even when it included gender atypical desires, allowing their child, in effect, to cross gender boundaries when the child chooses to do so and thereby indirectly expanding their son's or daughter's range of play. Both mothers and fathers offered this kind of response about daughters and sons; mothers, however, mentioned almost twice as many instances, and both mothers and fathers mentioned twice as many instances about boys. The latter pattern can be understood in light of the devaluation of femininity and the greater social costs for boys who cross gender divides. Both factors leave parents cautious about encouraging atypical outcomes for sons, but many are still willing to at least allow atypical pursuits that originate with the child.

Overall, indirect actions constituted less than one-third of the parental actions I coded as resisting gendered outcomes in childhood. This ratio may reflect the power of the gender trap at both the interactional and institutional levels, especially as social forces discourage children from originating gender-atypical pursuits as often as they originate typical ones. More common were direct actions, but the level of enthusiasm about undoing gender also varied, with mothers especially likely to report action with explicitly positive overtones. Fathers echoed such comments, though in smaller numbers compared to women, and those who did were predominantly men with only daughters. Fathers with no sons comprised about one-fifth of the fathers interviewed, but they accounted for two-thirds of the paternal reports of direct gender-undoing actions for daughters.[44]

Some fathers were emphatic about encouraging the kind of domestic skills, nurturance, and empathy that many parents considered atypical but positive for sons; mothers were even more likely than fathers to report this kind of direct resistance. Though many fathers reported actions they saw as counter to traditional gender expectations, they were more likely than mothers to express these actions with some caution or lack of enthusiasm. Caveats and limits emerged for sons, particularly when the outcomes involved not domestic skills and nurturance but icons of femininity. Pamela reports agreeing when her four-year-old son requested a Barbie doll, but she also noted that "we compromised, we got him NASCAR Barbie," referring to a Barbie doll that was dressed in a race car driver's jumpsuit and came with a stock car. Fathers talked about this kind of compromise, or other limitations, even more often. Some fathers, but no mothers, volunteered that they allow their sons to pursue toys or activities they consider unusual for a boy but that they would become concerned if that continued much past preschool age. Some heterosexual mothers who resisted gendered outcomes for sons did so only up to the point they believed would be acceptable to the boys' fathers.

The motivations parents offered for their actions help deepen our understanding of their choices and constraints as they navigate the gender trap. The motivations reflect both personal preferences and the wishes of the child. The two other motivations discussed in the previous section, inevitability and accountability, did not factor significantly into parents' explanations for their efforts to undo gender. This is not surprising, as the power of the gender trap made some parents feel pressured by inevitability or accountability, while only their own preferences, or their children's, would be likely to prompt them to avoid it.

Like a father who commented that he loved taking his daughter fishing, some parents explained their efforts to promote what they considered unusual gendered activity by referring to their own preferences. This kind of emotional response was about equally common for daughters and sons, and for mothers and fathers. Parents' enthusiasm for undoing gender, however, was greater regarding their daughters. Often overlapping with parents' personal preferences and beliefs are explanations based on following the child's preferences or contributing to the child's ultimate welfare. Miriam described how her four-year-old son refuses to go anywhere without his favorite stuffed animal, a manatee. She encourages his attachment, despite her sense that many would consider it atypical: "Really, why shouldn't he have what he likes?" Parents reported this kind of motivation even more often when talking about daughters, and mothers were especially likely to do so. One mother taught her elementary school age daughter basic home repair and plans to teach her basic auto maintenance when she is older, because she doesn't "want her to have to rely on a man" for such activities. Other parents linked this specifically to the belief that occupational knowledge is important for girls. References to the child's preferences based on individual rights are similar to those offered as explanations for reproducing gendered outcomes. Parents who encouraged, or at least tolerated, stereotypical interests, with phrases such as "we've just kind of given them the freedom to make those choices on their own," rely on an argument similar to Miriam's rhetorical question, "Why shouldn't he have what he likes?" But the focus on skill development, especially domestic skills and emotional capacity for boys and everyday maintenance and occupational skills for girls, is a distinct version of this motivation based on what the parent perceives to be the child's interests.

The Implications of Parents Undoing Gender

The parents interviewed for this book were not simply stepping into the gender trap but were also working to nudge and resist gender structures, thoughtfully considering the costs and benefits of that resistance for their children and themselves. Deutsch uses the following metaphor that refers to women who integrate traditionally male occupations and applies equally well to many of the interviewees who reported efforts to undo gender: they "may have to be mindful of how to negotiate gendered terrain, but at least they are on the hike."[45] Just as I have argued that reproductive actions have implications for gendered power, so, too, does resistance. By carving out "neutral" territory between the categories of "boy" and "girl," and allowing or encouraging cross-category outcomes, parents are "on the hike," chipping away at socially constructed gender categories, reducing their power as bounded, internally homogeneous determinants of behavior and attributes. The particular attributes and interests that parents identify are also important. In their efforts to discourage excessive emphasis on appearance, and to develop activity, competitiveness, independence, and knowledge of traditionally male domains such as science and construction for their daughters, parents clear some of the barriers to a greater range of adult opportunities for girls, particularly those often associated with higher pay and greater power in the workplace. At the intersection of workplace power and domestic power, those opportunities also have implications for women's power within heterosexual families and for their ability to support themselves in single-parent or lesbian households. At the same time, tolerating or promoting the development of domestic skills and emotional range in boys removes some obstacles to their options in the workplace and in families, as well as some of the limits to their expression of the wide assortment of human interests and capacities. The non-normative attributes and interests parents hope to cultivate, the way they try to do so, and the motivations they report indicate the potential for continued social change and outline some avenues for increasing the pace and scope of that change.

The hopes, beliefs, and resources that motivate and facilitate parental efforts to resist gender typing suggest openings for the further loosening of gendered constraints. The obstacles and limitations that impede such parental efforts highlight the need for collective action and institutional change.

Drawing on the building blocks introduced in this chapter—anticipation, beliefs about social and biological determinants, as well as actions and motivations—the next five chapters introduce case studies of the five types or configurations of parenting practice evident among the parents interviewed. Within the context of gendered forces at the individual, interactional, and institutional levels, these parents engage in a dynamic process of navigating tensions, a process that affects their children, themselves, and their larger communities and society, and helps us to better understand the prospects and hurdles associated with avoiding the gender trap.

TWO

"It's in Their Nature"

Naturalizers

Maya, a twenty-nine-year-old, low-income, African American mother raising her three children on her own, had scheduled our interview in the morning, before her office work shift began at noon and while her children were at a local day care center. We met in her small apartment, a tidy and well-organized space with a few toys neatly stowed in a bookcase in the sparsely furnished living room. Maya spoke in a quiet voice and seemed nervous initially. But she soon settled into a confident rhythm as she responded to my questions. At the time of the interview, I had not yet developed a specific analysis of how parents balance biological and social explanations of child behavior with reproductive and resistant actions as they navigate their children's gendered development. In retrospect, Maya's approach to balancing these tensions clearly illustrated what I came to view as the Naturalizer approach.

Maya: "It's The Way They Are Born"

Maya sees gendered outcomes as primarily natural and gender differentiation as a positive process. At the same time she reports various actions that reproduce and reinforce this differentiation for both her daughters and her son, who range from three years of age to five. Her position, then, is on the biologically determinist and gender reproductive ends of the belief and action tensions outlined in chapter 1. I expected that this would be the predominate pattern, the trend often assumed in the literature: parents reproducing through their actions what they perceive to be biological differences between their sons and daughters. Instead, however, only about one in five of the parents interviewed fell into this category, and even they added some socially constructionist beliefs and resistant actions, weaving these together with awareness of the social constraints surrounding themselves and their children.

This is the pattern evident in the way Maya is raising her five-year-old daughter, Keisha, the focal child of our interview, as well as her three-year-old twins Gina and Dwayne. Maya reported that her children's interests and attributes are sharply divided by gender. "They just seem so different. The girls just always want to be around me, the boy, my son, he just wants to be on his own." Early in her interview, Maya reported preferring a son for her first child for "traditional reasons." But she hoped to have daughters, too, as she believed they would stay closer to her in just the way she reports that her girls have done. When asked about the origins of her daughters' more sociable tendencies and her son's independence, Maya summarized her perspective in a phrase that captured what all Naturalizers believe: "I think it's just the way they are born, it's in their nature." She described Keisha's interests as typical for a girl:

> She likes dolls, she likes makeup, she likes girl things. She always goes to the girls' section at the store, she doesn't like the boys section. She never wants cars or anything, I think that's just, like I said, it's in her nature.

"I think girls are just much nicer than boys," she added with a chuckle. While Maya complimented her son's independence and intelligence, and clearly conveyed her respect and care for all three of her children, she was critical of what she saw as natural aggressive tendencies in boys, including her son.

> Boys are more aggressive and destructive. . . . It's a lot of work, and I think it's the way they are born. Boys are more difficult to raise. . . . You have to watch them more carefully. Girls will play quietly, boys

are always running around, if they aren't getting hurt, they are hurting somebody!

Like all Naturalizers, Maya combined this biologically determinist analysis with commentary on the social construction of gender, particularly noting peer influence as a source of some of her children's interests. For example, she mentioned that Keisha sometimes insists on buying or wearing clothes that she thinks will be accepted as gender appropriate by the other children at her preschool. By definition, biological explanations outweigh social ones in this group, and these parents are least likely to cite social sources. They are especially unlikely to mention institutional sources, such as media and society in general. Among the social forces I have described as interactional—parents, grandparents, other relatives, family friends, peers, and even strangers—peers are the only force that Naturalizers mention at about the same rate as parents in the other categories. They are also the group least likely to mention themselves as a source of gendering their children, even though they report many gendering actions. In Maya's case, as well as most others in this group, much of that gendering action is direct, and includes encouragement of typically gendered outcomes and discouragement of tendencies the parent views as atypical. For Keisha's interest in dolls and makeup, Maya provides what she can afford, viewing this as a matter of following her daughter's natural preferences, a behavior I have described as indirect gendering. But, like others in this group, she reports direct actions too.[1] She said of Keisha, "I wouldn't want her to be too boyish, because she's a girl, so I discourage that." In comparing how she treats Dwayne and Gina, she said, "I probably let [Dwayne] get away with more things. I set limits for both of them, but I let him get away with more." When I asked her to expand on why she does this, she added:

I want all of them to be responsible. But I would like the girls to be, I don't know how to say this, I mean, I want them to be more courteous to others, you know, like if somebody comes over, you say hello politely. Like I tell my older daughter, if she laughs too loud or yells, that's not the way girls are supposed to laugh or talk. She'll ask, "Is that okay for boys?" And I say, "Well, if boys do that, they can get away with it, but for girls, you know, they can't get away with it."

Despite the biological determinism underlying these responses, Maya also indicates her awareness of social rules that constrain behavior by gender. Dwayne, she told me, only likes traditionally masculine toys and activities, and she encourages this because she considers it natural. But when I asked how she would respond if he were to ask for toys or activities she considered more typical for girls, she focused on the *social* costs of nonconformity.

> If he's little and wanted a doll, that would be fine. But if he was 10 or something, I would be worried. But if he was little, I'd say okay, but I'd probably end up buying more cars for him, too, and just hope that he would be more interested in those.

> What, I asked, might happen if he didn't like cars more?

> I would worry if he had too many feminine characteristics. . . . I just want him to be a boy and play with the boys, not to like girl things. If he did that, the boys would think he's weird, and then he'd be lonely. . . . I would be worried about that, that he would be an outcast.

Here Maya indicates that her concern about the potential for an atypical interest extending into later childhood is not that it would somehow be unnatural but that the *social* costs to Dwayne would increase with age. This is a characteristic approach taken by Naturalizers. Maya falls into the gender trap by both encouraging gender-typical and discouraging gender-atypical outcomes. But in the foregoing quotes her emphasis is on discouraging atypical interests and tendencies. Encouraging gender typicality makes up the majority of the gendering action that parents spoke about. This is probably because so many social forces promote gendered outcomes that many parents do not face much atypical gender behavior to which they need to respond. The balance between these two types of action, however, differs for Naturalizers: the discouragement of atypicality makes up about twice the proportion of their overall reports of gendering action.[2] In crafting their children's gender performance, Naturalizers' motivations also differ. This group is most likely to report a personal preference for gender conformity and least likely to report such a preference for the attributes and interests which they think conflict with gender expectation. Unsurprisingly, doing gender with and for their children is partially motivated by their personal preference for gendered childhoods. Consider the remarks of Carole, for example, a thirty-two-year-old, white, middle-class, first-grade teacher in a heterosexual partnership who also falls into the Naturalizer category:

> My daughter [will] be a woman and whatever comes along with that she should be able to experience, and the same with my son. I think it's good to develop as a male and as a female and, you know, there are things that are good about being a male and things that are good about being a female. If you only stick in the middle, then you're missing out on the real highlights of each gender, that's why we have two genders.

Perhaps less predictable, Naturalizers are also one of the groups most likely to invoke concerns about accountability. An example is Maya's instruction to Keisha that girls "can't get away with" being too loud coupled with her worry that Dwayne would be "lonely" or "an outcast" if he failed to participate in traditionally boyish pursuits. These parents are second only to the group I call Resisters in the frequency with which they express fear or anxiety rather than just recognition regarding interactional accountability. Like the vast majority of parents who express that anxiety, it is more often in relation to boys, indicating their awareness of the pressures of hegemonic masculinity. When Christine's preschool-age son wanted to try on her makeup, she told him, "You need to know that people will look at you funny and you need to decide if that's important enough to you."

Maya generally supports all her children's gender traditional preferences for toys, clothing, and activities, and she encourages those outcomes. For her daughters, this includes providing dolls, dresses, and play makeup, as well as encouraging the kind of quiet, polite demeanor she considers natural in girls. Anna, a white, middle-class mother and Naturalizer, who wanted a daughter as a "soul mate," also commented on her two daughters' interest in dolls and quiet play. A stay-at-home parent who recently left her job as a pediatric nurse, this heterosexually partnered, thirty-four-year-old summarized her five-year-old daughter Kate's interests as follows:

> She loves to play with Barbies. She loves to play with dolls. She likes playing with her kitchen. I know boys are very rough in their play, and very loud and there's a difference when we get together with nephews and friends that have boys. She plays differently than them, the boys tend to be really rambunctious and loud and rough and that's not how Kate plays.

How, I asked, do you think these tendencies developed?

> I think that it's just part of the girl's makeup, she was born that way. I mean, I think it's boys and I think it's girls, I think we were meant to be different and I think it's just a part of them when they're born. I suppose some of it can be shaped, but I think for the most part it's just a part of them.

Just as Maya saw her daughters as naturally quieter, but still instructed Keisha not to be loud because girls "can't get away with that," Anna views Kate as naturally quiet and attracted to playing with dolls but also acts to shape those outcomes. At one point during our interview, Kate began to shake a large house plant, as part of a cheerful and active game she was enjoying in the background. Kate seemed content in her pastime, not seeking her mother's attention but just amusing herself. Still, she was harming the plant, and that caught her mother's eye. Anna's gentle admonition revealed her gendering action: "Oh, Kate, honey, please don't break my plant. Go get a doll and come sit with Mummy with your dolly. Go get your doll, angel, and please don't break my plant."[3]

Although Maya, Carole, and Anna encourage their children's gender-typical tendencies, they also want to be sure that their daughters are not limited in their aspirations. For example, Maya mentioned that Keisha "wants to be a firefighter or a policewoman," and she noted that her daughter "knows I say you can be whatever you want to be, she knows whatever she chooses to be is fine with me." Carole exposed her daughter to women's sports on television, and Anna is careful to point out female doctors to Kate. To the degree that Naturalizers resist traditional gender expectations for their daughters, it is primarily around access to sports and traditionally male occupations, not so much by pushing those pursuits as by making sure their daughters are aware of them and then letting them decide.

Maurice: "It's Hard-Wired"

Most of the Naturalizers among the parents interviewed were women, with the exception of two men, and represented a variety of backgrounds in terms of race, class, and sexual orientation. Maurice, though differing from Maya in gender, race, class, and sexual orientation, followed many of the same parenting approaches as Maya did. A white, upper-middle-class, gay man, Maurice and his partner have three children, daughters Jess and Sasha, eight and seven, respectively, and a four-year-old son, Casey. A hospital administrator in his late thirties, Maurice greeted me with a friendly, self-assured manner, conveying his assessment that we were peers. This was in notable contrast to many lower-income and working-class interviewees, who, like Maya, seemed slightly nervous when our interviews began. Eventually, all the participants settled into a comfortable rapport, given the familiar, everyday topics we covered and our shared status as parents. But Maurice seemed to feel that sense of shared status right from the outset, as we sat down at the conference table in his large, sun-filled office on a beautiful late spring morning. In describing what he sees as the origins of Casey's gender-typed behavior and interests, including his tendency to jump in puddles, Maurice used the term "hard-wired." At another point, he offered a similar assessment of Casey's fascination with dinosaurs in contrast to his daughters' focus on collecting trinkets and "sparkly things." He considers these interests gender-typical: "I think a lot of it is hard-wired, and that boys are just very different than girls." I asked for other examples of ways in which he views Casey as being "wired" differently than a girl, and he focused on emotional attentiveness and interest in mechanical objects.

> Casey's very much wired as a boy in the sense that he doesn't pay attention to the little things that are happening around him. If his sister is crying, he looks at her and walks by. Sasha's like, "Jess is crying," or if Sasha's crying, Jess will say, "Are you okay?" but Casey just kind of ignores that kind of stuff and he'll tend to walk by it. He's more interested in mechanical things, he loves the computer, he loves flashlights.

Social forces came up less often in Maurice's responses. And, regardless of their origins, he values gender differences, echoing Carole's theme that each gender has "real highlights": "It's wonderful to be a woman, and why should we want to deny that, and it's wonderful to be a guy, and why should we want to deny that?" He continued, explaining that he is glad that his children adhere to many typically gendered patterns: "There's aspects of gender identity that are wonderful and should be celebrated."

Maurice combines this positive assessment of gendered outcomes and biological outlook with various actions that suggest he plays an active role in crafting his children's gender. For example, he recounted offering a pointedly direct gender instruction to his son about trying on nail polish: "No, you can't do that, little girls put nail polish on, little boys don't." Maurice also told me that he treats his son differently than his daughters. Like Maya, he believes that boys require a different kind of discipline and also need to be comforted differently.

> I think I'm a little harsher with him. Like "buck it up," I think that's the attitude I take with him. We cuddled on Saturday for the first time in a long time, but I can remember when Sasha and Jess were four years old they were in our arms all the time. I just realized that . . . I think with him, I say, "These are the rules, you need to follow them." With the girls it's always been almost a suggestion versus a rule, you know.

Maurice combines this somewhat harsher discipline for Casey with more leeway.

> I think there is a tendency to think that it's okay for boys to be a little bit more aggressive. It's always bothered me a lot when Jess turned around and whacked another kid and I notice that I don't worry too much about Casey turning around and doing the exact same thing, you know in a kind of a play environment, as long as it's not anything that really hurts the other child. . . . When Jess was his age, if she turned around and whacked somebody, I lost sleep over it. It was like this is not girl behavior, what's going on here. Whereas, if Casey does something like that, he's being a boy.

This comment is similar to Maya's reference to letting her son get away with more than her daughters, a concession that both Maurice and Maya view as following, rather than constructing, a difference between boys and girls.

Along with his belief that Casey's interest in jumping in puddles is a hard-wired aspect of boyishness, Maurice spoke at some length about the different orientation he has to his children when it comes to outdoor play. He recounted these stories with a tinge of regret, implying that perhaps he was not being completely fair. But he also seemed comfortable with the compromises he was making in terms of the practical constraints of parenting, again framing his gendering actions as prompted by biological differences.

> Sasha went through a puddle of water the other day and I said, "Sasha, you're getting your sneakers all wet and then you're going to want to wear them tomorrow," and she's like, "Well, Casey ran through it," and of course I had seen Casey go through it and I didn't make a big fuss over it. So there it was, it was, "Yeah, well, Casey went through it but you know what, we have a different pair of sneakers for Casey, and for that very reason." Now we don't have backup sneakers for Sasha, so why is that? . . . She's a girl and she should keep her sneakers dry.

Casey we anticipate his getting his sneakers wet, so we have two pairs of sneakers always, so one can dry while the other one is being worn.

Maurice told me about a time when Sasha's sister, Jess, had asked if she could play in the back part of their yard in her bare feet, to avoid this issue of wet shoes. In his response to this request, Maurice interweaves his fundamental belief in gendered differences with actions that, I argue, reproduce those differences, although, from his perspective, he is not falling into a social trap but simply accommodating a preexisting natural tendency.

I told her, "Jess, you can't go down there in bare feet, you've got to put some shoes on." And she says, "Well, Casey's down there with his bare feet," and I said, out of my mouth, the words of my mother, "But he's a boy and I don't want you to get hurt, because if you get hurt, if you hurt your feet, you're going to whine about it forever." You know, Casey gets hurt and I don't hear about it, whereas Jess gets a hangnail and it's the world is about ready to end.

These are examples of direct gendering actions. Maurice talked about more indirect actions as well, where he and his partner offered their children the opportunity to choose for themselves, with results that followed typically gendered patterns.

When it came to decorating their rooms, . . . we let them pick out what they wanted. Sasha's room ended up with lots of pink, and butterflies and dragonflies on the walls. . . . Casey wanted it bright yellow and primary colors with dinosaurs. Those are good types of decisions, we were happy with what they picked out.

When I asked about what kinds of television shows, movies, or books Casey enjoys, Maurice reported following his son's lead toward media that struck him as typically boyish.

For movies, anything to do with dinosaurs is big, but the more action, the better. Casey can't sit to save his life, can't sit through *Beauty and the Beast* which the girls watched thousands of times. He can't sit through *Cinderella*, something the girls watched thousands of times, too. So we asked him what he wanted, and he wanted dinosaurs. Like the *Land Before Time* series, that's about dinosaurs, we got that for him, and he's watched that a lot and knows all the words by heart . . . the more action, the better.

Along with these instances of doing gender both directly and indirectly, Maurice shares with Maya, Carole, and Anna a pointed opposition to gendered constraints defining his daughters' occupational choices. With an even greater confidence that may be fostered by his class location, he followed up on his general preference to avoid "any kind of gender neutral environment" by offering an exception for Jess and Sasha.

In regards to their employment, in regards to their education, in regards to how they want to structure their lives, it's a completely different ball of wax. . . . As far as mapping out things, certainly career-wise the world is their oyster, whatever they want to do, there's nothing that's going to stop them from doing it.

For Casey, by contrast, Maurice did not report any actions designed to discourage gendered constraints or any emphatic feeling about openness to crossing boundaries. The only reference he made to gender resistance concerning his son was in his response to a question on whether Casey ever asks about social expectations for adult men and women. Maurice noted that their household structure avoids defining domestic labor as gendered, so he does not think Casey has developed any sense of differential expectations for women and men in family life. Moreover Maurice, the only gay parent in this category, differed from his fellow Naturalizers by the absence of heteronormativity. He made no remarks that assumed heterosexuality for any of his children, and in that sense did not reproduce the presumed inevitability of heterosexual orientation.

In his general preference to accept, value, and reproduce gendered childhoods, Maurice did not express the anxiety that many other Naturalizers conveyed regarding hegemonic masculinity or gender expectations. His motivations primarily centered on his own personal preferences and be-liefs, as well as his children's individual rights and interests. He did briefly suggest, however, that one of the reasons for encouraging his children to behave as others expect them to behave is that he sees positive benefits for them socially.

> Sometimes, I'll hear coming out of my mouth things like, "You don't want to do that, little girls shouldn't be doing that, or little boys shouldn't be doing that," you know? But that's partly because I prob-ably want to model with my children the type of behavior that will get them what they want. That will make them happy, make them feel comfortable, and a life without hassle and stress is probably a much easier life to live and more productive in the end.

The contrast between this remark and Maya's anxiety about the poten-tial for her son to be an outcast suggests both a gendered tendency among mothers toward greater anxiety about accountability as well as a pattern of racial and class privilege. Though constrained by his sexual orientation, Maurice generally feels confident about his place in the social world and ex-pects to pass this along to his children. He imagines Sasha, Jess, and Casey living "easier" and "more productive" lives if they follow social rules rather than fearing that they will be ostracized if they do not.

Pamela: "It's Testosterone"

Pamela, a white, middle-class, heterosexually partnered mother, is a thirty-six-year-old paralegal. What first stands out about her three-bedroom colo-nial home is the clutter; shoes, boots, and bags fill the entryway, along with infant and booster car seats for her one- and four-year-old sons, Danny and Evan. Additional rooms brim with laundry baskets, toys, projects in various states of completion, and piles of paper. What soon became apparent is that this disarray reflected a relaxed, informal attitude toward the hectic pace of family and work life, in a home that exudes a sense of contented and com-fortable chaos. When asked to speculate about how gendered patterns arise among children, Pamela focused on biological factors. With regard to Evan fashioning weapons out of cardboard rolls left over from wrapping paper, Pamela said, "It's a sword and it, you know, hits everything." She sees this as dictated by nature, concluding that Evan does this because "they're born that way, it's testosterone." She went on to talk about a television show she had seen.

> I saw something on TV, I saw it on a special. I think it was a *Dateline* or 20/20 kind of show, something like that, where they showed boys and girls and put them in a room together with the same toys and watched what they go for. At really young ages, they went for very different things. . . . I really think it's just inborn in them.

Also consistent with others in the Naturalizer category, Pamela sees gender differentiation and even gender separation as acceptable.

> I'm not one of these people who thinks we should make everything boy and girl, always together, I'm not like that. Like the Citadel [a military college], . . . "Oh, we've got to get women in there," but why? Why can't somebody have the choice to go to an all-boy or an all-girl school? I think they should be able to have that choice and not make everything the same.

Pamela's belief in gender differentiation was evident immediately in her responses to opening questions about preferences for having sons or daughters. "I wanted a girl more than a boy," she told me. "I wanted to dress her up and to buy the dolls and you know, all the things. Plus to take dance lessons and all that. A girl was someone that you could do all the things that you like to do with." Though she reported many actions that fall into the gender trap, reproducing the gendered patterns she views as positive and natural, Pamela also recounted more resistant actions regarding Evan compared to those reported by most of her peers in this group. Hoping to forge domestic skills, nurturance, and empathy for others, as outlined in chapter 1, she encourages her older son to care for his baby brother, noting that she would like to buy him a kitchen center to play with at home. She discourages fighting-oriented games that she considers typical for preschool-aged boys, including the same trading cards that began to shift my own thinking about my preschool sons' toys. But she crafts this resistance within the context of limits while encouraging certain aspects of hegemonic masculinity. For example, she remarked that she would probably encourage sports more for a son than for a daughter.

> I don't know how strongly I would encourage my girls to be in sports. They could if they wanted to, that would be totally fine, but I don't think I'd be encouraging them as much as I would a boy. We definitely want Evan to do that, he loves to kick the ball and play with the ball, and we're looking for a soccer team he can join. We really want to encourage that and when he's old enough, which I think is next year, he will go into soccer.

Pamela also mentioned that when Evan helps out with his baby brother Danny, he sometimes tells her that he would like to work at the day care center that he and Danny attend.

> He has said when he grows up he wants to be our day care worker's helper. That's what he wants to be. I tell him, like, "Oh, well, okay, maybe, but maybe not." Because you know, if it paid a lot of money I'd say, "Go for it," but I mean, it's not really the highest paid position he could get. He could never support a family doing that.

Their location in a particular social class marks the contrast between Pamela's concern about Evan's ability to support a family and Maurice's optimism that all three of his children will be able to pursue low-stress, happy lives. Pamela's concern for Evan's future is gendered, too, in that she expects him to take on the male breadwinner role. She is glad Evan wants to nurture his baby brother, but she hesitates to imagine him in a traditionally female occupation. And she notes that she would not be comfortable if he asked for items that are iconically feminine.

> I would not want him to think that he can't have a doll, but there are some things that I probably wouldn't buy him, because they are really

clearly girl stuff . . . like nail polish or makeup. . . . And I don't think
I'd put him in dance lessons. . . . I took dance lessons all growing up,
and I remember there would sometimes be boys and they hated it,
they were embarrassed by it. . . . That's nothing I would steer him
towards.

Two comments help round out a picture of Pamela's approach. She is the
mother quoted as buying a NASCAR Barbie as a compromise when her son
asked for a Barbie doll, a compromise, she later reported, prompted by her
own discomfort and her belief that Evan's father would object even more
strongly than she did. This compromise was typical of several Naturalizers
with sons. Accountability to her husband was also on Pamela's mind when
she reported her concern about the infant Danny being mistaken for a girl,
prompting her to "go straight to [her] husband" to say "I bought this in the
boys' department, I'm telling you, I really did, honestly, it's a boy's outfit."

Jerome: "Men Are Just Stronger"

Jerome's interview took place in the late evening, after his four-year-old
daughter, Louisa, and five-year-old son, Jack, had gone to bed. This white,
heterosexually partnered lawyer identifies as upper-middle class, and lives
in a stylish and carefully maintained two-story home overlooking a pond.
He views men as naturally stronger and more competitive than women,
and also sees boys as generally more physical, independent, and aggressive than girls. "I think as a rule most of that is inherited, it's already there,
it's more a biological thing," he explained. Jerome reported that he sends
both his son and daughter to the same karate and tap dancing lessons. Like
many Naturalizers, he is adamant that his daughter have access to a range
of occupations. Overall, however, his interview responses suggest that he is
crafting many gendered outcomes that he sees as natural, with that crafting motivated largely by his personal preferences and somewhat by his view
of the social costs to himself and his children from defying gendered expectations. Recall that Jerome mentioned he is raising Jack "to be a boy,
a man," and that he would view it as a failure if Jack grew up to identify as
gay. He also teaches his son that "if you decide you want [some] thing, you

are going to fight for it" and not "cry like a girl." As he reflected on his treatment of his son and daughter, Jerome concluded that he spends more time with Jack than with Louisa and their activities together differ.

> Now that I think about it, I think I've spent a lot more time playing with Jack and his stuff than I've done with Louisa. . . . When I was a kid, I loved Legos, and Jack has Legos. I like doing that with him. She'll play sometimes, she might come play with us when we're doing that.

When asked whether he ever initiated Legos with Louisa, he replied that he did not.

> No, I really don't. I sometimes initiate it with him, the Legos I mean, and like I said, she might come along, and we might all play together, but I assume it's really not as much of interest to her. She likes her kitchen set, she'll set the table and everything. She'll come to me and ask me what I want for dinner, and we'll play like that. But I probably wouldn't initiate that. It doesn't really interest me.

This description resonates well with Jerome's response to the questions about gendered anticipation: "I thought it would be easier to have boys." He explained that he "just thought things . . . would be simpler . . . like . . . going out and playing soccer or riding a bike and doing things like this, things a boy would like, rather than more girl things."

Several longer stories vividly conveyed his preferences and gendering actions, both direct and indirect. Typical of Naturalizers, however, they especially featured direct actions to discourage gender-atypical behavior. Expanding on how he encourages Jack to stand up for himself and feels disappointed when he fails to do so, Jerome recounted an incident in his son's kindergarten class.

> I know Jack has been in trouble several times in school, for fighting, and always to protect the girls. Like, one time, some boy was bothering one of the girls, and so he went and made him stop, he fought that kid, which to me is fine. This I don't have a problem with, it's

what I would expect him to do. If somebody is being mean to your girlfriend, and that's what they were doing, they were bothering his little girlfriend, he has a little girlfriend there at school, I would expect him to stand up and fight for that.[4]

As he continued relating this story, Jerome connected it to an incident during a family vacation, which fleshed out his hopes for his son.

We were on vacation abroad this summer, and we went to this outdoor plaza where there was this show with vultures. Big birds, they were really big. And those big birds were flying about four inches above our heads, they were flying fast and going back and forth. His mother was terrified, but Jack just stood up and looked up at the birds, as they were coming right at us. They go up high and they go down fast and at the last point they go in front of you. At that point, they're really coming right at your face, but he just stood there and looked at them and he was not going to move one inch. And that was the same way I felt, I've always been like this, I stand my ground and I like a challenge. His sister was hiding with her mom, but Jack was like standing straight and looking at every single bird, . . . and I told him, this is how I want you to stand tall. You will gain a lot more respect from somebody by looking at them right in the eyes, not by turning around or hiding or running away.

Jerome also expressed concern about his son's tendency to cry and occasions when Jack was passive in response to conflict with peers. He dislikes this kind of behavior and noted that he had been displeased when Jack wanted to join his sister, Louisa, in playing with Barbie dolls. But in a comment that captured thoughtful management of his son's masculinity and the limits many parents placed on an icon of femininity such as Barbie, Jerome reported that he decided it was acceptable:

He's not interested in Barbie, he's interested in Ken. . . . He plays with Ken and does boy things with him, he has always made clear that he likes Ken. . . . Louisa plays with the girl, the Barbie, and he plays with

69

the boy, he's the man, or the husband, the boyfriend, whatever, and she's the girl. So I let him do that. . . . If he was always playing with dolls and stuff like this, then I would start to worry and try to do something to turn it around. But he plays with Ken and it doesn't go much further than that, so I'm fine with it now.

Jerome also mentioned wanting a son first so that any future daughter would have a "big brother to defend her," thus anticipating a strong son and a daughter in need of protection. To some degree, Jerome extends his appreciation for traditional masculinity to his daughter as well. Like other Naturalizers, however, this primarily concerned occupational aspirations and a readiness to compete in the work world as an adult. He framed this in a way that assumed his daughter's class position:

I do want her to take on some masculine characteristics, I do, because that's what it takes, in my opinion. It depends on what career you want to have. I guess in some careers it's better to be very feminine, but in general, in college or anything in the professional life, especially, if you're more assertive and ready to go and have a good fight, you get more respect in the corporate world.

For his daughter as well as his son, Jerome preferred limits to this crossing of gender boundaries. In another story about the family vacation, Jerome shared his desire for Louisa to temper her competitive streak.

Well, on that same vacation, there was this one time when she was really putting up a fuss because she didn't get her way. And this older woman, she came up to Louisa and said, "Listen, little girls are on earth to be pretty, that's what little girls are supposed to be, pretty." That's what she told her, and she said, "When you fuss like that, you're not very pretty, and you're really a beautiful girl, so you have to stop." And Louisa just looked at her and stopped right away. . . . This old woman, she was like, "You're a beautiful girl and you have gorgeous hair and your dress is really nice but when you make a face like this you spoil the whole thing. So, pick yourself up and smile and you'll see, you'll be beautiful again." Really, in a way, her message was you'll get a lot more by being pretty and smiling than by screaming around. . . . It worked, what she said worked.

This is a significant vignette on many levels. Although the direct gendering action is not Jerome's but the stranger's, his acceptance of the stranger's intervention indirectly bolsters social expectations around gender. His basic goal is to get his child to stop fussing, a desire familiar to many of us who deal with young children. At the same time, the means to that end resonates so strongly with race- and class-specific cultural ideals of femininity, such as being passive, attractive, appearance-conscious, and oriented to pleasing others, that it is surely bound to reinforce those ideals.[5] More generally, his comment that "you'll get a lot more by being pretty" is much like his comment that Jack is more likely to get what he wants by fighting than by "crying and acting like a baby." Both are reminiscent of Maurice's argument that adhering to gendered expectations will, for his children, "get them what they want." The only two men in the Naturalizer group, both white and upper-middle-class, shared this kind of analysis, but so did some of the women in this group; the women, however, followed gendered expectations more often because they feared adverse consequences rather than the men's more positively rendered reasoning of "getting what you want" out of life. Another undercurrent in Jerome's responses was a devaluation of femininity that typifies hegemonic masculinity. Especially for his son, but to some extent even for his daughter, Jerome expressed a preference for interests and attributes more commonly coded as masculine. As he put it regarding Louisa, "I never wanted [her to be] a little princess, who was so fragile. . . . I want her to take on more masculine characteristics, too." He is skeptical about "fragility," "little princesses," and even games that involve cooking and serving food.

Actions that reinforced heteronormativity were, for many parents, brief or fleeting references of the kind introduced in chapter 1: the assumption that their child would eventually date and marry heterosexually, or the pleasure they take in viewing the child's other-sex friends as "boyfriends," "girlfriends," or potential spouses.[6] Jerome recalled an occasion when he offered a more detailed and direct reinforcement of heterosexuality.

71

One time I asked Louisa who does she want to marry when she grows up, and she told me she wants to be married with her brother. So I said, "Well, no you can't marry your brother," and she tells me, then she wants to be married to Rose, her friend Rose. So that's when I told her that boys marry girls and girls marry boys. Girls don't marry girls. So that's one thing I will tell them. Now if tomorrow they come and tell me they're gay, they'll still be my kids and they'll still be welcome home. I would not be happy with them, I probably wouldn't go around and tell my friends how proud I am of them, that they're great children, okay? But they'd still be accepted. But until then, I will keep telling them that boys marry girls and girls marry boys.

Perhaps Jerome's response will change as gay marriage spreads. At the time of the interview gay marriage was not legally available in Maine, which allowed him to assert as a simple fact that marriage always involves a male and a female person. In doing so he was able to reinforce gender difference, heteronormativity, and marriage, all interconnected aspects of the social construction of gender.

"I Try to Get Him Involved in Masculine Things"

Maurice's references to hard-wiring, Maya's to inborn traits, and Pamela's belief in hormonally driven differences all illustrate the Naturalizers' shared tendency to interpret gendered childhoods as a naturally occurring phenomenon. These parents especially viewed their sons' behavior as hard-wired or inborn. Asked if she considers his interests typically boyish, Jamie referred to her son as "all boy, a miniature man." She invoked brain differences by saying of boys, "I think even their minds work differently," and she went on to discuss what she views as the divinely ordained origins of gender differences. This twenty-five-year-old, white, low-income, single mother of one son, who works part-time as a freelance house cleaner, told me, "I just don't think we are built the same. . . . The Bible teaches us that the female is just much more delicate, the whole body structure is more delicate and the male is built stronger. Because of sin, the woman is supposed to have hard labor in childbirth, and the man hard labor in his work." Although not all her fellow Naturalizers referred to religion, Jamie's move beyond simply describing biological origins to viewing those origins as intentional or purposive was particularly notable in this group. This articulation takes biological determinism one step further, elevating gendered patterns as not just inevitable but also positive, adaptive for society or intended by God, and thus something with which parents or others should not interfere.

Along with their biologically determinist outlook, these parents report both indirect and direct actions that craft the same gendered outcomes that strike them as natural.[7] Similar to the other parents profiled in this chapter, Jamie said that she encouraged her son's interest in trucks, and remarked that her status as a single parent is one of the reasons she is particularly careful to steer her son toward such toys: "I bought them for him, and I point them out, like, 'Look at that tractor!' You know, I try to get him involved in like you would say masculine things, manly things, especially because the father's not around." She later recounted another direct gendering action: "When he screeches, I tell him not to screech. Boys don't do that, I tell him. . . . I don't want other boys, well, some boys and some men these days will think he's a wimp if he does that, you know?" These parents report some efforts to resist or adjust traditional gender expectations, particularly concerning occupational opportunities for their daughters and nurturance for their sons. But especially for sons, this is one of the groups most cautious about setting limits. Maya felt that some gender crossing might be tolerable for her son but only up to a certain age. Pamela "compromised" with a NASCAR Barbie, and Jerome accepted that his son played with dolls because it "doesn't go much further" than Ken.

Naturalizers expressed the highest level of personal preference for traditionally gendered outcomes and the lowest level of preference for undoing gender. Accountability to others was on their minds at notably higher levels than among Cultivators, Refiners, or Innovators. The sense of accountability came in the more positive spin offered by Maurice and Jerome, and in the fear-driven negative perspective more common among the mothers in this group. Either way, recognition of accountability highlights the power of interactional enforcement of the gender trap. Motivated by internalized preferences, but also by awareness of the social costs and benefits to their children, these parents are all united in their tendency to steer their children along a gendered path. Often they are leading, sometimes following the child. From their viewpoint, however, nature forges the basic direction in which their children are heading.

It is the Naturalizers whose responses most resonate with the literature on parenting and gender, which contends that parents often deny their own role in the gendering process. In reviews of existing research, Rhode, as well as sociologists Scott Coltrane and Michele Adams, concludes that many parents fail to see how they are constructing children's gender. "Most adults deny they are responsible," according to Rhode; Coltrane and Adams summarize the extant literature by arguing that "gender proscriptions and prescriptions . . . become so much a matter of habit that parents rarely are even aware of them."[8] These are the parents Messner is describing when he asserts that some parents "do not seem to read the children's performances of gender as social constructions of gender. Instead, they interpret them as the inevitable unfolding of natural, internal differences between the sexes."[9] Most of the parents I interviewed juggled competing interpretations of the origins of gendered childhoods, but only the Naturalizers struck the balance in the way these authors claim is a general tendency, by clearly foregrounding biological explanations. And as my analysis reveals, even this group expresses some awareness of social constraints.

Parents from a variety of class locations and racial backgrounds took the approach characteristic of Naturalizers. This group included not only heterosexual parents but also a gay parent. Mothers outnumbered fathers in this group, but both were represented. The women's responses differed from the men's, and contrasting the comments of Jerome and Jamie illustrates this difference in the key arena of hegemonic masculinity. Both spontaneously responded negatively to the possibility that their son might eventually be, or be perceived as, gay. Jerome specifically referred to this as a "somewhat selfish" fear, in that he would not be proud to tell others that his child was gay and would see it as a failure of his own parenting. Jamie, on the other hand, brought up the same issue in connection with the gendering efforts she makes, but, typical of mothers in this group, her negative response was driven by fear of the reactions of others.

I pretty much encourage him to stick to mostly boys' things, toys and clothes and stuff. . . . Like I wouldn't let him wear pink, because like I said before, I wouldn't want people to think he was gay. You know what I mean? They might think that if he's wearing some pink shirt or whatever. This stupid world cares about what we look like, unfortunately, . . . and you know, it shouldn't, it probably shouldn't matter. It's a piece of cloth, but that's the way the world is, and I wouldn't want him to feel out of place.

Jamie told me that "if [my son] was acting feminine, I would ask and get concerned on whether or not . . . I would try to get involved and make sure he's not gay." Here she refers to the possibility that her son might identify as gay and not just be perceived as such, but, again, she reports an action that is a likely response to such a "concern." Both Jamie and Jerome view childhood gender as primarily natural, but they also report negative responses to atypically gendered behavior and actions they would take to minimize such behavior. Another sense in which this pair of responses is typical, particularly of the Naturalizer group, is the focus on a son. The parents in this group predominantly had at least one son, and only one of the nine Naturalizer parents had only daughters. As noted in chapter 1, parents essentialized the behavior and attributes of boys somewhat more than of girls and were more emphatic in their reproductive actions aimed at boys. It is not surprising that parents of sons are especially likely to follow the pattern of beliefs and actions that classify some parents as Naturalizers.[10]

Naturalizers were most likely to reject the idea of treating boys and girls similarly or even consider that it was appropriate to do so. Much could be gleaned on this topic from parents' discussions of their beliefs and practices regarding their own children. But I also asked a more direct question on this subject:

Some parents try to encourage their kids to avoid tendencies that might be considered typical for their gender, like encouraging daughters to be more assertive and sons more nurturing, and avoiding clothes with gendered associations like pink for girls and blue for boys, while other parents don't think there's any need to do that. What do you think about whether parents should do that or not?

I always asked this question near the end of the interview to ensure that I was not raising specific examples in the earlier questions about whether their child's interests and attributes struck parents as typical for a girl or boy. The Naturalizers, defined based on their responses to other questions, also differed from the other groups on this one. This group, along with Cultivators, were most likely to dismiss the idea that parents should discourage gender typing. In this sense, the group's actions and beliefs are consistent with another claim that Rhode offers in her summary of the literature on gender and parenting: "most adults are uncomfortable with the prospect of a world without significant gender differences and are not preparing their children to live in one."[11] Though not the case for all the parents I spoke with, this does seem to be true for Naturalizers.

Another more indirect indication of their commitment to gender differentiation may be seen in their responses to a short question toward the end of the interview. Referring specifically to the preschooler who was the focus of the interview, I asked, "Do you tend to think of your son or daughter as a boy or a girl, or as a kid?" I did not follow up in any detail, as the question was simply prompted by my long interest in the claim made by sociologist Barrie Thorne that the ubiquitous use of the term "boys and girls" in schools perpetuates gender marking, continually reinforcing and constructing separateness and difference between children by gender through daily interaction.[12] This reasoning informed my own decision to avoid referring to my children as "boys." I call them by their names, not "the boys," and steer clear of phrases such as "good boy" or gendered language such as "handsome." That approach left me curious about how other parents viewed their children. Although their brief responses tell us only a little about parental gendering practices, they are consistent with other patterns reported in this chapter: Naturalizers were most likely to select a gendered term, *boy* or *girl*, when referring to their child. The Naturalizers are also unique in that they are most likely to talk about gender in terms of difference rather than inequality. Although power is central to the social constructionist perspective on gender that forms the foundation of my approach, it was not a common lens for thinking about gender among the parents in this group. Recall Pamela's argument that forced gender integration in education is undesirable because men and women are different. The celebrations of gender difference offered by Carole and Maurice also reflects the likelihood of parents in this group to interpret gender as a source of difference with no connection to power.[13]

In a nutshell, Naturalizers tend to fall into the gender trap, reinforcing gender differentiation and gendered childhoods. By legitimating and rendering inevitable gender structures through biological determinism, they also support those structures with positive assessments of their value and a tendency to ignore power or inequality as constituent elements of gender relations. They also reproduce gendered outcomes through their actions, including more reproductive action and less resistive action than any group other than the Cultivators. Through the particularly significant ratio of direct gendering actions and discouragement of atypical behavior, especially for sons, this group practices an approach to doing gender with and for their children that justifies and continues gender structures. Their beliefs and actions reproduce frameworks of accountability for their own children and others with whom they interact, and reproduce gendered outcomes more directly. They encourage their children to form gendered individual selves and engage in conventionally gendered interactions. Although these parents rarely identify themselves as the source of gendered structures, they do acknowledge the power of those structures in another way. Fathers especially steer their children toward attributes and behaviors acceptable to others and thus rewarded interactionally and institutionally, whereas mothers, in particular, steer them away from behavior that risks social costs. This suggests parents' awareness of gendered pathways, and their sense of agency in guiding their children through those pathways successfully.

As they balance the various tensions I have outlined, even this most traditionally oriented group expresses some recognition of social forces, and engages in some resistant action. To a limited degree, they encourage their sons to develop nurturance and basic domestic skills, to inhabit the revised version of hegemonic masculinity that, according to Messner and others, began to solidify in the 1980s and 1990s.[14] As Jamie recounted, those skills were on her mind when she allowed her three-year-old son to select a baby doll at a free toy swap they attended: "I thought about [stopping him] at first, just because of what I've been brought up as, that boys don't play with dolls, but then I realized that it's just not a big deal." As she put it, "Someday he could be a father, and he should know some of the parenting-type things." This revision of hegemonic masculinity does not extend, however, to encouraging a broader range of career choices for sons. The encouragement of a limited number of domestic skills for boys is coupled with more intensive encouragement for daughters to aspire to traditionally male occupations, especially by parents in more advantaged classes. This is promising for greater gender equality, but that promise may be diluted by the beliefs and actions that characterize the Naturalizers: construction and celebration of gender difference without attention to gendered power; limited recognition of institutional forces that structure gender inequality; greater willingness to revise gendered constraints on girls and women than on boys and men; and a fundamental belief that women's quieter nurturance and men's more active and competitive independence are biological. All this adds up to the prospect of a trap that sociologist Arlie Hochschild calls a "stalled revolution."[15]

In her influential analysis of the division of household labor in dual-earner heterosexual couples, Hochschild argued more than twenty years ago that expectations for women were changing faster than those for men, forcing women to layer a second shift of continuing household labor on top of their increasing responsibility for the first shift labor of paid employment.[16] Changes to career opportunities available to women and the number of hours some were working, especially heterosexual mothers, could not be viewed in isolation from men's behavior. If heterosexual men did not take on a greater share of nurturance and domestic labor, the changing expectations for women would come at little cost to men and great cost to women. This trade-off was felt inside heterosexual marriages, as women continued to absorb the second shift. It was also felt at the institutional level of organizations such as employers, schools, and day care providers, as well as in government policies. If men did not have to change their behavior in relation to family obligations, they would not pressure employers and other institutions to become more responsive to the competing demands of work and home, leaving women to juggle those demands with little institutional support.

In short, it is only in limited arenas that Naturalizers seek to resist gendered constraints for their children. They nudge their sons to develop some domestic skills and a nurturing orientation but only up to a point and primarily within the household rather than in their career options. They celebrate both traditional femininity and wide-ranging career opportunities for their daughters. Given that combination, they seem to view the daughters whom they presume will identify as heterosexual as agents who can freely plot a detour on the gendered path while their male partners stay closer to the traditional terrain. They are preparing their girls to take on domestic labor, exhibit nurturance, attend to interpersonal relations, be kind and relatively quiet, and limit any assertiveness they might display to only the sports field, cultivating an individual-level orientation toward what social scientists call "carework," and also reinforcing frameworks of accountability to this orientation for girls and women in general. Carework includes the unpaid family labor of caring for children, the elderly, and sick or disabled family members, along with the often low-wage labor related to the same social necessities, all of which are institutionalized in a highly gendered manner.[17] At the same time these parents send their daughters conflicting messages that they can aspire to and succeed in traditionally male occupations, "choosing" whatever combination of essential femininity and traditional male activities they desire.

Hochschild's analysis, and the substantial literature on balancing work and family that has followed it, convincingly documents the limits to such an approach.[18] Although a significantly different kind of masculinity may be of little interest to the Naturalizers examined in this book, their hopes to secure opportunities for their daughters cannot be separated from the traditionally gendered skills they encourage in those daughters nor from the fates of their sons. Without changing gendered expectations among both men and women, as well as the institutional and interactional constraints that create obstacles to such change, opening new opportunities while re-inscribing old obligations for girls and women creates only the illusion of options. More than two decades of scholarship shows that a second shift at home, whether their own or one resting on other women in heterosexual partnerships, will limit the ability of Jess and Sasha to have the world as "their oyster" in the way Maurice and many other parents imagine.[19] Given the complex, systemic links between economic, political, and domestic power, limitations in the economy constrain women's power in other arenas as well. Given the inseparability of race, class, and gender identified by scholars of intersectionality, these limitations will play out in ways that uniquely affect men and women according to race and class. Perhaps, for example, some financially advantaged women will ease the burden of the gendered second shift by employing low-wage domestic help, occupations typically filled by women of color or immigrant women, and offering little security, pay, or respect.[20] But even that approach, which exploits inequalities of class, race and citizenship to outsource some obligations assigned to them by gendered expectations, still leaves advantaged women with interactional pressures to consider. As sociologist Susan Walzer richly reveals in her analysis of gender and the transition to parenthood, mothers face the daily expectation that they will take on not just the physical labor of rearing children but also the less easily outsourced mental labor.[21] Through their essentialized sense of women as natural mothers, together with the kind of skills they are cultivating in their daughters, the parents in the Naturalizer category reinforce that gendered expectation in relation to babies, children, and carework more broadly.

The negative social sanctions that some Naturalizers fear for their sons, though possible to control through careful management of masculinity, pose risks for those sons if they find themselves unable or unwilling to live up to the ideal of hegemonic masculinity. When these parents not only teach their sons to follow that ideal but do so by rendering it natural and positive, they reinforce a set of structures and frameworks of accountability that could end up trapping their own children, and will certainly trap someone else's. The yardstick of hegemonic masculinity sets clear boundaries on individual freedom and capacity. Measuring sons by this yardstick discourages the development of the skills and sensibilities needed to share the obligations of both unpaid and paid carework, and reinforces frameworks of accountability that create interactional-level obstacles for boys and men who try to hone those skills. Deprived of the opportunities for human connection that carework allows, but also free of the responsibilities and effort of that carework and its negative impact on earning potential, men's power over women is reinforced. As Messner notes, this gendered power is inseparable from other forms of power. Hegemonic masculinity is "a symbolically displayed 'exemplar' of manhood around which power coalesces—and, it is important to note, not just men's power over women but also power in terms of race, class, and nation."[22]

Like all the participants who generously took the time to talk with me about their parenting, the Naturalizers thought carefully about their children's needs and interests. They are, for the most part, crafting strategies consistent with their beliefs and personal preferences, which, they believe, will benefit their children and themselves. But if one begins with the foundational assumptions presented in the introduction, their particular resolution will not, in the end, work ideally even for their own children. Moreover, it presents particular difficulties for those who seek more fundamental change to gendered structures and the intersecting structures of race, class, and sexuality-based power from which they are inseparable. On the other hand, these parents are also adapting to powerful structures that are difficult to resist and reform. They alone are not the primary instigators of the gender trap, though their approach enables the reproduction of gendered structures. Akin to all five configurations of parenting practice, Naturalizers strike a balance based on their own beliefs and their assessment of the interactional and institutional pressures around them, a configuration that has implications for their children and for society more broadly.

3

"I Think a Lot of It Is Us, Parents and Society"

Cultivators

Charles, a thirty-year-old, white, middle-class, small-business consultant, became a participant in this book when his wife, Susan, a stay-at-home mother, responded to a posting about my project. At the time, I had enough mothers participating but was still looking for fathers. Given Susan's interest throughout the interview, Charles likely volunteered because of his wife's desire to be involved in the project, but nevertheless he was attentive and engaged. His interview took place in their home, which was remarkably spotless and orderly given the presence of four small children, but in a warm and casual way.

Charles: "I Think It's Probably Parental Influence"

Although nervous at first, perhaps partly because Susan sat nearby rocking the baby and offering occasional corrections based on her greater familiarity with the children's daily routines, Charles soon became expansive, speaking with humor and thoughtful detail. He said he had always wanted a son, elaborating that "I think every father wants a son." Charles's first child was a daughter, five-year-old Sarah. She was soon followed by a son, Colin, four at the time of the interview, then another boy, two-year-old Byron, and then the infant Mary Kate, six weeks old. Charles described Sarah as "very much like a girl" and cited her talkativeness and love of dolls, shopping, and fashion, as well as her general disinterest in her brothers' toys. According to Charles, "from time to time she'll take one of the boys' toys and start playing with that, but I think it's more to irritate them than she really wants to play with it. . . . She's happier with her own toys, her dolls and all that." Four-year-old Colin also strikes his father as gender typical.

> He's very boyish. He loves his trucks and tractors. . . . My father owns a farm so he's got some cattle and does haying and things and so Colin loves to go with him and ride on the tractors and, you know, just kind of doing the boy thing.

Charles views these gendered patterns as socially shaped. For example, responding to a question about how his five-year-old daughter's interest in fashion developed, he said, "My wife buys her clothes, she wants her to look very girlish, and they pick them out together. Sarah loves to do all of that with her mother." He explained her interest in dolls, using a similar approach:

> Her interest in dolls? Oh, I think that it was probably us, I mean, she's had dolls ever since she was a newborn. You know we bought dolls for her, so I think it's probably parental influence. A lot of, you know, here's your dolly, go play with your dolly.

When he speculated about the origins of Colin's interest in more typically boyish endeavors, Charles did not hesitate to offer the same kind of analysis. He said his father invites only his grandson to participate in farm chores: "I guess he sees it as kind of the boy thing."

> You know if Mumma goes shopping, that's a girl thing. But if we're going to do the chores and take care of the cows then the boys are going. Grampa has influenced him that way, but he's been influenced by me I'm sure too. I mean, I'm very outdoorsy, you know, and on the weekends I might be cutting the wood or mowing the grass and Colin will be right out there. I always bring him out.

Charles envisions that this pattern will continue in the future.

I think that as the boys get older there'll be hunting trips or canoeing trips that I'd take the boys on. But probably the shopping trips and things like that, you know, the girls would go on with their mother. Those things would be different. . . . Maybe it's just because that's the way it was when I was growing up. My dad took the boys hunting and the girls didn't want to go hunting. They wanted to stay in the house where it's warm. And when the girls were going shopping, the boys were just happy to stay home and not have to go walk through the malls. Maybe it's just a stereotype on my part, but that's what I'm used to, that's how I see it.

Unlike the Naturalizers, Charles did not connect these gender differences to hormones or Darwinian imperatives. Like other parents I classified as Cultivators, however, he shared with Naturalizers a fundamental acceptance and celebration of gender differences; both groups expressed the highest positive regard for gender-typical outcomes and the lowest regard for outcomes they considered atypical. "I think it's great, she's doing wonderful," he replied, when asked how he feels about Sarah's typically girlish behavior. He is glad she enjoys fashion, and he thinks "she looks very nice, very well kept and pretty."

Lou, a thirty-five-year-old white, middle-class, heterosexually partnered small-business owner, and Cultivator, offered the same response after describing his enthusiasm for five-year-old Tamara's typically girlish interests, especially her kitchen center, dolls, and dresses. Like Charles, Lou sees Tamara's interests as socially shaped. "Her mom's a big influence and I think socially, too, her friends and day care." He views her pleasure in dressing up not as a natural female tendency but as a routine activity reinforced by social rewards. "She likes being in a dress, being dressed like a girl," he said. When I asked how he thought her interest in dresses develop, he responded:

I think people's comments when she does dress up. She takes notice of that, you know, how beautiful and you know, she likes to model for people, have them tell her how cute and pretty she is. She really makes an effort to look beautiful.

Lou appreciates Tamara's attention to her clothes, noting that "it's good, it's good, she's having fun and she just wants to look good."

Gwen, another Cultivator, also cited interactional influence to explain her five-year-old daughter Chloe's behavior. Though with less enthusiasm than Lou exhibited, and with a less direct approach, this forty-two-year-old business executive, a white, upper-middle-class, heterosexually partnered mother of one, accepted her daughter's gender-typical behavior based on her daughter's individual rights as well as peer influences.

> She prefers really feminine dresses. And I know there's a couple of girls in her class that kind of promote that, because when she walks into the classroom they'll get all excited and say, "Oh, you have such a pretty dress on today!" So I think it comes from those other girls.

When I asked Gwen how she felt about her daughter liking feminine dresses, she said, "That's entirely up to her. . . . She has her own development, and I think that's important for her to make those decisions."

Charles particularly values Sarah's interest in dolls: "I think that's healthy, I think that's fine, in fact it's great." He went on to note, "She's learning how to care for a baby, and I mean, I think it's really good too, because she's got a little sister now that she can help take care of, learn how to hold a baby the right way and all that." The subject of Charles's baby daughter emerged in relation to his two-year-old son Byron and in a distinctly gendered way. After characterizing Byron as somewhat aggressive, he noted a potential advantage to this characteristic:

> Byron, well, he's just a tough boy. Even around the house he tends to pick on the older kids. . . . I think that we're going to have to work with him a little bit to make sure that it doesn't continue too much, we're going to have to monitor that a little bit. I certainly don't think it's a good idea to have a child who's a bully, who's pushing around the other kids. It's important to be nice to the others and think of others and share a little bit. But some of that tendency, like to stand up for himself, is good, for himself and also, he's got a little sister he's gonna have to watch out for.

85

Whereas Charles envisions Sarah learning to care for her little sister by playing with dolls, he sees Byron "watching out for" Mary Kate by drawing on what Charles considers an appropriate level of aggressiveness. His expectation for Byron is similar to Jerome's reasoning that he wanted a son first so that any future daughter would have a "big brother to defend her." Both men are constructing girls and women as needing male protection. These fathers are simultaneously constructing boys and men as tough, independent, and strong enough to protect their weaker female family members.[1] As Schwalbe and his colleagues document in their analysis of processes through which inequalities are reproduced in everyday life, a common process in the subordination of women, people of color, and those of lower economic classes is "othering," or the routine and repeated casting of a group as separate, weaker, and in need of protection by the dominant group.[2] The process may be experienced as simple politeness or respectful daily interactions. But considered in the context of the history of gender inequality and its intersections with other forms of inequality, such protection elaborates sex difference in physical strength, creating a deeper gender difference and resulting in the subordination of girls and women.[3]

Along with his personal preference for gender-typical traits, Charles reports some discomfort with atypical behavior, but like other Cultivators (and Naturalizers), his discomfort primarily concerns boys, particularly if the behavior crosses conventional gendered boundaries to reach an icon of femininity. Neither of Charles's sons has asked for anything he considers typical for girls, but when asked to speculate about how he might respond if one of them did, he responded by mentioning a direct gendering action he would take.

Well, let's say it was something like a Barbie doll. I probably wouldn't think about it too much and I'd be like, "No." Then we'd go to the truck section. But you know, maybe I should back up, if they asked for a Barbie doll I would probably say more. Like I'd say, "You don't want a doll, girls play with dolls, boys play with trucks." I'd probably explain it that way. You know my boys, like I said before, have played with dolls once in a while and they like pushing around the grocery cart and things like that, but I think it's just part of growing up. I don't think it's a problem. . . . If my boys are thirteen and still want to play with dolls, I might be more concerned, but right now I'm not concerned.

When I asked whether parents should discourage gender-typed outcomes, Charles summarized many aspects of his approach as he answered:

I don't think it's necessary. . . . Because I think that girls ought to, well, because there are girl tendencies, you know, being more sensitive and nurturing and I think those are qualities, especially being the mother, that they need. It's not that it's not important for a man or a father to be nurturing or caring and sensitive too, but I think that the mother, it's more important that the mother is. And so I think that girls growing up that way, seeing their mother that way, and I think boys growing up seeing their fathers the hard worker, tough guy, is important. And discouraging that, I don't see the point.

This configuration is characteristic of the Cultivators in various ways. These parents resemble Naturalizers in that they are at the highest level of direct gendering and at a significant level of indirect gendering as they allow their children to follow gendered interests. They take pleasure in gendered childhoods, which they view as healthy and positive. They have little interest in what they perceive as cross-gendered attributes and interests, beyond the same skills and activities Naturalizers emphasize: for sons, basic domestic skills; for daughters, sports opportunities and a range of occupational options. And they have special concerns about boys' departures from gender-typical behavior.

By definition, the key difference between the reproduction-oriented parenting approaches of Naturalizers and Cultivators is that the latter view gendered patterns in childhood as social products to a significant extent. Among all the parents interviewed for this book, the greater the endorsement of biological determinism, the greater the tendency to report activities that reproduce gendered outcomes. As Cultivators demonstrate, however, biological determinism is not a necessary precondition to gendered parenting. Naturalizers execute the kind of approach that many in the literature assume is typical, reproducing gender while also perceiving the child's resultant attributes and behavior as natural. Parental gendering, however, is a much more complex balancing act, as demonstrated by the Cultivators and by the Refiners, Innovators, and Resisters profiled in the upcoming chapters. Most of the Cultivators do identify some biological factors, but they have primarily social explanations for the origins of gendered childhoods. They tend to acknowledge the full range of social sources outlined in chapter 1, but with particular emphasis on two interactional sources of gendering: parents (including themselves) and relatives such as grandparents, aunts, uncles, and cousins. Also unique to this group is its lack of concern with accountability. These parents recognize that gendered outcomes are shaped by social forces, including their own role, but they see the teaching and modeling of gendered expectations as a routine part of their parenting. Gendering does not feel like a trap to them but rather a process they engage in consciously.

Jennifer: "I Like the Girly-Looking Things"

Forty-one years old, Jennifer is an Asian American electrical engineer who identifies as upper-middle class, and she and her husband have three daughters, ages four (Lucy, the focus of our interview), ten, and twelve. She chose a small table in her neat but cluttered kitchen as the location for the interview. Before she had children, Jennifer had a culturally shaped preference for a son: "I wanted a boy, for my thinking it was like the typical family, a boy and a girl and the boy being the oldest. Probably that's the way from my background being Asian, with a lot of Asian background families, boys are important." This preference continued as all three of her daughters were born, but Jennifer reported that she and her husband do not plan to have any more children. Typical of Cultivators, she dressed each of her infants in a gendered manner. "As babies, I definitely dressed them so people could tell they were girls." She continues to dress four-year-old Lucy this way, noting, "I like the girly-looking things." All three of her daughters enjoy dolls and other toys that Jennifer considers typical for girls, and she cites various social factors to explain those interests: "Like commercials, whatever you show them, that's what they want, and it's a lot of times what their friends have already." Focusing specifically on Lucy, she said:

Since the older girls, her sisters, play with Barbies, she plays with Barbies. And she asks for these things, like when she sees her on TV she asks for like whatever Barbie accessories on TV. . . . She's influenced by what she sees on TV, and what she likes to watch is typically girls' stuff.

Although Jennifer views girls as generally more nurturing than boys, she did not mention nature as a determinant of that difference. She remarked instead that the difference results from girls spending so much time with their mothers, and therefore they become more familiar with domestic work. She thinks her own daughters observe what she does in the home and thereby develop a sense of women's responsibilities: "I know that they see that I do all the house stuff, the cooking, shopping, laundry, cleaning the house. I mean, they know I also work outside the house too, but I guess they see that kind of housework as for me and for them." Jennifer seemed wistful as she spoke about her responsibility for the second shift and her decision to reduce her weekly work hours from more than forty to thirty-two.

I mean, I do all the kid stuff, pick them up, organize their schedules, do everything at school, and he concentrates on his work, the yard, and money stuff, you know, and I think that would be true even if we had boys. I don't know why we have this division of labor, but if we had boys, maybe he'd be a little bit more involved in some of their activities at least, but probably not that much more so.

Jennifer reported that her husband occasionally told her that "doing heavy things around the house, . . . if we had a boy, he could help with that." Yet, along with her implied reservations regarding their gendered division of labor, she still encourages her daughters to play with dolls and assist her in domestic tasks. She also believes that, if she had a son, she, like her husband, would probably treat him differently.

I think I'm pretty easy on these girls, I help them out quite a bit. With boys maybe I would make them do more, yeah, I think so. . . . Discipline, I think I would be harder on boys, almost expecting them to do more I guess. . . . I think there might be a few different activities, like I think birthday parties would have to be different. With my girls I've had ice skating parties, or that Build-a-Bear place, but I don't think I'd do either of those with a boy. I think his friends, other boys, might make fun of that.

Jennifer reported some resistant gendering actions too, such as encouraging her daughters to participate in sports, which she views as more typical for boys but also an opportunity for girls to develop a more assertive attitude. Lou, another Cultivator introduced previously, struck the same chord about athletics for girls: "The more athletic the better, I think it's great. . . . We encourage them to be a little bit more aggressive, a little more assertive, independent, confident."

Similar views were cited by Olivia, a white, working-class, heterosexually partnered mother of three daughters: "Me and my husband both, we've talked about it, we want our girls to grow up doing sports. We don't care what sport it is as long as they're active and they're doing something athletic to give themselves courage and confidence." Drawing on interviews with volunteer coaches in youth sports programs, most of whom were parents, Messner demonstrates that "adults seemed to see boys' aggressiveness and competitive traits as a simple expression of nature, played out within (but not constructed by) sports, while girls were viewed as malleable, their softer natures reformable through sports participation."[4] Many interviewees, not just Cultivators, viewed sports in this way, encouraging sons as if it were self-evident that they should participate, whereas daughters were directed to sports as a means for developing confidence and assertiveness. Using sports to make his general point, Messner calls this tendency "soft essentialism." Boys' natures are seen as more fixed, whereas a softer essentialism aimed at girls "accommodates the reality of girls' and women's presence in sports, and public life more generally," while still reinforcing domestic pursuits as the first and most appropriate site for girls and women.[5]

Though Cultivators and Naturalizers tended to view boys and girls as very different, those with more than one son or daughter did sometimes note differences within a gender group. Jennifer saw variations in her three daughters with regard to their gender-typical behavior, with her youngest, Lucy, less feminine than her older sisters.

> She's very strong, you know, strong, and she has no fear, like jumping off things. . . . A lot of times she'll do something and we'll say to her, "Gee, you should have been a boy!" because it's something a boy would do. She takes more risks, she's very active, she's loud. She's just different from the other two girls, who are more ladylike. I mean, the things she does, she does it like a girl, she still acts like a girl, and she likes to dress like a girl. She does more girl stuff than what I would consider boy stuff, but she does some boy stuff too.

This comment suggests both an openness to Lucy's crossing what Jennifer perceives as typical gender boundaries, as well as caveats ("she does it like a girl") and the marking of those boundaries ("we'll say to her, 'Gee, you should have been a boy!'"). Implicit in Jennifer's joking manner is that Lucy's gender crossing is acceptable up to a point. If Jennifer had a son, however, she probably would not have lightly said to him, "You should have been a girl," if, say, his birthday party was not adequately masculine. Later in the interview she indicated this more directly. "It seems like it's not OK for a boy to be girly. . . . With girls, there's nothing really thought of as wrong by most people. But with a boy, if he wants to play with dolls or anything like that, that's frowned upon."

Like most Cultivators, Charles and Jennifer identified, respectively, as middle class and upper-middle class, and both have daughters. They vary in gender and race, as did the group overall, and are both heterosexual, as were all the Cultivators. Both cited tradition in explaining their original preference for having sons, and viewed their daughters' typically feminine attributes and interests as "fine with me" (according to Jennifer) or "great" (according to Lou and Charles). Though Jennifer recognized the social costs boys face if they deviate from gendered expectations, like most Cultivators she does not have strong feelings here. Though aware of accountability, these parents more often cite their own personal preferences and beliefs as the motivation for their gendering actions.

Karen: "We Gear It in That Direction"

In a rural area a few miles outside a small Maine town, a smiling family greeted me in the front yard of their home. Karen, a white, thirty-eight-year-old medical transcriber who identified as working class, had her nine-month-old infant, Amy, in a back carrier, while her five-year-old son, Michael, played catch with his father. I learned that, although Karen and her husband both work outside the home, they also raise a few cows and pigs. A welcoming atmosphere prevailed inside the house, with lively sights and sounds typical of a household with small children.

As was common among so many of the parents who participated, but especially Naturalizers and Cultivators, Karen's reminiscences about early preferences were shaped by traditional images of shared activities. She told me she always hoped to have a girl: "I think that I felt I would relate and connect with a girl more." When asked why, she replied, "I want to go shopping, and I want someone to go shopping with me!" She described Michael as "very boy-like" in his interests and attributes, citing a somewhat aggressive personality and "an early attraction to trucks and things like that." Although neither Charles nor Jennifer perceived biology as the main determinant for almost any of their children's gendered tendencies, Karen was more typical among the Cultivators, indicating biology as a contributing factor. She considers her baby daughter, Amy, "softer" and "calmer" than Michael was at the same age, and wonders if some of that may be a natural difference. "She's been a much easier nurser," Karen reported, "and she smiled at me at the hospital, I know she did. . . . And I think that comes with the gender, . . . just the fact that she's a girl."

Regarding Michael, who is old enough to have shown more definite gendered tendencies, she again mentioned nature: "I think some of it is just a natural thing, I really can't explain it a whole lot more than that." But, overall, she talked more often about social forces determining gendered outcomes, especially interactional-level forces. For example, immediately after commenting that it is "just a natural thing," she went on to note:

Of course, we did give him trucks and he is outside a lot, so we gear it in the direction of being a boy. We don't get him dolls, you know, or anything like that. . . . Yeah, he has his army men, a whole set up of that. He has a lot of trucks. . . . We get him toy guns and things like that. And he loves that stuff, he loves it.

According to Karen, Michael is greatly interested in his father's work for a local utility company, which provides him a uniform, a truck, and exciting equipment. Beginning with a desire to act out his father's work, he has expanded his interest to a series of occupations that include fire fighter, soldier, and construction worker. For each, his grandmother takes him shopping for whatever outfits are required. Karen said, "He has to be dressed exactly, in his mind, what he thinks they wear, . . . just dressed to the hilt." I asked her if Michael had ever commented about these jobs as typical for men. "We've had a few conversations about this lately, it has begun to come up, that he says these are guy things, yeah, he's distinguishing. And so I very gently tell him that that's not necessarily true."[6] Like Jennifer, and many other Cultivators, Karen regards the division of labor in her heterosexual household as the reason for some of Michael's ideas and interests.[7]

He spends a lot of time with his father. I think Ron and I are, in one sense, even though both of us can easily cross over, the overall, general way that we are is very masculine-feminine. It just comes with having a house and a family. So, he probably gets that right at home.

Gwen made a similar comment regarding her daughter's ideas about gendered divisions of labor. Whereas Karen is employed full-time, Gwen, after Chloe's birth, reduced her hours as a business executive to part-time, working twenty hours a week. When asked if her daughter ever questions social expectations for men and women, Gwen replied, "I think she perceives the difference of how her Dad and her Mom are, and the difference is, I can spend time with her but Daddy has to work. She's perceived that, she knows that men take a prime . . . role in the earning capacity."

Cultivators, with their emphasis on interactional sources such as role modeling by parents, were among those most likely to invoke a theme I introduced briefly in chapter 1: an articulation of social determinism that highlights tradition. As one parent put it, some people "are still living in the olden days." From this perspective, past practices continue on as a matter of tradition, not so much connected to any current structures of power as rooted in anachronistic patterns that will give way over time. Not all references to social determinants included any significant analysis of why social construction happens, but parents who did enlarge on this subject were clearly divided between orientations toward tradition or power. A focus on tradition was more common regarding interactional sources, more common among Cultivators, and primarily offered by fathers. Lou underscores this emphasis on tradition: "It's got to go back to the way that we heard our parents talk, and then it just goes on through now." Charles's earlier remark is similar: "It's just because that's the way it was when I was growing up, . . . that's what I'm used to."

In another example of the importance of tradition, Bob, a thirty-four-year-old, white, middle-class, heterosexually partnered father of two and also a Cultivator, argued that "it's a tradition that stems way back, . . . so we've got a lot of cultural baggage to sort through." These responses share the implication that gender differentiation is a leftover tradition from a bygone era, continuing out of habit. Though this orientation toward tradition was more common among fathers, Karen is another Cultivator who invokes tradition when she explains that a higher energy level and greater aggression among boys is a result of social factors, and she believes the tradition has gradually changed over time.

> I guess just our society as we've known it, that's where I think it comes from. I think guys have changed a lot, even since I've been growing up. How far back does that go? It could go back pretty far if you think about it, we're still very new at men being more sensitive, more nurturers too.

Most of Karen's comments indicated that her actions directly or indirectly encourage gender-typical outcomes for her son and anticipate such outcomes for her infant daughter. But there were also occasions when she discouraged outcomes she considered less typical. "One time we were in the store and he saw a Barbie something, I don't know if it was a Barbie suit-case, yeah, I think that's what it was. He wanted that, and I said, 'No, you can't have this, your father wouldn't like that.'" Karen continued on this theme by offering a hypothetical example:

Like if he wanted to take ballet, well, would I seek to have him be in a ballet class? No, probably not. But I would want him to know that it's okay for him to want to do that, I guess that would be okay. But we've pretty much leaned toward boys doing what boys typically do and the same with girls, so I don't think he's going to ask for that.

Karen did not refer to how others might react but rather to her own per-sonal comfort level. Her response regarding the Barbie suitcase clearly sug-gests that she feels accountable to her heterosexual partner's wishes, but, overall, Karen's motivations seemed more routine and personal. "I feel fine about it all, to me it's all very appropriate," she replied, when asked how she feels about the interests she described as "very typically boyish."

Other Cultivators also routinely discouraged behavior they considered inappropriately gendered. For instance, Gwen, like Karen, cites her hus-band as the source of a gendering lesson. Referring to Chloe, Gwen re-counted, "She's seen men with long hair and she's questioned it, and she's seen men with earrings. Her Dad is like, 'no way,' that's what he tells her, 'no way men with earrings or long hair.' He is very firm on that." Elaine noted that her husband discourages their four-year-old son, Theo, from seeking too much comfort: "He still looks for a kiss when he has a boo-boo, but he's socialized against that by, not so much by me, but his dad, he'll just kind of say, 'You're okay.'" Lou mentioned that Tamara sometimes wants to put barrettes in his hair as a game, but noted, simply, "I won't let her."

The feeling behind Karen's responses is much like that behind Elaine's, who provides another example of the Cultivator configuration of beliefs, actions, and motivations. Also the parent of one son and one daughter, Elaine perceives nature as an important source of gendered childhoods. Speaking about Theo, she remarked, "All that action, that's the male gen-der, tension/release, tension/release, it may have to do with their physiol-ogy. . . . It's their testosterone, they have an awful lot running through their veins." But she is quick to note that interactional social forces shape many of her children's interests and tendencies. Referring to her two-year-old daughter, Gabrielle, "We all have been socializing her that way." Later in the interview, speaking of both her children, she echoed this view:

> I think my kids seem to be pretty much our culture's stereotype of a little boy, you know, the snakes and toads and frogs, and little girl with the, you know, the little ribbons in her hair and reading stories and playing with her dolls. I think they just got to be that way because I think that's how my husband and I are, so I think they've picked that up from us.

Lou made parallel comments about Tamara's interest in dolls. First he noted the influence of estrogen and testosterone: "She's got more estrogen and boys have testosterone, I think that explains some of it." But in the end he concluded that he thinks environment is even more critical. "You still have that tendency to raise a girl as a girl, boy as a boy, I know I do."

Another aspect of the routine reproduction of gender is heteronormativity, with this group of parents offering the most comments that take for granted a heterosexual orientation. Elaine expects to stay closer to her daughter than her son in the future, as once her son "takes a wife" that woman will become his primary emotional anchor. Gwen noted how "cute" it is that the boys in her daughter's preschool have begun talking about which girl they want to marry. Bob explained that he and his wife encourage their daughters to enjoy cute dresses, hair accessories, and dolls, because he thinks "it can be very healthy to have gender stereotypes." In explaining this more fully, he indicated his expectation that his five-year-old daughter, Vanessa, will identify as heterosexual.

> I think it's healthy to celebrate that we're different people. . . . It's okay for a woman to be the executive in a board room and at the same time to be a very feminine woman in her personal life with her husband, her mate. I want my daughter to know she can have that. I think if we don't celebrate that we're different those kinds of good things can be broken down.

Cameron: "No Way My Boys Are Going to Be Like That!"

Whereas eight of the ten Cultivators had at least one daughter, Cameron only had sons, four-year-old Ethan and one-year-old Zachary. A white, middle-class, heterosexually partnered, thirty-seven-year-old father and an industrial manager, he noted that he often cooks for the family, and he was folding a heaping basket of laundry as we set up for the interview. Both children were still awake and playing downstairs during the early evening period Cameron chose for our interview, so he suggested we talk upstairs in Ethan's room. Surrounded by his four-year-old son's trucks, balls, indoor-sized basketball hoop, and stuffed animals, Cameron began by saying he had preferred to have a son in order to pass down the family name and share an interest in athletics, the kind of gendered anticipation particularly common among Cultivators. He described Ethan as less traditionally masculine than some boys but with only limited tendencies in that direction.

> Ethan, well, he's a very well-behaved little boy, he's not overly aggressive, he's not rude, but he's not sissy-like either. . . . You know, he doesn't throw fits, he doesn't talk back a whole lot. He's very bright and can reason well. To be honest, I wish he was more interested in sports. I mean, I know he's only four, I've got to keep saying that to myself, but I really do wish, yeah, I wish that. It's kind of disappointing to me, I mean, not overly so, but definitely kind of disappointing.

Cameron also noted interests and attributes he considers more typical for a boy, mentioning Ethan's interest in vehicles and certain sports. When asked how he thinks those interests developed, Cameron cited parental influence as well as Ethan's own lead.[8]

> You know, we would buy him the car sets or we got him that basketball hoop over there, we got him like a construction site thing, we bought him a lot of stuff like that. But we didn't choose that for him just to push it on him, he was really into that stuff.

Most of the other parents classified as Cultivators spoke about their children the same way Elaine did, describing them as fitting "our culture's stereotypes" of a girl or boy. Cameron was one of two parents in this group who had only sons, and both men described one of their sons as less masculine than they preferred. Given that all the other parents in this group had at least one daughter, or only daughters, this may suggest a pattern related to social determinism. Perhaps identifying social sources for gendered outcomes is more attractive to parents of daughters, as they generally invoked biological determinism less often compared to parents of sons. But social determinism may also be attractive to fathers of sons who seemed less masculine than the father preferred, as it allowed room to maneuver toward tendencies the fathers valued more highly. Perhaps these fathers would have held socially determinist beliefs in any case, but their sons' performance of masculinity prompted them toward a greater range of reproductive actions. Notably, however, the only parents in this group with no daughters, Cameron and Derek, are fathers with sons they consider somewhat more "feminine" than they prefer.

For Cameron, the attempt to manage Ethan's gender performance includes encouraging patterns he considers typical for a boy, such as engaging in sports, playing with trucks, and being assertive, as well as discouraging gender nonconformity. Cameron expressed his own dislike of cross-gender behavior and was more concerned about the opinions of others than any parent in the Cultivator group. At one point he offered a brief report I considered an instance of undoing gender. After telling me that his son "wanted a Barbie so we got him a Barbie," he expanded on the incident, indicating the clear limits he places around gender-atypical behavior.

> Like I said, Ethan was asking for Barbies constantly and we finally got him one. But even then, it's got a sports theme, it's a basketball player theme to it. So it's not totally, you know, in a little frilly dress and all that. Sad to say, that makes me feel better, it's kind of a more masculine type of Barbie.

Cameron went on to report not just the kind of compromise represented by the basketball Barbie but also more direct gendering action:

He asks for, you know, all the little things that are in commercials, including stuff that's just for girls. Period, anything, whatever the thing is, he says, "I want that," and I'm like, "Ethan, you can't get everything and by the way, that's for girls honey, you know, and you're a boy."

When asked to speculate on how he might treat a daughter, Cameron reflected on the differences.

If I had a daughter, I'd probably be more protective in some ways, just because it goes back to the idea that girls are supposed to be these little frail things, I guess. I don't know, I just don't think I would go send my daughter out to throw rocks with the boys or play football with them. I think we'd put girls in the traditional dance and gymnastics things, as opposed to the boys going to baseball, football, soccer, things like that.

In response to my question as to whether he would sign the boys up for dance or gymnastics, Cameron replied:

Personally, I wouldn't be at all in favor of it. Gymnastics, I don't know, maybe I wouldn't mind so much. But not dance, I just, well, it's probably my own selfish feeling of like, "No way, no way my kids, my boys, are going to be like that."

When asked if he thought that would be a reflection on him as a parent, he responded, "As a male parent, yeah, I honestly do."

Besides Cameron's personal preference and comfort level—which he summarized by noting, "I don't want him to be a little quiffy thing, you know?"—his concern about how others might react is evident in his belief that Ethan's gender performance reflects on Cameron "as a male parent." He is also worried about how peers might treat Ethan if he fails to live up to conventional expectations: "I don't want him being femmy and perhaps getting teased or roughed up or anything like that." At another point, Cameron focused again on the social costs his son would face if he wanders off the gendered path.

I think we'd all be better off without some of the stereotypical beliefs we have, girls do this and boys do that, sure, we'd be better off. But the problem is, they exist, they exist and I don't want to be the one taking all of that on. I'm not going out there with my picket sign saying, "Barbies for Boys, Barbies for Boys!" No, I don't think so, not me.

Cameron was clearly giving careful thought to his answers, and as the discussion about Ethan continued, he spontaneously brought up the connection between male-gender performance and sexual orientation:

Like I said before, every toy commercial that comes on he says, "I want that!" and I say, "Ethan, that's for a girl." I guess that's part of me saying, "No, you're not going to have a little tea set and baking set and stuff like that." . . . I don't know why I do that, there are things that are meant for girls, but why would it be bad for him to have one of them? I don't know, maybe I have some deep, deep, deep, buried fear that he would turn out, . . . well, that his sexual orientation may get screwed up. It's probably, I'm probably being very stupid in thinking that, but hey, I don't know, so why risk it?

Like Jerome, a Naturalizer who also mentioned the possibility of his son, Jack, being gay, Cameron seems to imply that he could prevent this unwanted outcome by carefully attending to what Ethan is allowed to play with and carefully crafting his masculinity. Jerome noted that he would see it as a failure if Jack turned out to be gay, as he is "raising him to be a boy, a man." The linking of gender performance and sexual orientation, coupled with the assumption that parental action can control both, is evident in Jerome's comment as well as Cameron's fear that playing with toys "meant for girls" might *cause* Ethan's sexual orientation to "get screwed up." These connections were evident only regarding sons, especially among Naturalizers such as Jerome and Jamie, and Cultivators such as Cameron and Derek.

Derek, a middle-class, heterosexually partnered, thirty-one-year-old Asian American computer programmer and father of two sons, reported various direct gendering actions he took to encourage his five-year-old son, Caleb, toward typically boyish behavior and discourage attributes and interests he views as inappropriate. He described Caleb as enjoying many activities commonly associated with boys but also referred to him as "kind of sensitive," and noted, "I would like my sons to be more masculine." Asked to elaborate, he replied:

> Sometimes under pressure he'll kind of break down. . . . Just as an example, he was at play group one time and one of the other kids said something to him and he was so upset he kind of walked away, just walked home. All because one of the girls had called him stupid or something like that. And I spoke to him about that, about his feelings and how he should act about that. I guess as opposed to just breaking down and crying, walking away would be the next best thing if you couldn't cope with it, and in terms of being a more masculine way, I'm glad he did that. But I'd like him to be able to cope with it, not to need to walk away like that.

The link between gender performance and sexual orientation, and the role of parents in crafting both, came up at the end of our interview, not as an answer to a specific question but rather in response to my asking whether Derek had anything else to add to our discussion. He gave the following reply:

> Well, most of your questions are gender-related, and as a parent, I guess you wonder if your kid's going to be gay or not or things like that. And I guess you know, he is my son, you keep an open mind to it. It's not something that I'd want, I hope he's heterosexual, but if he isn't I'd still love him. So I guess maybe in the back of my mind, and I'm sure a lot of other guys' minds, that's why they'd push their children to the blue shirt over the pink shirt and things like that. . . . I don't think I'd fret over it [his son wanting a pink shirt], but it would put a spark in me that way. I don't try to push him too much to being masculine, but like I said I would steer him away from a pink shirt as opposed to having him wear a blue shirt.

Both Cameron and Derek associate icons of femininity—such as the color pink and Barbies—as well as emotionality and passivity in boys with the potential for a non-heterosexual orientation. With a touch of concern, disappointment, and direct gender instruction similar to Derek's in the play group example, Cameron said:

> Sometimes I get so annoyed, you know, [Ethan] comes [crying], and I say, "You're not hurt, you don't even know what hurt is yet," and I'm like, "Geez, sometimes you are such a little wean," you know? But again, I've got to keep saying this to myself, "He's only four, he's only four," so I guess we'll see how it develops.

These comments, taken out of context, might suggest that these fathers are casually dismissive of their sons, but that would be a mistaken impression. Cameron and Derek clearly knew their children well and spoke at length about their parenting in thoughtful ways. They offered warm and genuine praise for many aspects of their sons' personalities and interests. But their concerns are so consistent with what scholars of hegemonic masculinity view as key tenets of the normative ideal—homophobia and rejection of femininity—that the traces of that structural component of the social construction of gender are hard to miss. Through their beliefs and actions they augment the trap of hegemonic masculinity, but they surely did not originate it. In that sense, they may be trying to prepare their sons to navigate the gendered world outside their homes as much as they are trying to live up to their own personal sense of successful gender accomplishment; that personal sense, however, is likely forged by the structural power of hegemonic masculinity.

"A Lot of Influence of Stereotyping"

Though he was anxious about Caleb's gender performance and future sexual orientation, Derek mostly treated the social construction of gender as a routine aspect of raising children. Comparing his sons to a female cousin, he said that she is much calmer, quieter, and neater. "She'll come into the house, take off her shoes, wash her hands, while my kids just run through the house and run their muddy hands across the wall." When asked why he thinks those differences arise, he nodded to nature but pointed more directly to social forces: "I would say it's probably some nature but more so it's a lot of influence of stereotyping." He went on to explain that he thinks his niece is being raised differently, and, if he had a daughter, he would raise her differently as well. Although Naturalizers and Cultivators regard gender differentiation as positive, Cultivators see it as largely a social construct and generally articulate social determinism in terms of tradition. For them, gender is a source of difference without connection to power. Bob typifies that outlook. After mentioning that five-year-old Vanessa has asked why her mother is at home with her and her father goes off to work every day, he explained how he and his wife, Debbie, responded.

> We answer her very factually with what our situation is, which is that I have more income potential than Debbie does so that's why I work and she doesn't. There's additionally the fact that Debbie has much more ability to be with the kids than I do and maintain patience and that sort of thing. You know, I get a few kids running around and I lose my mind completely. They could just be doing normal kid things and it drives me crazy.

Bob seems to view the differential in income potential and patience with children, which explain their decision, as simple facts that are unique to their individual household and not the outgrowth of a larger set of structural forces and inequalities. He noted his desire for Vanessa to know that some day she could be a powerbroker in the board room and still be feminine with her husband; presuming that she will share her mother's patience and domestic skills, however, he also wants her to know that she has the option to be a stay-at-home mother.

> I think our culture doesn't see as a part of that conversation the option for a person to say, "I am a woman and I want to stay home with my kids." I would seek to have that be an option for Vanessa as well. That it's not just about doing this and that to get a career, I mean, that's fine, but there's also other options for her.

Although Bob uses the word "person" in his comment, it is immediately clear that the person he has in mind is a woman. And that woman presumably has a male partner with sufficient income to support her full-time care-giving work, implying outcomes constrained not just by gender but by class and sexual orientation as well. Like Naturalizers, Cultivators assume their daughters' suitability for domestic responsibility, constructing both the potential for individual-level orientation toward nurturance and the interactional-level pressures that Walzer outlines for new mothers.[9] On the foundation of this presumed domestic orientation, these parents then layer an offer of "choice," to add paid employment or not. But as sociologist Pamela Stone lays bare in her study of upper-middle-class mothers in heterosexual partnerships, that choice is deeply constrained by both interactional and institutional forces.[10] Many mothers in professional occupations are surprised to discover how difficult it is to combine the second shift with the demands of a fast-paced career that is often structured with the assumption that someone else is handling the carework.[11] Stone describes the women she interviewed as trapped in a double bind that is like quicksand, sinking deeper as they try to escape, with the "true parameters of constraint . . . concealed by the rhetoric of choice."[12] In contrast to the domestic skills parents see as important for their daughters, the emphasis for sons is on different skills as the foundation for adult life, skills that involve the central elements of hegemonic masculinity: a competitive spirit, toughness, independence, and an ability to resolve conflict assertively. Other required skills are the careful avoidance of feminine attributes, activities, or items, including displays of vulnerability or excessive emotion other than anger. These emphases lay the groundwork for an orientation toward achievement outside the home and family, which is particularly evident among middle- and upper-middle-class men, according to research by Stone and fellow sociologist Karen Pyke. This orientation also includes the suppression of the complex range of human emotions and aesthetic pleasures, which, Connell argues, hegemonic masculinity idealizes.[13] But there is more to the gendering process described here than the individual transmission of social expectations. Cultivators also reinforce frameworks of accountability to hegemonic masculinity ideals, which may trap not only their own children but children generally while also reinforcing gendered structures at the institutional level. As scholars of masculinity demonstrate, the intersection of these various levels of gendered social influence have a profound negative impact on male health and well-being, even as they simultaneously privilege some boys and men, especially those in more advantaged locations in the hierarchies of race, class and sexuality.[14]

Consistent with their views on the appropriate life skills for men and women, Cultivators engage in actions that reproduce gendered childhoods, motivated more by personal preferences for, or at least comfort with, gendered outcomes than by concern with gendered accountability. Some discouragement of gender nonconformity is apparent in this group, especially by the two fathers who see one of their sons as insufficiently masculine. But to a greater extent than even the Naturalizers, their reproductive actions focus on routinely encouraging gender-typical behavior rather than discouraging atypical behavior. From trucks and building toys and sports for their sons, to dolls and crafts and a preoccupation with personal appearance for their daughters, Cultivators promote the kinds of toys and activities that foster different capacities in boys and girls. As psychologists Isabelle Cherney and Kamala London point out in their review of the literature on childhood play, "stereotypically masculine toys tend to promote the development of spatial abilities," whereas typically female toys "tend to encourage the development of verbal rather than visual-spatial skills . . . and promote nurturing behavior."[15] The parents profiled in this chapter are relatively aware of their own role in shaping these outcomes, and they consider the resulting capacities as necessary to enable their children to occupy their adult roles in an appropriately gender-differentiated world.

Like all the parents interviewed for this book, Cultivators balance reproduction with resistance. But if they allow or support behavior they consider gender-crossing, it is primarily to encourage daughters to pursue sports and be aware of nontraditional career options. Though less adamantly than many Naturalizers, Cultivators still emphasized occupational opportunities for their daughters, as illustrated by Olivia's comment that, "the other day Nina even said she wanted to be a fireperson. And I said, 'Oh, great,' you know, because it's something that can go either way. I mean, most jobs are either way, and that's the way they should be." Like Olivia's observation, noted previously, about the courage and confidence fostered by athletics, this remark conveys her desire for her daughter to have some less traditional options. Cultivators, on the other hand, made fewer attempts to undo traditional gender expectations for their sons; occasional references were made to empathy or keeping the son's aggression within some limits, but relatively few intentional efforts were made to build domestic skills or nurturance. And, like Olivia, even for daughters their less traditional efforts are combined with encouraging a wide variety of gender-typical outcomes. As Olivia told me:

> As a baby, [Nina] was definitely dressed as a little girl. . . . When she was a toddler, we loved to ask her, "Are you our pretty girl?" and she'd go like this, shake her head yes, really strongly, it was so cute. . . . She and her sister they both love makeup. She's gotta have her Chap Stick or whatever, that's her thing. . . . They pretty much love dolls, all three of them, like I said, I really never had the trucks and the boy stuff for them.

Nina's parents help to support and even craft her interest in appearance, praising her as a "pretty girl" and encouraging an interest in makeup and colorful clothing. Though other parents also reported this kind of action in relation to daughters, Cultivators were especially likely to do so and they were especially enthusiastic about it. As exemplified by Charles's assessment that Sarah's interest in clothing and shopping is "great," Lou's feeling that Tamara "is having fun and just wants to look good" and Karen's enthusiasm about shopping with her daughter, all the Cultivators with at least one female child spoke positively about fashion and shopping for clothes as an activity for girls and their mothers. As Elaine explained in relation to two-year-old Gabrielle, "We buy her little purses, earrings and jewelry and pretty clothes and we go shopping, she loves to go shopping with mommy."

Certainly there are benign aspects to an interest in the aesthetic pleasures of clothing and accessories, but, as scholars of gender have argued, a commodified overemphasis on appearance can be constraining for girls and women, and thus I consider it a component of the gender trap. Russell and Tyler contend that for "young girls particularly, the pursuit of ideal femininity seems to be honed largely through the capacity to function as effective consumers."[16] And much of that consumption is oriented toward enhancing appearance, encouraging even young girls to judge themselves by restrictive standards of "prettiness" and to focus time and energy on how they look to others.[17] Media reinforce these messages as well, constructing ideals of beauty that are not only gendered but inflected with racial and class implications.[18] Several of the Cultivators casually referred to media as a source of their daughters' interest in fashion, makeup, and "beautiful princesses." As Jennifer said, "my girls, they watch those shows on Disney, and Disney movies, all those movies for girls, and they love the stuff." Olivia similarly commented that Nina and her sisters developed their interest in nail polish and "cute outfits" through "those shows with the music and the girls and all that glittery stuff, they just love it." These connections are consistent with the literature documenting that children's media often represent boys as active and achievement oriented and girls as passive, nurturing, and appearance oriented.[19]

In many ways, the Naturalizers and Cultivators exhibit similar actions, distinguished primarily by their beliefs about the origins of gendered childhoods, and to a lesser degree by what motivates their actions. Both groups express high levels of support for gender differentiation, but Cultivators draw more of their reported motivation for reproducing that differentiation from their personal support, whereas Naturalizers meld that support with a notable dose of accountability to others. Cultivators put less stock in the costs and benefits or navigation of structural constraints and consider gendering a routine part of parenting. In Derek's words: "I think my wife agreed, or maybe it was more so me, that you just wouldn't put a pink shirt or anything like that on a boy, so that's that." Cultivators see themselves and other social sources—especially the interactional kind, such as parents, peers, and relatives—as responsible for much of the gender crafting in their children's lives, and they feel comfortable with that.

Among the study participants, men are slightly more likely than women to be Cultivators, with women outnumbering men in the Naturalizer category. Combining the Naturalizers and Cultivators, those tendencies average out to a gender distribution that is similar to the overall sample. Cultivators, however, stood out at least somewhat in others ways: all were heterosexual and more likely to identify as middle or upper-middle class. About one in eight participants who identified as low income or working class followed the Cultivator configuration, compared to nearly one in three parents who identified as middle or upper-middle class.

My commitment to an intersectional approach leads me to speculate on race, class, and sexual orientation patterns when they arise, albeit cautiously and in the context of the scholarly literature. Perhaps, as in Bob's case, those who favored the traditional division of labor by gender were apt to be heterosexual and in a higher socioeconomic class. Their ideology is consistent with what Pyke documents among middle- and upper-middle-class, heterosexual couples in her study of class-based masculinities.[20] According to Pyke, the ideology that she terms the "hegemony of the male career," "rationalizes the primacy of the successful male career in marriage as economically efficient and in the best interests of all family members." She goes on to argue:

> This class-specific ideology adds an additional layer of legitimations to practices that emphasize gender differences in ways that obscure the gendered nature of inequality. . . . By obscuring gender inequality in ideologies that appear gender neutral, logical, and practical, the embeddedness of masculine privilege in institutional life becomes less vulnerable.

In Bob's "very factual" analysis, Debbie's patience and skill with children, as well as her lower earning potential, are rendered as individual attributes, separate from the context of gendered structures, as are Bob's income-generating capacity and his impatience with children. Obscured in this analysis, as Pyke observes, are the power differentials that shape gendered phenomena such as patience and earning capacity, and the further power differentials that result from gendered divisions of labor that often trap heterosexual women into being financially dependent on men. The particular earning power of middle- and upper-middle-class men allows for this hegemony of the male career, and thus she argues that hegemony is a key example of "how marital powering processes vary across social class in ways that reflect and (re)construct larger structures of inequality."[21]

Consistent with both their class location and beliefs about gender differentiation, the Cultivators, among my participants, are most likely to include a heterosexual couple where the wife does not work outside the home for pay or works only limited hours. They are also the parents least likely to use paid child care, even if a mother does work part-time, relying more on overlapping shift work or non-paid care from grandparents. I designed the brief questionnaire that preceded the interviews primarily to document basic background information, including the number and ages of children, racial and class identification, work hours, partnership status, and the like. But I also included an opinion question, drawn from the public opinion literature on gender-related attitudes. I asked participants whether they think that married men and women with children are often better off if the mother focuses on child care and the father on paid work. The alternative choice was whether both parents should share equal responsibility for child care and paid work. Three-quarters of the Cultivators believed that it is preferable in a heterosexual family when the woman focuses on child care and the man on paid work, far more than among any other group. Their responses to this brief question reinforce what their detailed interviews document: Cultivators value the hegemony of the male career and their actions tend to reproduce it.[22] The implications of this finding are similar to those I discussed in the last chapter, where we saw that nurturing responsibility potentially limited heterosexual women's power and autonomy. For many of the Naturalizers, the gendered future they seemed to be aiming their children toward raises the specter of the second shift. For the Cultivators, on the other hand, what comes to mind is the more class-specific gender trap of the hegemony of the male career and its particular risks for women. As Pyke argues,

This view assumes that family life is organized around family interests rather than the interests of more powerful members. However, this assumption ignores the costs that many wives pay for limiting their own job involvement in support of their husbands', particularly on the loss of a spouse to divorce or death. . . . It may be in the best interests of married women to focus on their own job development and economic independence, because the majority of them will be supporting themselves when their marriages end (due to divorce or widowhood). This capacity to impose a definition of reality that masks the real interests of their wives is indicative of the power of higher-status men, who benefit most from this ideology.[23]

Another distinguishing feature of this group of participants was that al-most all the Cultivators had at least one daughter (eight of ten parents); the Cultivator configuration was especially common among parents with daughters only, but almost all the Naturalizers had at least one son (eight of nine). Among parents inclined toward more reproduction-oriented prac-tices, the approach among those with sons was predominantly marked by biological determinism and concern about accountability, whereas those with daughters were influenced largely by a socially determinist and rou-tine outlook. Given that many parents believed that gendered account-ability imposes stronger constraints on boys than girls, and that many are more comfortable with gender-atypical outcomes for girls than for boys, the gendering of girls probably feels more routine and less fraught for parents who tend to reproduce gendered childhoods. The behavioral pattern among Cultivators especially celebrates nurturance, emotional attentiveness, and connectedness, as well as consciousness of fashion and appearance among daughters. Feminist analysts have long argued that Western culture steers girls and women toward serving others and viewing themselves as objects for others to gaze upon.[24] It is this kind of femininity that many Cultivators are crafting for their daughters, even more pointedly and casually than is done by Naturalizers. In view of the devaluation of femininity accompany-ing hegemonic masculinity, and given the implications of the second shift and the hegemony of the male career, this particular articulation of femi-ninity carries limitations for girls and women in households, the economy, and political and cultural arenas. The effort to open sports and traditionally male careers to girls is a positive step in offering them a greater range of play and a fuller human experience. The value of that opening, however, is limited by the potential trap of the deeply traditional options simultane-ously encouraged for girls and the lack of corresponding openness to boys entering into traditionally female domains. Cultivators direct their sons away from femininity and toward greater independence, toughness, sports, and outdoor play. Combining all that with routine heteronormativity, these parents ease their children toward gendered selves and toward a conven-tionally gendered path that reinforces, across a wide variety of arenas, ac-countability at the interactional level and class-inflected, gendered power structures at the institutional level.

4

"We Try Not to Encourage It, but I Know It Gets in There"

Refiners

Ben, a white, heterosexually partnered parent, is thirty-five years old and considers himself upper-middle class, an identification consistent with his luxurious home in a tree-lined neighborhood of similar houses. On the evening of our appointment, his wife was in the kitchen making tea and scones as we sat in the dining room talking about his experiences raising two sons and two daughters, all under the age of six. Ben concluded his assessment of the origins of gendered childhoods by saying, "If I had to throw something out there, I'd say sixty/forty, sixty environment, parents. . . . I do definitely believe that quite a bit is hardwired into a kid when they're born, that innate knowledge of how that gender's supposed to be that I talked about before, but more of it is environmental." In this comment, Ben typifies the Refiners, parents who combine roughly equal parts biology and society in explaining gendered childhoods, and roughly equal parts reproduction and resistance in their gendering actions. This melding highlights the way parents juggle and combine a variety of approaches that might, at first glance, seem unlikely to go together. Thinking about and acting on children's gender is an intricate balancing act with far more variation and complexity than could be captured by a model focused on individual-level socialization or unconscious rote reproduction. Gender structures do not simply predetermine parents' interpretations or behaviors. Rather, they shape a range of options for parents based on a mix of individual, interactional, and institutional factors. Refiners represent an approach that is at the center of the tensions I highlight: they are comfortable, up to a point, with typical gendered patterns but also consider gender differentiation at least somewhat problematic, and they are optimistic, to some extent, about their ability to disrupt that differentiation. Like their Naturalizer and Cultivator peers, they tend not to view gender categories as sources of structural power. More so than those peers, however, Refiners often view gendered expectations as unwelcome limitations on individual choice and obstacles to the development of skills and capacities which they believe their children need in their adult lives. Some degree of gendering based on biology, their own personal preferences, and their inclination to follow their children's lead strikes them as acceptable and desirable. Along with this acceptance, however, Refiners want to smooth the sharp edges of the constraints generated by the gender trap, moderating their influence and refining their content. As Ben put it, "I don't want to see strict dividing lines by gender, I don't think that's useful."

Lisa: "I Try to Emphasize That Whatever They Want Is Okay"

Another Refiner, Lisa, is the single parent of five-year-old twin sons, Dylan and Alex. She is white, thirty-two years old, and identifies as working class. Employed as a child care provider, Lisa has watched countless preschool-age children pass through the child care center where she works. It was at the center that she requested her interview take place, over her lunch hour, and as I watched her deftly field questions from coworkers and children, it was clear that she is an essential figure there. Based on her employment experience, she perceived that both biology and social influences shape gendered outcomes in childhood.

> I have watched classrooms and, you know, we will have ten girls and ten boys. I might have one girl that misbehaves, but I will have eight boys that have tendencies to make it to timeout once a day because of hitting or being physical or that kind of stuff. There has to be an inborn difference between boys and girls, I mean, there really, for the most part, just has to be. . . . They are all from similar families, similar backgrounds, they have all had experiences here in our center, some

112

have siblings and some not, but the group of boys will have the higher tendency to be more aggressive, physical, louder, play harder, and then the girls will tend to be more quiet.

Lisa also believes that parental influences have a role in developing gender differences.

I think that both the boys and girls would get dirty, however, I think clearly parents have said to the girls, you know, I don't want you dirty today. I think society is saying that girls shouldn't be dirty, that's how they are being brought up. . . . I think that is how their moms teach them. If you are a little girl, you stay in your dress and you stay on the swings and you stay clean, that is all you should do. . . . For boys, I think there are some days when those same parents just think, "Stay under control today, just listen today, sit in the circle and don't punch anybody and I'll be satisfied."

Although she began by talking about cleanliness, ultimately she referred to the same kind of physicality, loudness, and aggression she previously cited as natural, now implying that perhaps parents allowed it and thus played some role in shaping it. This combination of biological and social explanations was typical of the parents I classified as Refiners: neither biology nor society seemed to outweigh the other but were combined in ways that often seemed inconsistent but also highlighted the power of biological determinism to influence even parents who believe in the significant role of social determinism.[1]

Lisa offered a similar analysis of Alex and Dylan, describing them as "definitely acting like boys" and citing a range of high-energy activities as examples: "it's always bikes, sandpit, swings, hiking in the woods, climbing trees, that's the kind of behavior they show, active little boys." In her beliefs about the origins of those tendencies, Lisa again mentions "inborn differences between boys and girls." She also spoke about social factors such as classmates and her own actions. Like other Refiners, her socially determinist responses focused especially on interpersonal sources, including parents, peers, and relatives.

I have to think the environment is part of it, too. I can't help thinking that because I have that tendency myself, as a parent, to say, you
know, "Let's get trucks and cars because that's fun and all the other
little boys in the class have it too." . . . I've certainly bought them a
box full of trucks and ambulances and fire trucks.

Besides buying trucks and the like, Lisa also reported other reproductive actions. For example, in designing activities at home, she gave up on
certain nurturing-focused activities because "those just didn't hold their
attention" compared to activities involving the solar system, dinosaurs, or
gross-motor movement. Lisa sees herself as following a path already forged
by biology to some extent but also as adding to the gendering of that path
through her actions. In response to a question about whether she thought
her approach would change if she had a daughter, she again pointed to biology and her own actions.

If I had a daughter, yes, I bet you I would treat her differently in
some ways. And I bet you she would be different too. . . . My sister
has two boys and two girls, and her little girls have got the high-
heeled shoes and the hair styled up and the earrings and the dresses
with the flowers and the tights. I would love to do that, so yes, I am
sure I would.

Together with her sense that trucks and cars are fun for boys, this idea
that she would love to dress up a daughter suggests a personal preference
for some aspects of gendered childhoods. She also mentioned that, "as a
parent with little boys it's just more fun to do something like solar systems,
but I don't think I'd feel that way with little girls, I'd probably pick something else." On the other hand, Lisa engages in a series of both direct and
indirect actions that undo traditional gender expectations for her sons. She
is explicitly trying to encourage domestic skills and nurturance in Alex and
Dylan, buying them baby dolls with bottles so they can practice rocking and
comforting a baby, and showing them how to cook. Lisa also views the capacity to be empathetic as less typical for boys and takes direct action to
encourage it:

We have this chart at home and it is really important that we have "feeling talk," that we sit down and talk about how we feel today. "I am happy because of this, I am missing so and so." I really try to put that piece in and talk about your feelings, do some of that nurturing kind of work, and I hope I am really offering that piece that is not always offered for boys. . . . I think it is so critical as a person to know what is going on inside yourself.

These examples are consistent with what many parents considered acceptable gender atypicality for boys. But Lisa was the most resistance-oriented of the Refiners. Whereas most parents who resisted traditional career aspirations did so by noting that traditionally male careers should be open to women, Lisa emphasized the appropriateness of nontraditional careers for a boy: "For a while Dylan was going to be a doctor and Alex was going to be a nurse, and there did come up a question where girls are nurses because of books they'd seen, but I said, 'No way, you can be a nurse if you want to be, absolutely you can.'" She also engaged in the indirect undoing of gender by allowing her sons to explore even iconically feminine activities and objects when they expressed a desire to do so. In one such instance, she reported an event that had occurred before she was divorced. "They both wanted Barbies, and, of course, their dad did not want to go get them, so I am the one who had to go buy them, and I did go out and buy them." Lisa allows Alex and Dylan to explore their interest in dress-up as a play activity in a way many other parents consider inappropriate for boys.

They want to put my lipstick and my makeup on in the morning; of course they end up getting it all over the place. Well, I just say, "Take my old lipstick not my new lipstick," but I let them go ahead. And, you know, I tell them, of course, that girls wear makeup but sure, I will share it with you if you would like to try it. And usually girls wear dresses, but if you would like to try my dresses on, that's fine. . . . I know some don't agree with that, but I think it's fine.

With Lisa's motivations revolving around both personal preferences and her children's interests, she spoke of finding various gender-typical pursuits "more fun" not just for the children but for herself. She believes that expressing feelings and empathy is part of a child's healthy development and that her children need to know that "boys can do whatever they want to do." In explaining her encouragement of both the high-energy pursuits she associates with boys and the calmer nurturance and empathy she associates with girls, Lisa referred specifically to these characteristics as necessary for healthy development. "Having that range, it just makes you a better person, better able to get along with other people and enjoy life because you are a little more well-rounded." Accountability was less of a motivation for Lisa than for other Refiners, but she did acknowledge negative judgments. She commented on the disapproval expressed by some boys' fathers at the day care center if they saw their sons playing dress-up or other dramatic activities, and she believes that many parents would disagree with her willingness to let Dylan and Alex try on high heels and makeup.

The mothers who were Refiners were most likely among all the mothers to mention accountability to fathers, whether or not they heeded that pressure. Grace, another single mother in the Refiner category, cited the role played by accountability to fathers and male relatives in relation to sons when she recalled that her teenage son, Matt, had objected to the toy kitchen center, baby doll, and toy high chair she purchased for her preschool-aged son, Tyler:

I tend to think that you have the most difficulty when you have fathers around, they're the ones, you know? I had Matt to deal with when I had Tyler, you know, but I have the final say here. But when you've got a husband to deal with, it's harder. And those old stereotypes are going to continue to stay. "What are you trying to do, make a girl out of him?"

Lori, another Refiner, similarly described her husband's potential reaction if their infant son, Sean, eventually expressed interest in a traditionally female profession: "I think if Sean told him he was gonna be a nurse, my husband would probably faint." Lori also noted her husband's approach to their three-year-old daughter, Alyssa, compared to the infant Sean.

I know he's happy that he has a little boy. He'll make comments, "Oh, I can't wait until I can take him to, you know, Red Sox games," and I'm like, "Well, you can take Alyssa too." . . . Because it doesn't matter if she's a girl, you know, and if our son wants to play with dolls, he can. I don't think my husband agrees though, he's just like, "Well, I *guess* that's true."

In a comment that may reflect personal preference or concern about accountability rather than simply acknowledgement, Lisa did report reservations about her twin sons' interest in the iconic activities of Barbies and dress-up: "Sometimes I do think to myself, why do they want that? Yeah, I think, 'Oh, my God.' But of course, most of the time I try to just think, 'Okay, it's okay, you can try it out.'"

Brianna: "Not Too Much One Way or Another"

Brianna, the mother of a three-year-old daughter, is a white, upper-middle-class, forty-nine-year-old surgeon in a lesbian partnership. We spoke in her quiet, comfortable, and impeccably organized office, where she watched the clock to ensure our conversation fit within the one-hour time slot she had allocated. Brianna responded thoughtfully but pointedly in the interview, telling me that she preferred having a daughter because she felt she could relate more to a girl, although she also mentioned that she herself was not particularly feminine. After remarking that her daughter, Haley, has always liked dolls, both baby dolls and Barbies, she began to speak of biological factors:

It's made me think a lot more about sort of genetic influence, the fact that she's got two X chromosomes, . . . and it's not a more recent thing, it's all along she's been very nurturing with her dolls.

Brianna added that, in her view, neither she nor her partner, Lynne, steered Haley in that direction.

We don't push the Barbie stuff at all, in fact I would prefer her not to have it, . . . so I'm intrigued at how even though I sort of do that mid-

117

dle road, she nonetheless is veering over toward being more feminine or stereotypically feminine, that's why I think it's genetic.

Brianna's articulation of biological determinism, introduced in chapter 1 as the "fallback" position, is evident in her conclusion that nature must be combating her parental efforts of trying to follow "that middle road," since Haley was nevertheless veering toward stereotypically feminine behavior. The Refiners were most likely to use biology as a fallback, which was also evident in Lisa's argument that the gender variations in a classroom are likely the result of nature, as the boys and girls all come from similar households. Yet she later argued that parents treat boys and girls differently within households. For Brianna, too, the fallback to biology was somewhat inconsistent with other comments in which she highlighted social forces. For example, she subsequently mentioned that Haley enjoys makeup, hair styling, and fashion, interests Brianna considered socially cultivated.

We don't introduce that kind of stuff except by mistake, but Linda, the day care person, does introduce it. She'll do Haley's nails or she'll have an afternoon where the girls all comb her hair. There's only about three girls there, and they all put pigtails in each other's hair and put clips on each other's hair, she loves that.

Brianna spoke about other social sources of gendering, focusing particularly, as did most Refiners, on interpersonal sources:

I have a sister who does a fair amount of that. . . . She gives Haley gifts that are overly, almost in a joking way, you know these really frilly purses or all this fake jewelry. . . . I sometimes think she feels perhaps that we are not going to raise her niece in a feminine enough way, and she wants to make sure she has that influence, but she tries to keep it light by making it almost in a joking way.

Refiners may be especially inclined to "fall back" on biology because of the overall configuration of their beliefs and preferences. They tend to view gender differentiation as at least somewhat problematic and to prefer

118

resistance to some extent. But they also see biological explanations as part of the story and express preferences for some degree of gender typicality, viewing gender more as an issue of difference than of power. As they try to craft a refined version of gendering, which they consider healthy, they do so while believing in biological determinism, providing a ready explanation should one of their refinement efforts fail. Following the same pattern Marie, a white, middle-class, thirty-four-year-old, stay-at-home mother with two daughters, told me at one point in our interview, "Oh, yeah, I do think there are some differences. I never, you know, before I had kids I wouldn't have wanted to say that, but I find myself saying that now . . . I cringe saying that, I hate to say that, but I really do find that's the case." Like Brianna, Marie recognizes social forces but seems to discount them once she sees gender-typical behavior, especially when it arises despite her efforts to discourage it. Refiners often indicate a baseline acceptance of social determinism that has been shifted by their parenting experience, even though that experience could be explained by the social forces they acknowledge.

The gendering actions Brianna reported were largely indirect and followed what she sees as her daughter's lead but were laced with shifting assumptions about her child's agency. After noting, for example, that Haley prefers dolls to trucks or construction toys, Brianna went on to explain that she would happily buy the latter items if Haley wanted them: "If I thought she was interested in building or working with that kind of stuff, I'd be running out and buying that . . . But, you know, she's just not at all interested in it." Brianna also described two instances in which she claimed to have followed Haley's lead concerning a typically gendered activity and item. Each highlights Brianna's indirect, perhaps slightly reluctant, reports of doing gender with and for her child.

> She has expressed some interest in doing ballet, and I'm thinking, well, sure, at this age, we will put her in some little ballet class when she's four. . . . Pink, she loves pink. That's her favorite color. So you know, like for Christmas time I bought her this little pink plastic purse, which wasn't my first choice, but she was pretty excited. So I try to buy her pink stuff.[2]

119

Like other Refiners, Brianna sometimes discounts her child's agency and turns to biology as an explanation; she assumes that gendered tendencies do not emerge because Haley acts on the social cues that Brianna acknowledges but instead result at least partly from natural tendencies beyond Haley's control. She also believes that she is following Haley's lead but steering her toward the "middle ground" while respecting her agency and preferences. Through indirect gendering, Brianna reinforces the social structures that shape expressions of Haley's agency, even while she shifts between perceiving that agency as flowing from nature or social influences imposed by her peers and day care provider. Brianna does not view child rearing as only about parents; she believes that it also involves granting her child's preferences primacy in ways that lead Brianna, as a parent, indirectly into the gender trap.

Despite the reluctance she implies, Brianna said that she is comfortable with Haley's generally traditional interests and that she had never requested toys or activities more commonly associated with boys. If Haley had made such requests, however, Brianna said that a limited amount would be fine but that she prefers that her daughter is at least somewhat typical.

> I think I would feel uncomfortable, if she really were to go toward race cars and to be more male oriented, stereotypically male oriented. I would think, "Hmm, that's interesting, I wonder why that's happening?" Would I not let her do that? No, I wouldn't not let her do it, but I guess I would wonder about it and feel some concern.

Thus Brianna expressed some personal preferences, but overall her primary focus throughout the interview was on Haley's preferences and the desire to make her child happy.

> I don't think it's fair to restrict something. . . . And it really does seem like she's gravitating more toward the Barbie and that stuff, and that's okay. . . . I'm not trying to push one thing or another. . . . I mean, I think if you try to push something that's your agenda rather than the kid's agenda, that's a mistake.

120

At the same time Brianna reported encouraging outcomes that she considers not "stereotypically female"—an undoing gender approach more direct than indirect.

> We are raising her with sort of, you know, like it's okay to hold worms, this morning she wanted to hold a worm, look at the worm, and that's great. We're raising her with "let's go hiking" and "I'm a good hiker Mommy, aren't I?" And we'll go camping outside in a few weekends, so we do a lot of stuff that's not stereotypically female. . . . I know there are families whose girls are dressed in pink ruffles every day, all that kind of thing, and I would say, "Oh, the poor kid." I think a kid is healthier, I think an adult is healthier, who is more androgynous rather than too much one way or another.

Like Brianna, Lori also invokes this assessment of what is healthier during childhood and into adulthood. But in her case, like Lisa, she invokes it in reference to boys.

> I think, when they grow into men, they'll be better fathers and husbands if they are taught when they're young, if the parents, you know, show them that it's okay to cry, it's okay to love somebody and to show it, don't keep your feelings all bottled up inside you. I think it just makes a happier person as an adult.

Seeking a middle ground that they consider a healthier place Refiners are most likely to invoke gender neutrality of the sort introduced briefly in chapter 1. Rather than identifying gender boundaries and working to cross them, their responses are focused more on ignoring boundaries, with explanations such as "I comfort and discipline my son and daughter exactly the same way" or "I don't take gender into account at all." This "gender blind" approach is consistent with Refiners' preference for a compromise that potentially challenges gendered structures by refusing to fall into the gender trap defined by those structures. But just as sociologist Eduardo Bonilla-Silva argued that color-blind ideologies ultimately cannot disrupt structures of racial inequality, and MacKinnon argued

121

that purportedly gender-neutral laws cannot adequately redress imbalances of gendered power, the potential of this gender-blind parenting approach is limited by insufficient recognition of the strength of entrenched gendered structures.[3] Building on previous analyses of racial inequality in the United States, Bonilla-Silva contends that ignoring deeply rooted inequalities allows them to continue unabated. In her influential analysis of legal systems in the United States and internationally, MacKinnon reveals how ignoring gender allows male dominance to continue. Lorber calls this the first paradox of degendering, "a period of self-conscious attention to gendering has to come first. You have to be aware of gendering to degender."[4] Attempts at gender-neutral parenting run the same risk, particularly when combined, as they often are among Refiners, with a willingness to follow a child's gendered lead. The problem with teaching children that, in Brianna's words, "You can do whatever you want to do" is that myriad social forces shaping children's desires—some of which are perceived as natural—often mean that parents follow them into the gender trap.[5]

William: "A Little Bit More Well-Rounded Approach"

Unlike Lisa and Brianna, who each have only sons or daughters, most Refiners have both. William, for instance, is a forty-three-year-old, heterosexual father with two teenage sons from a previous marriage who live with their mother a distance away, as well as three children with his current wife, Amy. White, identifying as middle class, and employed as a banker, William lives with his four-year-old son Brian, the focus of our interview, as well as Brian's eighteen-month-old brother Connor, and eight-year-old sister Faith. William was casual, confident, and outgoing throughout the interview, which took place in the cozy living room of his modest, early twentieth-century frame house. He said that before having children he hoped for a son in order to continue the family name and forge the father-son bond he wished he had with his own father. When his first child was a son, he was, in his words, "pretty pumped." He views males as generally more aggressive than females, and females as more nurturing. "I think it's genetically predisposed that way," he told me, and spoke about an anthropol-

122

ogy course he took in college. "I think it comes back from hunter-gatherer times. You know, I have spent a bit of time looking into anthropological aspects of it and really taking a look at that and there's something to be said for that. That's part of our humankind genetic makeup."

Along with their tendency to believe in the fallback articulation of biological determinism, Refiners joined Naturalizers as most likely to identify some intention or purpose behind natural sex differences. William did so when he referred to the "anthropological aspects" of gendered variation in aggression and nurturance. Male aggression was explained similarly by Marie: "I think it has something to do with testosterone and the abilities that God gave men way back when, the survival instincts and having to hunt to protect the family and that whole thing, I think it's part of their biology." Ben noted that "every kid is born with certain innate knowledge of how that gender is *supposed to be*."

This purpose-driven biological foundation still leaves room for significant societal influence, as evident, for example, in Teresa's analysis. This thirty-one-year-old teacher's aide, a working-class, white mother of two in a heterosexual partnership, observed:

> I do think part of it is the way that we raise children, the girls to be good caretakers and boys need to be tough and protect the family and all that. But then I do think also, I just think there's something that they're born with. I mean, why would there be two different sexes if they were going to be exactly the same?

William combined his purposive biologically determinist outlook with a belief in the value of "shaking things up," trying to soften the edges of male aggression and harden the edges of female nurturance.

> I think a nurturing environment is more likely to let that line get blended. And that's the position we're in, that's what we want to do. Unfortunately we have kind of a stereotypical male-female role here, with Amy being home with the kids, but we try to break that up and shake it up and confuse it purposefully. Just so that there's a little bit more well-rounded approach.

Four of the Refiners used the term "well-rounded" to describe what they value in avoiding too much gendered constraint. Only one participant outside this group used that term, suggesting that it captures a particular aspect of the goals and preferences of Refiners. William, for example, sees himself as encouraging a well-rounded set of interests when he teaches his four-year-old son to cook, a pastime William himself enjoys. He also engages both Brian and the younger Connor in gardening, including cutting flowers in the family's garden, an activity he considers somewhat unusual for boys and thus an opportunity for letting "that line get blended." William also views efforts he and Amy made to involve eight-year-old Faith in active outdoor pursuits as a chance to avoid gender-typical patterns.

> She'll do girl things with her girlfriends. She will play quietly in her room, do art things, be creative. But she never really played with dolls a lot, she likes playing rough. I think that was part of our relationship, hers and mine, you know, because we've always roughhoused and tumbled around and I would swing her around by her hands and that kind of stuff. She was our first, so we did a lot of stuff, backpacking, hiking, bicycling, canoeing, skiing. . . . We wanted to keep things moving, not just leave her sitting playing with dolls all the time. . . . And now Faith plays soccer and she's very aggressive, and she's an aggressive skier too, which is good to see.

William views his youngest son, eighteen-month-old Connor, as especially gender-typical, a child, William said, who "came out knowing he was a boy." Even so, William identified in Connor a mixture of biological and social influences.

> He is incredibly stereotypical. His grandfather is a fire captain, fire chief, and you walk around and there are fire trucks everywhere, which he loves. And he's into tools and doing things like fixing stuff around the house, you know following me or his grandfather fixing things. Yeah, he is total boy. . . . I think a good part of it's genetic. I really do. I think environment has something to play too and certainly role modeling and that sort of thing certainly comes to play. . . .

I think a lot of it's genetic early [on]. I think environment impacts more and more as time goes on, but you're not going to kick that genetic code.

William also described four-year-old Brian as typically "boyish" but not to the same extent. Though he talked about being completely comfortable with whatever his children's sexual orientation might eventually turn out to be, and in that way was among the least heteronormative of the heterosexual parents, William's openness to what he called "crossing lines" was tempered by biological determinism and the limits to his own personal comfort level. He defined the limits in relation to Brian:

Lately, Brian has asked for things I think would be more for a girl. He's seen the ads on TV, and I want to tone it down a notch. For example, if he wanted a Barbie doll I might get him a doll but not necessarily a Barbie doll. If he wanted a little girl's play set, I might get him something very similar to that but a little more gender specific. I don't know why, but that's how I feel.

William also suggested that his own feelings delineate those limits. Like Brianna, Refiners are not consistently motivated by their own personal preferences, often focusing on the preferences of their children. But whether expressed as motivations for their actions or not, this group of parents' personal feelings are the most equally distributed in terms of reproduction and resistance. They strike a middle ground not just in their actions and explanations for gendered childhoods but in their feelings as well. William's ability to balance his feelings is evident in the pleasure he experiences teaching Brian to cook and his satisfaction in teaching Faith to be active, even aggressive, coupled with his desire to "tone down" Brian's emerging interest in toys more typical for girls.

Celine, a thirty-two-year-old part-time restaurant hostess, made similar remarks in discussing her four-year-old daughter, Ariel. She told me that Ariel enjoys catching frogs and playing with Barbies and referred to that combination as a "blend" of typically masculine and feminine interests: "She's got a good focus on things, that blend feel, I love it." This white, working-class, heterosexually partnered mother of four is pleased that her daughter enjoys frogs and snakes, which Celine has encouraged, but also delighted to see her maintaining more typically feminine interests as well. Like William, she becomes concerned more quickly when her two sons cross conventional gender lines, as she believes that playing with dolls is "not normal" for boys—in her words: "It's not in their gender." Ben, introduced at the beginning of this chapter, is more open to that kind of play but, again, only to a limit shaped by his preferences and sense of how others might react.

> You've got to be steering in the right direction, so to speak, given the norms. . . . I just think there's a certain age at which you have to remind them that there's a certain direction in which they're supposed to be going, and do what you can to steer them in that direction. So, does it bother me when Lucas [his three-year-old] and his friend Allen are holding hands? No. No, you know that's what teachers teach the kids to do when they're on field trips and all that, I can rationalize it at this point, I can handle it now.

William expressed greater comfort in blending gender lines than Ben or Celine did, but he, too, wants to keep them somewhat intact.

Belinda: "Exposed to All Options and All Sides"

Belinda, another Refiner who used the phrase "well-rounded" to describe her child-rearing goals, is a white, middle-class, heterosexually partnered mother of two who had been a pilot but became a full-time homemaker after the birth of her first child, seven-year-old Elizabeth. When Elizabeth was four, Belinda had a second child, three-year-old Robert, the focal child of our interview. In her own gendered path and her approach to her children's, Belinda believes that biological differences affect work and family, but she is also in favor of women entering traditionally male careers and opposes socially enforced gender expectations. Typical of Refiners, she recognizes the social sources of gendering, particularly interactional sources as opposed to institutional sources. Belinda cited members of her extended family as an important source of her children's interest in gender-typical toys.

> There is an expectation from family members about boys and girls and things they'll like. . . . They always buy Barbies, all my in-laws and all the family, my house is filled with Barbie at Christmas, plus trucks. It's Barbie and trucks, Barbie and trucks, like there is nothing else.

Another defining feature of the Refiner approach is the belief in biological determinism. While both children were at camp on a summer morning, Belinda sat amid the toys cluttering her spacious living room and talked about biology as a factor.

> Elizabeth didn't show as much interest in trucks and vehicles as Robert did, he really took to them much more than Elizabeth. Even though Elizabeth was exposed to all the airplanes and stuff like that she wants to be a teacher, she wanted that even before she went to school and really started being influenced by school. Robert wants to be a rocket ship pilot. I mean, he loves Star Wars, that's the big thing. We get them Legos. But Elizabeth will build a house with her Legos, Robert will build a rocket ship with his Legos. . . . I don't know how much that was socialized and how much of that is just biology. We try not to encourage the socialization aspect of it, but I know it gets in there anyway. But also, I really think some of it is just natural.

Belinda also reported various actions that reproduce typically gendered outcomes. Although she considers Robert's interest in cars and trucks natural, she also concludes that the specific form of his interest is socially shaped: "I really do think it was natural. But I also think if it had been a Barbie car that we handed him it would have been just as interesting as a truck at first." She goes on to talk about encouraging Elizabeth's interest in dolls: "I do some of the stereotype thing, I give her dolls. I want her to play with dolls. I want that nurturing, loving aspect. . . . I want her to be feminine." She also encourages ballet, an activity she considers more appropriate for girls, and takes Elizabeth thirty miles each way for frequent lessons. With Robert she plans to focus more on sports, and reported that his "obsession" with Star Wars was something his father cultivated but did not encourage for their daughter. Belinda spoke at length about a role-playing game Robert and Elizabeth play together, based on Robert's love of Star Wars. She said the children often end up in conflict over the fact that "only two good female parts" are available in this game, Princess Leia from the older movies or Queen Amidala from the more recent ones.[6] Thus Robert has an array of choice parts, whereas Elizabeth has only two. Belinda was creative in coming up with ideas for how Elizabeth could execute one of those two parts in new ways, but it seemed not to have occurred to her that her daughter could act in a male role.

At the same time Belinda is careful to comfort and discipline her son and daughter similarly, basing her approach on their age, and she wants her children, especially Elizabeth, to have opportunities beyond those often ascribed to each gender.

> I am much more aware, as a woman who was very much in a man's profession for a long time, about building Elizabeth's self-esteem, building her awareness of opportunities out there. We'll go to the aquarium and . . . if there's a woman diver, then I'm gonna be there and I'll stand there at the tank until the lady comes up for air. I am very conscious about exposing her to different fields.

When asked if she tries to do the same with Robert, she replied, "I guess it could probably be good for Robert, but . . . not so much, it's [more] for Elizabeth, I know I'm very conscious of it." She prefers that Elizabeth is exposed to a blend of traditionally feminine, as well as a broader range, of interests and activities. She disliked the level of interest her seven-year-old daughter was showing in very girlish clothing, and she and her husband discouraged this.

> We're keeping her well-rounded. I think we've had an influence that's kept her from being overly feminine. . . . I tell her she can do whatever she wants. She can be a test pilot for a while and then become a stay-at-home mom and then she can go back to doing something else later

like I plan to do. I just want her to know, I want her exposed to all options and all sides.

Belinda wants her daughter to be feminine and nurturing, graceful and balletic, but she also seeks to avoid an "overly feminine" focus on fashion and wants her daughter's options to include a traditionally male career. Belinda and other Refiners couched this twofold goal in an overarching commitment to individual freedom: "She can do whatever she wants." For Robert, too, she is open to some crossing of typical gender lines, as he plays along with some of his sister's games. Belinda allows this in a way that many Cultivators discourage. "He will let his sister put makeup on him and play with dollies, because we've never told him that boys don't do that." But she also acknowledged limits as a result of accountability when she further commented: "He doesn't know that that's not okay to some people, but he's also only three, he's never been laughed at for doing that." Belinda implies that eventually someone will laugh at Robert if he does not stop on his own, so one way or another, through loss of interest or the pressure of accountability, he is likely to stop.

Most Refiners were distinct in how they responded to a general question near the end of the interview. "Are there any particular things that you're trying to teach your kids about boys and girls or men and women?" The responses tended to fall into five categories. Some participants said no, they were not trying to teach anything in particular. Others mentioned teaching about physical aspects of reproduction or anatomical differences (such as teaching that women can have babies and men cannot), or about physical safety (for example, several parents noted "good touch" and "bad touch," interpreting my question in sexual terms). Cultivators predominated in these first two categories. Some parents, mostly Naturalizers, spoke about a third focus, teaching their children traditional gendered structures. Jerome, for example, repeated his earlier comment that he is teaching his children that "boys marry girls and girls marry boys," whereas Jamie replied that she is teaching her son how a gentleman ought to treat a lady. Another group reported that they are teaching their children to reject gender expectations and even inequalities. This fourth category was most common for Innovators and Resisters, whom I discuss later. The fifth and final category of responses may be termed the "individualist response"; these are parents who are teaching their children that they "can be, or do, anything they want." Seven of the ten Refiners were in this category, and the lesson they have in mind runs parallel to their previously discussed tendency to engage in actions that are gender-neutral. Lori noted that despite her husband's likely reservations about their son wanting to be a nurse, her own response would be different: "as long as he was happy and doing whatever he wanted that would be fine." Belinda's answer struck a similar chord in relation to her daughter:

> I don't want her to think that, you know, you have to have a career and things like that. I want her to know that being a stay-at-home mom is okay, too. I want her to know that she has all options. To me the big thing is self-esteem; I want her to know that she's capable of doing anything.

Belinda, in commenting on gendered divisions of labor and her desire for her daughter, but not her son, to consider options that include full-time homemaking, conveys the individualist sensibility that Refiners exhibit, along with the class-based gender expectations common to some of these parents. She also expresses the Refiners' less consistent, but still frequent, tendency to frame gender relations as a matter of difference rather than power. Naturalizers were the most likely to offer this framing, followed by Cultivators and then Refiners, who again occupied a middle ground between parents oriented toward reproduction and those oriented toward resistance. Belinda mentioned that her son asked "why so many mommies are home and so many daddies go to work." Her response was similar to that of Bob, a Cultivator described in the previous chapter, who pointed to individual differences in income-earning capacity and patience with children. In a briefer version, she still explained that the division of labor by gender involves difference, not power: "In our house it's because daddy works very hard so that . . . we can afford for mommy to stay home and be with them [the children]." Another example comes from Ben, who wondered what he would say if one of his children ever asked why their mother is home with them all day and he is not.

I wouldn't want to make it seem sinister. I'd just want to give a nice answer that they could understand without getting too much into it. It just goes way back, like I've talked to Jacob, we've actually talked about the way it used to be when the man would go out and kill the animals and the woman would stay with the kids and do the domestic stuff. So I could talk about that as far as saying how it came to be that men work more often than women.

A few Refiners do refer to gendered power, as illustrated by a comment Brianna made about her daughter: "I do have the concern that sooner or later she'll have to encounter the reality that women are somewhat oppressed, . . . but I'm not too worried." Marie also expressed concern about her five-year-old daughter, but, like Brianna, it apparently does not shape her parenting practice at this point.

The Little Mermaid, I feel, sends a horrible message, this woman has to change her whole being to be with a man. It bothers me, but I do let her [my daughter] watch it, we have it on DVD. I'm not saying that it's not a subtle message that might reach her, but I really think that goes way over her head at this point.

Overall, Refiners gravitate toward a compromise on this dimension, too. The few who are concerned about gendered power do not view it as a major issue, and although the group as a whole is critical of too much gender differentiation, it views differentiation as acceptable up to a point.

"If I Had to Throw Something Out There, I'd Say Sixty/Forty"

Moderation was a theme in how Refiners responded to a question focusing on children's interests: "Do you think kids today would be better off without as many gender-related expectations, or do you think these kinds of expectations just fit pretty well with what kids like anyway?" Three sample responses illustrate the typical attitude among Refiners.

I do think that to some degree those expectations seem to fit, things that go more with girls than with boys and vice versa. So I don't think that the whole concept of it is a negative concept, it's just gone too far. (Marie)

I think it would be better if they didn't have so much of it, if they could just kind of pursue their own interests as they arise. . . . I mean, some of it is just going be a natural inclination, but I don't think that it should be pushed onto them so much. (Teresa)

I don't think they'd be better off without them at all, I just don't think there's a need for a strict adherence to them. . . . I mean, I don't think it's helpful or necessary to beat a particular gender into a child. (Ben)

These views capture the Refiner approach of providing a solid foundation of direct and indirect reproductive actions, as well as encouraging some crossing of perceived gender divisions. They seek to prepare their children for a refined version of the conventionally gendered path, hoping that in the process they will gain a wide range of choices. Individual choice is especially important to this group. They emphasize their children's interests through a focus on the "healthiness" of a refined path and their desire to let their children "do anything they want."

Clearly this desire potentially can chip away at gendered constraints in childhood and beyond. Through their efforts, Refiners may weaken the gender trap for their children and loosen the pressures of interactional accountability on other families. These parents, however, limit their own ability to live up to that potential fully; they emphasize following their children's lead and fall back on biology when their relatively gentle resistance fails to capture their children's interest. They may underestimate the extent to which social influences shape their children's preferences, especially institutional-level pressures, and overestimate the strength of their own undoing efforts, making gender-typical outcomes seem more natural or more freely chosen than they actually are. Consider, for example, Marie's comments, as we explored the interests of her five-year-old daughter, Lauren. Marie spoke about how she and her husband offered Lauren a range of activities and toys early on. "You know, we tried to go out back with her and play baseball, say just for an activity, you know, hit the ball with the bat when she was a toddler. And I bought her little toys that were trucks. We consciously wanted to buy her toys that people would think were for both sexes." Now that Lauren is five, however, all this changed.

> I'm home with her more and I have to say that it's not as if I'm trying to get outside with her and play ball with her every day. And I don't sit down with her and try to play trucks. . . . She plays independently really well, so I think some of it is just kind of who she is, you know? But I'm sure if I tried to do more of that outdoor sports type of play she probably would be into it more.

As the conversation went on, Marie talked about her hopes for Lauren, which she conveyed as giving Lauren more choices. "I want her to be well-rounded, I want her to have physical flexibility and I want her to enjoy sports and be able to have the confidence in sports so that if she chooses to want to play, she can."

Marie views Lauren's interest in sports as an option that she wants for her daughter but not one that requires her direct influence.[7] But when asked whether she might raise sons differently, sports promptly came to her mind. "I wonder if we would play more sports, you know, if we would be more inclined to try to do that more frequently, I think we might." This set of hopes and actions, and this emphasis on choice and following her daughter's lead, all came together in a story Marie told about enrolling Lauren in a soccer camp the previous summer.

> I got her involved with the little summer soccer camp, just a four-day thing. But she thought it was a lot of work and she was tired everyday and I saw that by the end she'd be chit-chatting with a girlfriend of hers, you know, and other people were still in the game. So she was not really into it at all. . . . I felt a little bit disappointed just because, like I said before, I really wanted her to be exposed to a well-rounded background and I'd like her to be interested in some sort of sporting activity, just to make her a well-rounded person. And I offered

her that, I talked with her about playing soccer in the fall with the local recreation department, but she really just wasn't interested at all. She's also taken dance lessons for the past two years and has preferred that, so we'll focus on that instead.

This story exemplifies how parents may fall into the gender trap by reading socially shaped gender patterns as individual choices, sometimes even as choices shaped by biology. Refiners are especially likely to do so, probably because they merge biology and society in their beliefs about the origins of gendered childhoods and tend to view gender differences without analyzing institutional structure and power. Marie regards herself as trying to open a new option for Lauren, but she also believes in fundamental, individual-level sex differences, what she refers to as "the biology piece," "testosterone," and "survival instincts." When her offer to give Lauren options fails to capture Lauren's interest, she is willing to shift gears and take a new path that she views as forged by Lauren rather than by broader interactional and institutional forces. Sports and dance each offers rich opportunities for fitness, self-expression, and social interaction, but the pattern evident in Marie's responses reduces the likelihood that a given child will gravitate either to sports or dance based on temperament, personality, or individual preference rather than on socially constructed gender expectations.

A similar configuration of reproduction and resistance characterizes a story Ben told about his family following a period when construction workers had been in their home working on a kitchen expansion.

There's this particular construction worker, his name was Fred. . . . He and I would sit down in the back and have a beer and talk about, you know, the day. And you'd see Jacob walk by, playing dress up in his sister's Cinderella outfit, and I'm thinking, "What must Fred be thinking of this?" . . . He's walking around in ballroom gowns and Cinderella outfits, and we'd get a laugh out of it. Fred would say, "What's going on here?" and I'd say, "Just early training, making sure he's as docile for his wife as I am for my wife." And Fred would say, "Hey, Ben, I think you better step in here and put your foot down." . . . And Fred has seen Lucas, my other son, my three-year-old, holding hands with his little friend Allen, while Jacob dances by in that princess outfit. Yeah, that's a little harsh to take. That's a stigma I have to live down, I suppose.

Ben told this story in good humor, laughing as he described the encounter, but it revealed the tensions parents have to balance as they navigate the gender trap. Ben views a Cinderella outfit as appropriate only for Jacob's older sister to own ("his sister's Cinderella outfit"), a routine act of gendering consistent with other comments he made in his interview. For example, at one point he said that it is hard to stop "the Barbies or the Disney stuff" from coming in as birthday gifts to his daughters: "There's really nothing you can do." Perhaps the Cinderella costume was one of those Disney items that could not be stopped because it had been a present, but he also mentioned that he and his wife bring home similar items for their daughter.

If from day one we didn't expose Leah to, for example, the Disney princesses and all that, I don't think she would've had nearly as much interest in it. It's hardly the biggest thing in her life, but you know, she likes it a lot. If you were to go upstairs you'd see her sheets are princess sheets from Disney, her pillowcase too. That was some influence on her parents' part, specifically, and I don't object to any of that stuff. But, you know, I certainly didn't go after Leah's princess or Barbie stuff and show it to Jacob once he came along.

Scholars of gender and childhood have noted the power of princess imagery in general and especially the Disney princess narrative.[8] They have argued that it often reinforces not only gender inequality but intersecting inequalities of race, sexuality, and nation.[9] This reinforcement takes place through its focus on beauty, passivity, and female dependence on a prince, which resonates with what Connell calls "emphasized femininity."[10] Ben views princess-themed items as appropriate only for Leah or her toddler sister, reinforcing those connections. But playing in their sister's outfits or holding hands with another boy is perfectly acceptable for his three- and four-year-old sons, thus refining the stricter gender constraints that many Cultivators would simply dictate for their sons. He wants to allow his sons to express themselves, to have fun and enjoy their childhood. Ben's comfort with this crossing of gender lines is framed, however, by a number of constraints: heteronormativity ("making him docile for his wife"); accountability to others who expect him and his son to appear masculine ("a stigma I have to live down"); and a willingness to "steer" his children in the "direction they're supposed to be going," if such crossing continues past a particular age.

Ben's encounter with Fred also has class implications. He casually defends his son's gender performance to the construction worker renovating the kitchen of his expensive home; the two men bond across class lines through masculinity performance, with the less powerful man challenging his employer about his sons' behavior and the more powerful man laughing at himself for being docile for his wife. These dynamics are reminiscent of Pyke's notion of class-based masculinities. The worker tells Ben that he ought to "step in" and "put his foot down," but Ben appears confident and casual as he defends himself jokingly.[11] Ultimately Ben suspects that his class-based brand of masculinity performance is adequately well respected, that he can refine it up to a point and begin "steering" only when it becomes necessary. In recent decades, as Messner has argued, white, middle- and upper-middle class men "began to symbolically distance themselves from . . . traditional masculinity and forged new, more sensitive forms," but these forms are still bounded by the basic parameters of hegemonic masculinity.[12] Following Connell's work on hegemonic and subordinated masculinities, Pyke asserts that working-class men exhibit a "compensatory masculinity" based on physical strength and more explicit domination of women to "symbolically turn the tables against" higher-class males, "whom they ridicule as conforming 'yes-men' and 'wimps' engaged in effeminate paper-pushing kinds of labor." Pyke also observes that "middle- and upper-class men, on the other hand, who display the more civilized demeanor of polite gentility, express disdain for the ostentatious displays of exaggerated masculinity and misogyny among lower-class [men]."[13] In the process she concludes, "The gendered power advantages of higher-class men" are obscured, "camouflaged by an aura of merit and righteousness that accompanies their privileged position."[14] The exchange between Fred and Ben, though not as dramatic as the deeper discourse Pyke describes, is a gentler version of that tension in which Ben is both vigilant and reasonably confident as he nego- tiates his sons', and his own, masculinities by recourse to humor and ac- knowledgment of his accountability to the worker's normative conceptions of gender but buffered by his relatively superior class position.

Other Refiners also raise the issue of accountability, more so than Cul- tivators do, partly because they are more likely to allow or even encourage atypical outcomes that reveal accountability pressures. But Refiners tend to express only a modest amount of concern about that accountability. Moth- ers' expressions of accountability to fathers arise more often in this group than any other, with paternal pressure one of the moderating influences for the many heterosexually partnered women in this group. But instead of reflecting a high degree of concern over this pressure, mothers more gener- ally negotiate with their husbands, especially if they have sons, refining the situation, rather than resisting it, in order to remain within their husbands' comfort range. Reports of accountability to people other than fathers are similarly articulated, with some degree of concern but little anxiety. Teresa spoke of accountability to significant others who exert social influence by giving presents, especially what she called fighting toys, to her four-year- old son, Austin. Though she sees male aggression as partly biological, she feels that social forces push children "too far," into violence. She prefers to keep Austin away from such toys but is frustrated in her efforts. "I'm not really respected when I tell people that's not what I want for him, they still give it to him anyway, so the best I can do is I just kind of compromise and take some of the little parts off, like if they have swords or little guns." Teresa resists to an extent but strikes this compromise, going as far as she feels she can within the constraints imposed by biology and social account- ability. She tries to "round out" Austin's interest in fighting games by buy- ing toys that encourage empathy and nurturance.

Refiners are from a variety of class backgrounds, but all are white and most are heterosexual (nine of the ten interviewees in this category) and female (eight of the ten). Responsiveness to accountability pressures from male partners may partly explain the tendency for heterosexual women to fall into this category, but several single mothers are here as well, and most of the heterosexually partnered mothers report more motivations related to personal preference than accountability. In this group as a whole, per-

137

sonal preference motivates their reproduction and resistance, as well as a desire to do what they believe is in the best interests of their children. Together with their acknowledgment of a socially constructed component to gendered childhoods, and their efforts to refine by combining reproduction and resistance in their actions, their configuration of beliefs and practices potentially avoids the gender trap. As I have noted, however, the foundation of their belief in biological determinism often leads them to underestimate the power of social forces and restricts their ability to realize that potential.

When asked toward the end of the interview whether they think it is possible to reduce the amount of gender typing kids engage in, Refiners were second to Innovators in saying they do consider it possible, and their responses suggest that they view this goal as relatively simple to achieve. As Grace put it, "Oh, yeah, it's possible, because it's only a mind-set," and Belinda replied "Yes, definitely, you just have to control what they see and who they interact with, and I think parents have a lot more control in that than they realize." The Naturalizers, in contrast, tend to view any significant reduction of gender typing in childhood as undesirable and unlikely to succeed given the determining role of biology. Cultivators also tend to consider it undesirable, and many of them responded with confusion about whether it is possible, as the question seemed somewhat irrelevant. Refiners, meanwhile, are already taking action to reduce gender typing. Given their relatively modest goals for refinement, their recognition of interpersonal sources of gendering, and a more limited focus on structural barriers, many of them probably see the possibility as quite real. Together with their tendency to follow their children's lead and to want all options open for their daughters but fewer for their sons, this pattern suggests that the Refiner approach has built-in limitations. Their children, responding to an array of social forces, often lead them down conventionally gendered paths lined with dolls and princess imagery for girls, and trucks and high-energy activities for boys. Their beliefs about girls' and women's biological tendency toward nurturance, articulated often with presupposed intent or purpose, reinforces gendered divisions of responsibility for carework of the sort discussed in chapter 3. That reinforcement includes the individual level, as daughters are encouraged to see themselves as nurturing and to develop those skills. The responsibility assigned to women for carework is also reinforced at the interactional and institutional levels. As a result, that responsibility may become less the "choice" these parents were hoping for and more a structured obligation that traps their daughters and other women within institutional barriers and under interactional pressures.

Given this possibility, parents' plans to give daughters myriad options can succeed only to the extent that parents also encourage sons to shift their options, a shift they endorse only to a modest degree. From Hochschild in the 1980s to Stone two decades later, researchers studying gender inequalities in the workplace and the home have concluded that any significant change to women's opportunities also requires change in societal expectations for men.[15] Cultivators, as noted in chapter 3, hoped for new and broader options for their daughters but sought little change for their sons; Refiners seek more change in how masculinity is constructed, and yet they still emphasize relaxing gendered constraints more for daughters than for sons. Clearly the policing of gender boundaries is more salient for boys than for girls, especially in view of phrases such as "tone it down a notch," "my husband would probably faint," and "you have to remind them that there's a certain direction in which they're supposed to be going." But unless boys and men are more fully prepared for carework, paid and unpaid, it will be difficult for Elizabeth to "choose" freely between being a test pilot or a stay-at-home parent in the way her mother envisions. Whether Elizabeth identifies as heterosexual or not, whether she is partnered or not, she may find herself constrained by interactional and institutional forces that make it difficult for women to choose freely. And if only daughters make those choices, with sons, by definition, heading down a gendered path toward full-time employment in non-carework occupations, women will continue to experience the lifetime earning penalties of occupational gender segregation, as well as part-time and interrupted employment.[16]

Greater recognition of social construction and its powerful effects on their children's preferences, and more attention to gendered power structures in place of individualism and gender neutrality, would allow the parents profiled in this chapter to succeed more often in their efforts to sidestep the gender trap and provide a wider range of opportunities for their children. Given their focus on children's individual interests and healthy

139

development, and their belief that gender expectations have some foundation in nature but are also imposed by socially constructed obstacles to individual choice, their approach has prospects for loosening gendered constraints. But even without the internal tensions of their approach that reinforce the gender trap, Refiners are ultimately interested in refinement, not significant change. It is the Innovators and Resisters who aim to shift gender structures more significantly, and it is to these parents we turn now.

5

"You Applaud All the Other Stuff"

Innovators

Anthony, a white, working-class, heterosexually partnered father of three who works as a sales representative, belongs in the group I classify as Innovators. His small, neat, and carefully maintained gray duplex, nestled close to its neighbors on a densely populated side street, was the site for our interview. Like his fellow Innovators, Anthony believes that parents can raise children in less gendered ways, a belief shared with the Refiners profiled in the previous chapter. But Innovators are more confident than Refiners that they can achieve this outcome and are willing to go to greater lengths to succeed. These are parents who express little belief in biological determinism, in fact the least of any of the groups. They focus mainly on social sources of gendered outcomes and report actions that are more resistant than reproductive. Their motivations cluster around personal preference and their children's interests, recognizing accountability to others but barely concerned about it on a daily basis. They frame their resistance with a strong endorsement of working to avoid the gender trap. They also adapt that resistance, scaling it back based on their comfort with certain gender-typical outcomes, their desire to follow their children's preferences, and a cheerful acceptance of the inevitability of some gendering. Innovators offer more structuralist readings of childhood gender compared to Cultivators or Refiners, but not to the same extent as Resisters. Twenty-nine-year-old Anthony illustrates many of these commonalities, as he was a stay-at-home father for the first two years after now five-year-old Nathaniel was born.

Anthony's other children with his wife Linda include three-year-old Christopher and eighteen-month-old Molly.

Anthony: "It Has to Be a Concerted Effort"

Anthony spoke with quiet enthusiasm about his experiences as a parent. He preferred to have sons, not wanting to "have to go shopping and get all those pink dresses and tights and all of that," and he ended up dressing both his sons and his daughter primarily in the same simple blue jeans, T-shirts, and sweat shirts. He encourages his sons to develop nurturance and domestic skills and urges his daughter to embrace sports and matchbox cars. He engages in some reproductive actions, but like most of his fellow Innovators, he tilts these more toward encouraging gender-typical behavior than discouraging nonconformity. He promotes crossing gender boundaries but also some gender-typical patterns. He is pleased that three-year-old Christopher is interested in learning to play ice hockey, a sport Anthony enjoys, and he bought a net for practicing hockey shots in their driveway. He enrolled Christopher in skating lessons, though only after Christopher asked. Anthony and Linda enjoy dressing Molly in "little pink dresses and hair ribbons, most certainly some stereotypical girl things." Both parents support mixing these tendencies with those they consider more unusual.

> We made it a point to be sure all our kids have had doll and doll-like toys to play with. . . . They have a little play kitchen upstairs that they play with, as well as a work bench. The work bench, their grandparents got them, the toy kitchen we got them, so we try to get it to balance out.

Anthony observed that Nathaniel likes both pink and purple clothes. "He's worn pink, he's worn purple. Actually he looks really good in purple, and Christopher looks great in purple, too. We never tried to avoid certain colors." The shift in focus from pink to purple may indicate Anthony's attempt to avoid the most iconically feminine color, an adaptation in his resistance. Nevertheless, he was enthusiastic about purple, a color most parents associated with girls. Commenting on a major snow storm the pre-

142

vious winter, which caused a power outage, he recounted efforts to teach Nathaniel not to connect particular occupations, such as repairing power lines, with men or women.

> He had some questions particularly during that blizzard, that was a wonderful educational thing, to show him that men and women can fix things. We needed to have the power fixed, and he knew someone will come and fix the power. He asked me if a man would come do it, and I said, "Maybe, or maybe a lady, it doesn't matter." He said something like, "Oh, okay, a lady can do it, too?" and I said, "Yes." . . . Even the books we choose are not sexist books, we try to pick pretty diverse books that show different kinds of people doing all sorts of things.

Anthony also talked about being careful not to get ahead of his children by assuming traditional interests. "Wherever their interests lead them, we're going take them. We don't care if our girl likes baseball and our boy likes dance, it's actually kind of working out that way. That's not a concern for us." Consider his comments related to eighteen-month-old Molly.

> It could be something as simple as this, to give you a feel for what I mean. There's a line of dolls called the American Girl dolls, and they have one named Molly. At first we thought, "Wouldn't it be cute if we got that for her?" But then we said to ourselves, "No, what if she doesn't like dolls?" Sure, it is a collectible, but we should let her choose. When she's eight, she can look at the catalogue and if she thinks Molly's really cool, then we'll consider getting it for her then.

Anthony tries to keep his gender-typical actions in the domain I call indirect gendering, and in this example he is careful to tease out whether his daughter is really expressing an interest or if he is directly instilling that interest on her behalf. Anthony believes that gendered variations exist, but he sees their origins in social terms, a trap that requires hard work to resist.

> You know, you look at the commercials for kids, for a middle school kid and even younger, and boys are running around on skateboards

143

with baggy pants and girls are wearing crop shirts and bellbottoms playing with the little electronic diary things. Boys are sneaking in stealing some kind of cereal from the old ladies and girls are baking things.[1] So they pick those things up subtly. . . . And Nathaniel, he gets it from day care, too. You know, he will come home and we'll be watching TV or something and a commercial for Barbie will come on and he'll say, "Oh, that's a girl toy," and we'll say, "No, boys can play with that, too," and he'll say, "No, it's a girl toy." So you have to go into this whole long discussion with him, we've worked very hard on that in this house.

He offered a briefer example after mentioning that some people consider aspects of Molly's demeanor typically girlish. "She's very aware that she is a cutie pie. She knows how to work her smile and she will snuggle right up to you, but any kid can learn that." This is a tendency that some Cultivators and Refiners noticed in young girls. Grace noted that her newborn daughter did "something with her eyes, it was almost like a little flirt, just before she smiles she does that, and the boys didn't do that, never." Karen sensed that her baby daughter smiles and interacts more lovingly than her son. These were patterns both saw as indications of biological sex differences. To Anthony, a similar tendency seemed a learned behavior, one Molly picked up from daily interactions. "Girls aren't these delicate little flowers that, you know, are going to fall apart. And by the same token, boys aren't rock pillars. I really think it has to do with environment, the way they're raised."

Anthony also believes that the division of labor in his own household serves as a model to his children. Owing to circumstances at his and his wife's jobs at the time Nathaniel was born, Anthony stayed home, as noted, to care for the new baby full-time.[2] After Christopher was born Linda took a short parental leave, and then the two children were enrolled in day care while both parents worked full-time outside the home. From Anthony's perspective, the years he spent as a stay-at-home parent helped ensure that once they both were employed, he and Linda would continue to share the parenting duties equally. "Everything really is fifty-fifty here. I get up with one kid, you get up with the other kid. If I do this, you do that." Just as heterosexual men who are as involved or more involved than their female partners in parenting are unusual in the contemporary United States, Anthony was unusual among my participants.[3] Also consistent with the literature on gender and parenting is Anthony's description of the effects of his experience. Whereas many heterosexual fathers in my study referred to their female partner's greater patience, natural nurturance, or greater knowledge of the children's daily needs and interests, Anthony spoke about the connection and awareness he developed through time spent with Nathaniel.

> For more than two years, I would be the one that would get him up, get him dressed and get his meals, we played together, he would help me with all the housework throughout the day. We spoke our own little language and I knew what he liked and didn't like, you know? On the weekend, we'd be making lunch for him and I'd say, "Nope, he doesn't like that," and Linda would ask, "Since when?" and I'd say, "Last week." It's little things like that that might be part of why he's always been my child so to speak, he calls out for me first if he's hurt or if he wakes up in the night.

In this short vignette, Anthony conveys one of the arguments of Risman's book, *Gender Vertigo*. Based on her contention that gender is socially constructed at the individual, interactional, and institutional levels, Risman hypothesizes that men who take on primary care of their children will develop the kind of nurturance skills so often thought of as natural in women. Risman predicts that "the consequences of gender structure at the interactional level, the situational demands, and the clearly expressed need of young children to be nurtured will create behaviors in men that are usually called 'mothering.'"[4] To account for the potential effect of only the most nurturing men selecting the experience of becoming full-time caregivers, Risman studied what she calls "reluctant" single fathers, those thrown into the position through divorce or spousal death. Anthony was not in the reluctant category, but the change he noticed parallels what Risman generally found. When men engage in the intensive child care activities normally assigned to women, they come to see themselves as more nurturing and child-oriented, and are more likely to engage in the kinds of behaviors that a biologically determinist view explains as a woman's natural abilities.[5] Walzer looked more specifically at the division of labor among heterosexual couples who are new parents.[6] She, like Risman, argues that women's greater responsibility for daily care creates rather than reflects the greater mental labor they invest in parenting, and thus their tendency to know more about the baby's daily needs and preferences. Both Risman and Walzer conclude that women's apparently essential nurturance is a product, not a cause, of their daily work as parents. Anthony's experience is consistent with this social-constructionist argument.

The backdrop to his efforts to resist gender expectations through direct actions and role modeling, and to his socially determinist beliefs, is Anthony's lack of concern regarding accountability. For example, when Anthony's grandmother "had a hissy fit" after he purchased a doll for Nathaniel, Anthony ignored her reaction. When asked if he tended to dress Nathaniel, when he was a baby, so that people could tell he was a boy, Anthony was nonchalant. "We didn't stick a baseball cap on him every time we went out just so they'd know he was a boy, and sometimes people would say "what a beautiful girl." We'd just say, "Oh, he's a boy." But it didn't bother us." He also spoke of another occasion when he was unaffected by accountability pressure from his brother-in-law.

> When all the boys got out the doll case at [their grandmother's] house, and they're playing that, one particular cousin's daddy came along and said, "Let's go get some other toys, these are sissy toys." Meanwhile, there sits my kid playing with the doll, combing the doll's hair, and he has caught on to that, to so-and-so's daddy thinks that's wrong or bad. But it doesn't bother us at all, you know? Absolutely not. How then are they going to learn to take care of their children if they don't?

Anthony sees neither his efforts to resist gendering his children nor his willingness to ignore accountability pressures as sufficient by themselves to dismantle socially constructed gender patterns. Unlike the optimism of many Refiners—for example, Grace's comment that "it's only a mindset"—Anthony believes that deeper changes are needed to avoid the gender trap.

I think it is possible, because me teaching my three kids to do that will have a very small ripple effect. They will teach their two or three kids or whatever, who in turn will teach their two or three, and on it goes. But that's not enough. . . . It has to be a concerted effort. It can't just be one person or one family, or you can't say, "Well, we'll only teach it in school." You can teach it in school and then when you go home your mommy and daddy aren't acting that way, you turn on the television set, you go to the movies and it's back, you pick up a comic book and it's back. That's not going to work. It takes that concerted effort in a lot of places at once.

Anthony is optimistic that multiple social forces ultimately will converge to reduce gendered patterns but stresses that it takes *work*. He considers that work an important element of parenting. It is not surprising, then, that Anthony's answer to the question of whether he is trying to teach his children anything in particular about men and women or boys and girls invoked not physical differences but gendered constraints.

We're really going out of our way to try to teach equality, equal opportunity, respect. Mommy and Daddy may disagree, but Mommy and Daddy may never have a knock-down, drag-out fight. We've been able to, unfortunately through some neighborhood instances, tell them about domestic violence, and tell them it is not okay, that is not right in any way. And then, like I said, we have gone out of our way to try and include things like gender neutral language, that boys and girls can do whatever they want, you know, there's no reason why Molly can't someday play hockey just as well as Chris can play hockey.

Gendered power is implied in this response, in the references to equality and domestic violence, but Anthony referred even more explicitly to inequality shortly thereafter. He used the term "gender neutral" to describe what he is trying to teach, but then he added, "But . . . here's the thing, how can you teach them to respect the sexes, give opportunities to the sexes, without pointing out that there is a difference? If you're just gender neutral, why then do you need women's *equality*?"

147

Miriam: "If They Want Sparkles They Can Have Sparkles, What Do I Care?"

Anthony's emphasis on resisting gendered expectations, and his dismissal of everyday accountability pressures, is shared by Miriam, a white, upper-middle-class, heterosexually partnered mother who is home full-time with her four children. Miriam has two sons and two daughters: five-year-old Rachel, four-year-old Seth (the focal child), three-year-old Eli, and one-year-old Sarah. From the dining room of her elegant home, over coffee and homemade muffins, she recounted how she had always hoped to have a large family and that her first child would be a girl, as she believed she would have a closer relationship with a daughter and share more interests. Consistent with this preference, Miriam reported feeling comfortable with some gender-typical outcomes for her children, including her acceptance when Rachel "made a beeline" for the girls' section of the toy store. As Miriam noted in chapter 1, "How could I avoid it even if I tried, and how could they either?"

Miriam was equally comfortable with gender-atypical attributes and interests and was pointedly disinterested in certain aspects of typical boys' culture. When her children were small, she "bought only unisex toys." She encourages an interest in science and nature in all her children, and tends to dress them all in the same color every day rather than selecting gender-differentiated colors. Miriam seemed pleased that her sons "don't care about baseball, they don't care about hockey, they don't even know what it is." She further noted, "I don't even know if they could, like if they saw a ball from each sport, I don't think they could identify it." She dismissed what she considers a typical boyish fascination with vehicles and construction equipment, offering a rationale that invoked her class-based expectations for Seth.

> I can't see really how knowing about dump trucks is going to help you in college. Seth knows, well, for example, there's this computer game we have that has these little groups of animals that you have to sort into mammals, mollusks, all that kind of stuff. Seth can do that whole thing, he can identify them all.

Innovators stand out in that none of them mentioned believing that boys face particular social pressures to stay within normative gender boundaries. Innovators recognized accountability pressures on boys but did not specifically raise the specter of those pressures being greater than comparable pressures facing girls. Miriam, for instance, told stories about accountability in relation to her sons but rarely felt any need to yield to those pressures.

> I do like to buy different colors for the boys, I don't want all brown and blue. And it is so hard to find yellow or orange for boys. I was shopping once, and I saw this beautiful outfit for Seth. It was this deep, deep orange. And the sales lady came over and said, "That's a boy's outfit." And I said, "Oh, I know." And she said, "It's a very strong color for a boy," really kind of advising me, maybe you shouldn't get it. And I said, "I know. That's actually why I want it, because it's different."

Miriam keeps notes each day to document interesting occurrences that she wants to share with her husband when he comes home, and one of the stories was an even more dramatic instance of accountability.

> There was this little boy my son absolutely loved at the park we go to every afternoon, a little boy named Timothy, and we'd often seen him there with his father, Steve. One day he shows up with his mother, and I tell her, "These two love each other so much, and I am going to such and such a park on Wednesday, would you meet me there because it would be so much fun for them to have a little play date outside of just chance meetings?" . . . She said okay, and I said, "Give me a call so I can give you directions." She never called. . . . Later, another friend who knows them told me that Steve was not too thrilled with Seth. You see, Steve is making Timothy into a tough guy, you know? Timothy is wearing like real boy's boy clothing and he doesn't have a jacket on when it's 45 degrees. He and his father throw balls back and forth, like real boy's boy activities, too. And Steve told her, this friend, he told her he "nipped that [friendship] in the bud." . . . I was

149

livid, because Seth had been rejected based on the type of little boy that he is, that his interests are a little too intellectual and his clothes are a little too unusual. I can see the distaste Steve has for Seth's type of little boy, and he has told some of my friends that, too. But you know what I think? If a guy like Steve doesn't like a boy like Seth, then you know you're doing the right thing! I wouldn't change Seth for anything.

When questioned about whether any of her children ever asked for items or activities she would consider more typical for the other gender, she told several stories indicating that they did and that she was happy to comply. An example was Seth's request for an easy-bake oven: "[These ovens] were in the girls' aisle next to the doll strollers, all done up in pink boxes with pictures of girls in pink all over them. One of the boys wanted to do it, Seth did, and so of course I pursued it. It doesn't hurt anyone, they're learning, it's creative, I thought it was great." Miriam was similarly open to crossing gendered boundaries for her three-year-old son, Eli. She had previously mentioned that Eli sometimes conflates gender and age. His sister is the oldest child in the family, and he sometimes talks about growing up and becoming a girl, assuming he will be more like Rachel when he is as old as she is.

> He loves doing what his sister's doing, and she has this Barbie pool. He'll go out there and play with it with her, just like she's doing. One day, he said to me, he said, "Someday, when I'm older and I'm a girl, can I have that Barbie pool?" So I said, "Eli, you'll never be a girl, but if you want that Barbie pool you can have it!"

This story implies that Eli has only been casually discouraged from his belief that he will someday be a girl. Miriam is clearly less bothered than many other parents I interviewed would have been about her son's claim that he will be a girl when he is older, and she happily let her sons have iconic feminine items. She is equally casual in telling her son that he will "never be a girl," suggesting the hegemonic assumption that gender is fixed. Given increasing attention to transgendered youth and adults in the contemporary West, that may change over time.[7] Currently, however, it is not surprising that a parent of a three-year-old, even one as resistance-oriented as Miriam, might respond in this way.

Along with her lack of concern about whether her sons exhibit conventional masculine behavior, Miriam is pleased that Seth is nurturing and attentive toward his baby sister, Sarah. She made no comments about any natural tendency for five-year-old Rachel to care for her younger siblings but did remark on Seth's efforts, which she connected to role modeling:

> They all love her, but Seth's the one who really goes the extra mile. . . .
> I think it's because of his father, he sees his dad doing all the domestic
> duties I do. So I think he has a strong role model for an involved male.

Although Seth was the focal child for the interview, Miriam also spoke of resistive actions she has taken regarding Rachel. She told another story about an incident that she viewed as gender-typical for a girl and which she considers socially constructed and problematic.

> Last year, when Rachel was in preschool, she was sitting in the tub
> one night and all of a sudden she got this very, very sad look. She's
> sitting there and I said, "Why do you look so sad?" I mean, it was re-
> ally marked, I noticed a change of her expression out of the blue, just
> like a wash came over her face of something sad. So I said, "What's
> wrong?" and she said, "I think Diana's prettier than I am." Well, I
> can't even tell you how upset I was. I never, ever comment on any-
> one's looks to her, never, and I was so upset that she would think or
> care about that, . . . but that's what the girls talk about at school, and
> that's what the teachers let them get away with.

Miriam went on to say that she is generally willing to intervene, to "fight" this kind of gendered pattern that she sees as limiting for Rachel, which she did in this case by bringing it up with Rachel's teacher the next day.

> And do you know what she said? She actually said this, she said, "Oh,
> you're kidding, Rachel is so much prettier." And I said, "No, that's not

my point." I said, "Now you think I'm telling you the story because I want you to tell me that Rachel's prettier." I said, "Wait, wait, no! That is so not what I'm saying, my point is that I can't believe at four years old that she'd even notice that." I tried to tell her, in a nice way, that I think there's something going on there in the classroom that she might want to watch out for, try to discourage among the girls. . . . I always try to fight against things like that.

This story conveys what Miriam understood to typify girls' peer cultures, which she preferred to keep Rachel away from as much as possible: "cattiness," with shifting social alliances and competition over who is prettiest, most popular, and best dressed.[8]

Like the Refiners, who spoke of a less gender-typed childhood as "healthier," many Innovators were motivated in their undoing of gender by the belief that this effort served their children's individual welfare. Miriam shares this resistant version of the individual rights narrative; recall her response to my rhetorical question, noted earlier, about the beloved stuffed manatee Seth carries with him everywhere, "Why shouldn't he have what he likes?" Some parents in all five groups connected a less gender-typed childhood with a healthier childhood, but this belief among Refiners, Innovators, and Resisters was expressed to a much greater extent. Miriam's comment that an easy-bake oven is creative and educational for her sons is an example, as is Anthony's belief that playing with dolls helps prepare Nathaniel for fatherhood. Miriam made another, similar observation in a story in which she reveals an implicit sense of accountability and reiterates her willingness to "fight."

I took the kids to this plaster place, Plaster Creations, where they pick a plaster mold off the wall and they paint it and decorate it. Rachel picked a little kitty, Eli picked an alien, Seth had a turtle. But they all chose pink paint. They chose six or seven colors each, but the boys also chose pink to include in theirs. And when it came time to put this fixative on it, the boys wanted sparkles. But the woman clearly seemed to think those were there for the girls, because she said to Rachel, "Do you want sparkles on yours?" And she didn't ask the boys, she just skipped right by them, but they both called back to her and said, "We want sparkles on ours!" She didn't hear them, so I went back and got her, because I would always fight something like that. If they want sparkles they can have sparkles, what do I care? I mean, how is their life going to change because they had a sparkly turtle at Plaster Creations when they were little? You know, Seth's like, "Well, I'm in therapy now at 36 because I had sparkles on my turtle?" I don't think so, just the opposite, it's creative, it allows him to develop and express his creativity, to appreciate colors and textures and beauty.

Miriam views her sons' opportunity to fashion their plaster molds however they choose as an individual right that has potential implications for their development. This story brought to mind another aspect of Risman's *Gender Vertigo*: besides addressing issues such as men's primary caregiving, Risman's overall argument is that gender inequality rests on socially constructed gender differentiation. Her prescription is not to discard playful or creative impulses that sometimes underlie gendered self-presentation, but instead to make them available for people to employ regardless of gender. All people, in Risman's view, need "easily accessible means to use their creativity, their sense of color, coordination, and panache." And she adds, "We must not forget that pleasure matters. For after all, don't we care about inequality because we want to equalize our opportunities for pleasure?"[9] What Risman calls creativity, color, and panache may be important elements of what draws many parents I interviewed, especially mothers, to the clothing and accessories available for girls, and it is certainly what Miriam wishes were more readily available in boys' clothing. But in her response to the sparkles for Seth's and Eli's creations, Miriam expresses the same basic idea Risman advocates: she wants all her children, not just her daughters, to have a chance to play with color, to express their creativity, and to show a little panache.[10]

Miriam resists gendered expectations, but, like other Innovators, that resistance is adapted to her own personal preferences, her children's interests, and the social world around her. She is casual rather than distressed when she gives in to what she sees as the inevitability of some of Rachel's gender-typical requests. Miriam has filled Rachel's room with icons of

femininity, including "millions of Barbies" and pink tutus and princess costumes, even as she remains baffled by her daughter's focus on prettiness.
By contrast, Seth's room is brown with a dog theme, something she volunteered she "wouldn't really do in a girls' room." She has always kept both
her sons' hair short, but she likes Rachel's to be long and adorned with stylish accessories. Miriam was one of a small handful of parents who, like the
Refiner William, spontaneously declared that it would be fine with them if
any of their children eventually identify as gay.

> One day, we were sitting at lunch and Rachel said, "I'm going to marry
> Noah," her good friend from preschool. Then Seth said, "Well, then
> I'm marrying Evan," a little friend of his. I said, and this is the truth
> because I'm very supportive of homosexual marriages, I said, "In
> this state, in our state, you can't. But in other states in our country
> you can." And I was telling somebody that story, and they said, "Oh,
> wow, you're not going to get into that with him are you?" And I said,
> "Well, sure, it's the truth. It's not going to make him gay to tell him
> the truth. . . . He's going to fall in love with who he falls in love with."
> It wouldn't be my first choice simply because I'm afraid of society's
> reaction, it's a harder life with all the discrimination and sometimes
> even violence, and no one wants anything to be hard on their chil-
> dren. But I mean, all I really hope is that they meet a person they care
> about and have a long-term relationship with somebody who makes
> them happy.

In contrast to William's response, Miriam's openness is limited by fear
of the reactions of others. For that reason, perhaps, or simply because she
assumes that her children will identify as heterosexual, her resistance is
accompanied by the same kind of routine heteronormativity that was evident in all groups but the Resisters. Miriam referred to Rachel's interest in
marrying Noah as "adorable," and noted that she often jokes about it with
Noah's mother and even his extended family. "But I'm only joking, because
I don't want her to marry the first person she meets. Later, when Rachel's
twenty-five, and she's with a man I don't like, I'm going to say, 'Remember
Noah? He's what I had in mind, you should have married him!'"

Overall Miriam stood out from nearly all the other parents I interviewed in the degree to which she embraced gender crossing by her sons and dismissed the reactions of others. In a particularly dramatic story, however, she conveyed her recognition of accountability to institutional power. After describing how Rachel likes to dress Eli in costumes from her dress-up trunk, Miriam recounted an incident that occurred the previous year, when Eli was two years old.

> So, Rachel had dressed him up again, he was looking lovely. And Eli was so happy with the way he looked that he did this little jig and danced out of the room, he was kind of moving his head from side to side and he wacked his head right into the door. Like smack on, and he split his head open. So we went to the hospital with him. He was wearing like pink pants, a pink princess costume over those, and on top a frilly apron that had been mine when I was little. There were all these sort of brawny, youngish, twentyish kind of good-looking orderlies or whatever, helping us with him. And I said to my husband, "They're all looking and giving him double takes." I said to my husband, "Just tell them why he's dressed like that, that Rachel did it." . . . People can be so uptight about things, I was worried they were going to think I was some kind of nut and next thing you know, send a social worker in. . . . In a hospital, someone has the power to go make a phone call to a social worker or someone, someone who doesn't realize he's two years old and it doesn't matter. . . . It was totally obvious that it was a little boy dressing up in silly clothing but there are people out there who would think that's really wrong, and I was afraid.

In her day-to-day parenting, Miriam's efforts to undo gender are motivated by her personal preference for loosening gendered constraints and her belief that this serves her children's best interests, in her case especially for her sons. Although Innovators had their own individual reasons for dismissing accountability pressures, Miriam's seemed to be based on class privilege, which bolstered her confidence in the face of interactional pressures from people such as the Plaster Creations instructor, the clothing salesperson, Timothy's father, and Rachel's preschool teacher. Considering the institutional power of hospital social workers, however, even Miriam worried about the social costs of straying too far from the gendered path. As an upper-middle-class parent raising four children on one income, in an elegant home that allowed each child his or her own room, Miriam had the resources and values that coalesce into the particular gendered approach to parenting that sociologist Sharon Hays dubbed "intensive mothering."[11] According to Hays, intensive mothering affects women across class lines but is especially influential among white, affluent mothers. As Hays puts it, the ideology of intensive mothering dictates that "correct child-rearing requires not only large quantities of money but also professional-level skills and copious amounts of physical, moral, mental, and emotional energy on the part of the individual mother."[12] Far from the only mother interviewed whose approach resonated with this description, Miriam was different in the degree to which she had the resources and inclination to carry it out: she was familiar with expert advice to parents in various arenas, devoted extensive time to planning and organizing activities, parties, and play dates for her four children, and carefully thought through many of the details of her parental philosophy and practice.[13] I suspect that this thoughtfulness, and the high degree to which she was able to meet the difficult standards of this intensive mothering ideology, contributed to Miriam's general confidence. Intensive mothering in no way assumes gender resistance—in fact, quite the contrary. I consider Miriam's approach to gendering her children a separate matter, but her confidence in executing her approach to mothering may be based on her race and class resources, as well as her heterosexual privilege. Even Miriam, however, with her strongly held individual beliefs about undoing gender for her children and her willingness to ignore many of the interactional accountability pressures she encounters, is not immune to the institutional power of a bureaucracy such as a hospital. Her fears about the hospital were never realized, neither in the particular visit she recounted nor, amazingly enough, in a second incident where Eli was again dressed in his sister's costumes and had to be taken to the emergency room. These events did not change Miriam's outlook overall, but they do indicate the limits to her confidence in resisting gendered expectations and her awareness of the potential costs.

156

Walt: "There's Just Too Much Prejudice
Around, We're Not Going to Do That"

In a qualitative sample of parents, it is inappropriate to generalize every modest association, but it is appropriate to consider each participant's social background in understanding their parenting behavior. For Miriam, as we have seen, racial-, class-, and sexuality-based privilege may explain her confidence. Another potential role of intersecting inequalities might have emerged among several parents of color interviewed in previous chapters, but none spoke explicitly about how their race may have shaped their approach, except in brief comments such as Jennifer's indication that a preference for sons was common in her Asian American community. Race did play a significant role, however, in the way another parent of color described his approach. Walt, a working-class, heterosexually partnered, African American father, pointed to racial inequality specifically as a motivation for his efforts to undo gendered constraints for his sons, four-year-old twins Michael and Justin. Walt welcomed me to his small ranch home with a friendly smile, dressed in a sports-logo T-shirt and athletic shorts. A full-time supervisor in a small manufacturing facility, Walt works from six in the morning until two in the afternoon, but he is particularly passionate about his part-time work coaching high school teams after school. Athletic activity forms a major component of his family's life, as both he and his wife, Dalia, were successful multi-sport athletes in their schooldays. He is confident that he would be just as enthusiastic about sports if he had daughters, and his part-time coaching involves both male and female athletes. He drew on that background in answering my question about whether he ever had a preference for a son or daughter. He expressed only a vague preference for a son, indicating that he had done volunteer coaching as a teenager with coed track teams and always felt comfortable with both boys and girls. He surrounds Justin and Michael with sports-themed clothing and sports equipment, and the children spend time at sporting events. According to Walt, this has exposed them not only to boys' athletics but to girls' athletics as well: "They come to a lot of my practices, so they see girls running, they'll go watch some of the softball games, they'll see girls' lacrosse and field hockey, they know girls do all those things." When

Michael and Justin were babies, Walt enjoyed picking out typically boyish clothing, and he clearly conveyed personal preference as his motivation: "I was picking things out for sons, yeah, sneakers, Nikes, sports stuff, those tiny little Nikes, things like that—I loved going shopping for them, and I still love it." But he was unequivocal in interpreting his sons' interest in sports as socially constructed, and, in fact, all his responses regarding the origins of gendered patterns were pointedly social. Walt was emphatically cautious, however, about not forcing them deeper into the sporting culture than their inclinations might take them.

> The fear I have for my two boys is that I was pretty good at sports and they're four now and a lot of people are putting pressure on them right now to be like Dad, but they might not want to play football or run track. . . . I don't want them to have that pressure, because they aren't even in school yet and a high school coach I know is saying, "I can't wait to have your two boys playing football for us." And, you know, people think I'm crazy sometimes because I say, "Oh, they could play field hockey." But why can't they? Just because they're boys they should play football and run track? That's not fair to them.

Like other Innovators, Walt made few references to accountability, and those he made, such as the brief comment "people think I'm crazy," seemed to cause him little concern.

Walt also spoke about interests his sons have that he considers gender-typical, including their fascination with fire trucks and with Batman and Robin, which, he believes, he fostered and encourages through the DVDs, toys, and games he purchases. Though he believed that if he had a daughter he would expose her to sports just as he did his sons, he also thought that he would treat a daughter differently, such as being more protective of her than of a son.

> To me I just think boys, well, you let boys get away with more than you do girls, you know? And I don't know why, I just think that's the society. So I do think I'd be more protective of a daughter. It's not to be sexist or anything like that, I just think boys know how to defend

themselves and Daddy always wants to protect his girl. I think that a lot of fathers think that way.

This protective impulse has more concrete implications when expressed by fathers of daughters than of sons. But it carries a corollary assumption, explicit in Walt's case, about the ability of sons to defend and protect themselves. That assumption contributes to frameworks of accountability that also promote the gender trap for boys. Responses from other participants suggest that Walt is correct in assuming that "a lot of fathers think that way."[14] As I argued in chapters 2 and 3, which focused, respectively, on Naturalizers and Cultivators, this emphasis on male protection and female vulnerability reproduces gendered outcomes by constructing boys as tough and sufficiently fearless to watch over their weaker sisters.[15]

Walt's efforts to allow and encourage what he considers unusual attributes and interests outweigh his reproductive actions. "As long as I'm broadening their horizons, I'm happy, you know? I would like for them to take tap [dancing] and I'll introduce it to them this year, now that they're four," he said. The family has neighbors with two daughters a few years older than Justin and Michael, and Walt reported how pleased he is that his children enjoy playing typically girlish games with them. "It wouldn't bother me at all," he said, "if they wanted a Barbie or something like that," and he also noted that he was glad they had received dolls as gifts.

> I think it was when they had just turned three, they got dolls as a gift from someone. I didn't think anything of it, in fact I thought it was great. If they learned how to dress a doll, that's good. And they still sleep with them, especially Justin, he pretends his is a baby and he rocks it so nice and sweet.

Colors were another topic Walt brought up when asked if his sons ever request anything he considers more typical for a girl.

> Justin likes orange, so I get him an orange shirt or I always look for anything orange I can find. Some people wouldn't think that's a boy color. I would never say no, there is to me too much about gender op-

posites and things like that. I think that's why we have some of the problems we have in the world today. I want to teach them that, hey, just because you wear this certain color of clothes doesn't mean anything, you're just being you, you know? . . . If he wants to wear orange or pink or purple, he likes purple and wears that a lot. He has purple shirts and he matches up pretty good, he looks great and he likes it.

Throughout the interview Walt offered brief but thoughtful responses. At one point he spontaneously connected his thoughts about gender to his experiences of race and became especially animated about gender issues.

There's just too much prejudice around and we're not going to do that, I don't want them to do that or think that way. Just because if they see someone wearing a different color, that's not a boy's color, I don't want them picking on that person, you know? I just can't have myself teach my kids anything that's prejudiced, knowing that I'm black myself and I know I don't want anybody else to do that to me. And down the road my boys being black, they may have that problem too, but at the same time I want them to know that, hey, just because somebody treats you that way it's not the right way, we're not going to treat people that way. . . . They might run into people that might not like them because of what they are, but they shouldn't be prejudiced against anybody else.

Walt, unlike intersectionality theorist Hill Collins,[16] was not linking racial or gender prejudice to an underlying form of domination, but he was comparing these prejudices in a manner consistent with intersectional theory.

A related aspect of intersectional theory was invoked by Thomas, another African American father and Innovator. In speaking about his three-year-old daughter Jasmine, this working-class, twenty-three-year-old, heterosexually partnered man, a clerical worker and part-time student, noted that gendered experiences can vary by race. Instead of comparing race to gender, as Walt did, Thomas considers gendered experiences to be potentially race-specific, just as Hill Collins and others argue.[17]

My daughter, she's going to come across some trials and tribulations and discriminations and things as a female, and if I ever have a son he is going to come across some trials and tribulations and possibly discriminations as a male. And actually, it's not just that, not just as a female or a male, but as an African American female or an African American male, because that brings along its own issues that are unique.

As Walt continued the line of thought in which he compared racial and gender prejudices, he introduced another dimension of inequality to expand his intersectional analysis, broadening it to encompass sexual orientation.

I think it would be a much better world if people just didn't worry about what other people were doing sometimes, not being biased about what colors anyone is wearing or about other genders, other sexes, or who's loving who, you know? Who cares? It's just as long as you're happy, as long as that person is happy with the same sex, so what? Like I say, that's how I treat my boys and want my boys to treat other people. If someone of the same sex likes the same sex, you treat them the same as anyone else.

I asked Walt if there was a particular reason why he brought up the topic of same-sex couples.

We have in our family a cousin who is gay. And eventually that's going to come up. And I'm going to let them know that just because someone is gay or whatever doesn't mean they're different from us. That's all it is, it's just them living their life in their way, we're not going to treat them any different, we're not going to be prejudiced against them in any way. I have people who work with me that are gay, too, and I treat them the same as everyone else. Like I said, being black myself, I know how important that is, I don't want anybody else being prejudiced toward me, or down the road my kids having that problem.

The kinds of intersectional analyses both Walt and Thomas volunteered were not evident among Naturalizers, Cultivators, or Refiners. Two other Innovators, however, joined Walt and Thomas in connecting gender and other forms of inequality, so that four of the eight parents in this category made at least some reference to such associations. Two other references came from Anthony and Marcus, both white, working-class, heterosexually partnered fathers. Anthony commented about using "non-sexist language" and noted that he and his wife also try to use "non-racist language," implying comparability between racism and sexism. Marcus, the father of one daughter, was in the armed forces before becoming an appliance repair person. He had seen what he called a "troubling pack mentality" among his male peers in the military, and noted that women were usually the first victims of that mentality of "macho harassment and disrespect" but it "could be minorities, too."

The fathers of color among the Innovators showed greater recognition of intersectionality, but even these short comments by white fathers convey awareness of the potential connections across dimensions of inequality that were not raised by Naturalizers, Cultivators, or Refiners.[18] Because of the small number of parents of color interviewed for this book, it is impossible to generalize the role race played in shaping the likelihood that a parent will view gendered childhoods through an intersectional lens, all the more so because I did not ask any questions about intersectionality. Given the different patterns of response among parents, however, race and an orientation toward gender resistance certainly appear to be associated with parental tendencies toward an intersectional analysis.[19]

Eric: "Just Expose Them to as Much as You Can, Don't Squelch Anything"

Innovators also stand out in the degree to which gender issues are framed to include power or structure. More than half the Innovators offered at least one such framing; none of the Naturalizers did; and only one of the Cultivators and two of the Refiners did. Among Innovators, for example, Anthony noted that gender neutrality was not enough; he wanted his children to understand the need for "women's equality." Another example is

Kevin, a thirty-nine-year-old white, middle-class, heterosexually partnered father of a three-year-old son. This construction manager is cautious with language, referring to female coworkers as "women" rather than "girls" and avoiding both "language that undermines girls in any way" and any actions that "objectify women." Eric, another Innovator who invoked power imbalances, spoke of his five-year-old son, Nicholas, whom he encourages to participate in various domestic chores.

> I don't want him growing up to become a pig-headed male, or just what I call a useless male, you know? Those guys who don't know how to take care of themselves, can't live on their own, can only eat out of a can, can't do laundry or anything, you know, in the real world. They go from a mother to their wife and expect her to take care of them. . . . Plus some of the guys where I work, they look down on women, they are just degrading, and I don't want him to be like that.

Though more a critique of individual men than of the structure of gender inequality, Eric's comment acknowledges and criticizes male power over women. Like the "pack mentality" disparaged by Anthony, Eric's comment seems to focus on the "compensatory masculinity" that Pyke identified among lower-income men.[20] She argues that too much focus on this kind of behavior obscures and legitimates the subtler but more extensive class- and gender-based power wielded by economically advantaged men. Still, the critique of attempts to undermine, objectify, exploit, or degrade girls and women offered by Innovators, more so than Naturalizers, Cultivators, and Refiners, expresses a different and potentially resistive analysis of gendered patterns.

Eric, a thirty-nine-year-old white construction worker who identifies as working class and is heterosexually partnered, has two children: five-year-old Nicholas and an infant daughter, Madison. We sat down at the dining room table in his log-sided house on a large lot out in the countryside, where Eric told me that he had no gender preference before Nicholas was born. As he explained it, "I figured either one would be a blast, it didn't matter to me, I figured as long as they can help bring in the wood and stack it, I don't care if it's a boy or a girl." Eric was the least resistance-oriented of the Innovators, but this early comment was characteristic of his over-all approach. He was very comfortable with gender-typical behavior for his son and described Nicholas as "all boy," enjoying that they share an interest in hunting, fishing, tools, and cars. He also saw these interests as socially shaped and made no reference to biology or nature in explaining gendered outcomes. He rejected efforts to discourage girls from sharing boys' inter-ests or to discourage boys from participating in activities he viewed as more typically feminine. "A lot of it," he said, "is shoved down their throats." He went on to voice concern about some negative ideas he thinks Nicholas picks up at his preschool.

> He'll come home and say stuff like, "You know, girls do this and boys do that," he comes out with that stuff sometimes. . . . That's outside interference, and I tell him that's not true. I say, "Now wait a minute," you know, and I try to correct him on those things, because I see too much of this kind of stereotyping, especially with some parents and some kids he's going to school with.

The toys Eric and his wife, Kim, purchase for Nicholas primarily seem gender-typical, such as toy soldiers, vehicles, toy police gear, and the like. But Eric also approves of his son playing with other kinds of toys, thus en-gaging in indirect resistance and displaying a contrast to many reproduc-tion-oriented fathers. "He gets together with his cousin, she's a girl, and he's in playing with Barbie and the Little Mermaid stuff, playing with the little kitchen sets and stuff like that, he does that and he says he has a blast with it, which is good." A similar openness is evidenced by his efforts to discourage Nicholas from making gender-typed associations: "He was going on about how pink is a girl's color and all that, and I said, 'No, no, colors are what you make them. . . . Whatever color you like is a cool color, it doesn't matter.'" Eric noted that his baby daughter, Madison, not yet six months old, is "getting girly things shoved at her, you know, she's dressed in pink a lot, poor girl," and said he plans to treat her in just the same way he treats Nicholas. He hopes she will enjoy hunting and fishing, and expects her to learn the same chores as Nicholas, such as carrying in the wood. Eric sum-marized his approach when he said,

I think it's important to balance them out, just pointing out things. No, that's not necessarily a girl's color or a boy's activity, whatever. . . . Make them aware that things don't have to be so different. . . . Just expose them to as much as you can, don't squelch anything. If you see the boy going out playing with the Barbie dolls, don't jump down their throat and say, "Hey, you know, that's girl stuff," or vice versa.

Eric is at least somewhat inclined to incorporate a critique of gendered power into his outlook. But his references to power, like those of half the Innovators, all white fathers, often included tradition too in explaining why gendered patterns continue. Though it is most common among Cultivators, Innovators and Refiners are the second-most likely to offer tradition as an explanation, while Naturalizers rarely offered this reasoning because they were focused on biology. Eric explained that he is only somewhat optimistic about reducing gendered constraints in childhood:

I think ignorance is part of it, handed down through the years, you know what I mean? It's an old, old unwritten law that's finally start-ing to get a little change, which is good, but kind of hard to break old habits. . . . Some people just can't shake it, can't see beyond it.

Marcus offered a similar analysis, identifying intergenerational trans-mission of gender expectations: "You've still got grandfathers and grand-mothers, you know, that lived the historicals, that believe that's the way it should be." This kind of explanation suggests that, with effort, patience, and the passage of time, outmoded gender patterns will fade away. The In-novators' tendency to combine their power analysis with a gentler refer-ence to "old habits" and tradition may explain the relatively high level of optimism they voice about the possibilities for change, as long as people are willing to work to make it happen.

"Choose More Inclusiveness and Make an Effort"

Not all the Innovators believed that reducing childhood gender constraints was possible, but they all considered it a good idea and most were optimistic, as long as the steps taken involved the "concerted effort" Anthony described. Walt mentioned the need for television images to change, and others felt that change was possible if parents were willing to take on the effort. According to Kevin:

> I think parents can do a lot, if they make an effort, . . . encourage them to do things and don't make a big deal out of it that it's a boy or a girl thing. . . . You don't just applaud the boy behavior and being tough and all that stuff, but you applaud all the other stuff that might be considered girlish.

In the phrase "you applaud the other stuff," Kevin reflects the distinction between indirect and direct undoing of gender, implying that the latter is necessary to avoid the gender trap: just *allowing* gender-atypical behavior is insufficient; he advocates going a step further to applaud it. He went on to point to gender-segregating activities which, Thorne argues, construct gender boundaries in childhood, expressing his belief that parents, schools, and other groups should "choose more inclusiveness."[21]

> They go to boy scouts, they go to girl scouts—it seems like it should be more inclusive. Even when you get to kindergarten, my middle son was doing a project where they had crowns and all the girls made believe they were queens and all the boys were kings. I mean, there should be less emphasis on the girls and boys stuff. I guess I would choose more inclusiveness, make an effort to do things that both boys and girls can do together.

Thomas also objected to this kind of separation and spoke about its potential longer-term effects.

> It'll limit their interests in life, stop them from wanting to explore other things. It often separates brother and sister, male friends from female friends. I don't think you should do that because then we get into bigger complications when they're older, you know? Like women thinking, "I don't want to do construction work, that's for men," or

men who say, "I don't want to be a nurse, that's for women." I really, really oppose teaching them differences like that.

In contrast to Naturalizers, Cultivators, and Refiners, Innovators were especially likely to speak not just of opening traditionally male occupations to women but the reverse as well. When asked if he is trying to teach his children particular things about men and women or boys and girls, Ed, a thirty-six-year-old, working-class, white, heterosexually partnered customer service representative with three children, favored males and females crossing traditional occupational lines. Like Kevin, he seemed to do more than just tolerate the thought of nontraditional outcomes for his son; he celebrated the possibility.

I want them to know they all can pursue whatever careers they want. If Spencer decides that he wants to be a stay-at-home dad, God bless him. And Kendall, if she wants to go off and be the CEO with some company, I think that's great, too. I think they have to find their own paths. One thing that I really want to do is to encourage whatever the interests are and help them pursue them and not to judge.

As Innovators reflected on what they hope to teach their children, about half of them framed their response in terms of individualism, letting their children choose whatever they wish. The other half wanted their children to resist gendered constraints more actively. Ed's response reflected elements of both.

Seven of the eight parents in the Innovator group were fathers. The predominance of men in this group may stem from the largely female composition of the Resisters group, discussed in the next chapter. Among the two resistance-oriented groups, Innovators and Resisters, the men tended to execute the more confident, casual resistance of Innovators, with limited anxiety or sense of accountability to others. Given that all the fathers in this group are heterosexually partnered, their female partners may have been in the background shaping just enough gender conformity to eliminate paternal anxiety. But it also seems clear that these men have a different outlook on gender issues than do Naturalizer, Cultivator and Refiner fathers, many of whom take on the gender policing role that scholarship on gender and parenting has widely documented for fathers.[22] And their presence reminds us that not all fathers are policing gender boundaries in the way much of the literature paints them to be. Even if fathers are more likely to do so than mothers, it is important to highlight the fathers profiled in this chapter. This group identified largely as working class and included two fathers of color, so perhaps their experience of subordinated status along other dimensions of inequality intertwines with their outlook on gender inequality to make them particularly resistant. The patterns in each of these people's biographies are important to consider, as are the connections between the patterns among my interviewees and the broader patterns found in scholarly literature. Just as I believe that class privilege shapes Miriam's confidence, class disadvantage and racial disadvantage may shape some of these fathers' desire not to construct additional confining features in their children's lives. It may also be that their social class discourages them from accepting the ideology that Pyke identifies as the hegemony of the male career, which is common among middle- and upper-middle-class families, and leads them to a more flexible attitude about acceptable behavior for boys and girls, men and women.[23] Among the partnered, heterosexual parents in my study, the Innovators were least likely to include the traditional family structure of an employed father and homemaker mother, and the only group to include a heterosexual father who spent time as a primary caregiver. Some scholars of gender and family have concluded that working-class heterosexual men are more likely than their middle- and upper-middle-class counterparts to take on significant child care responsibilities.[24] That pattern of undoing gender in their partnerships makes it all the more striking that among the men I interviewed, those who identified as working class were more often in the Innovator category, whereas middle- and upper-middle-class fathers more likely were among the Cultivators or Refiners.

Motivated by personal preference, beliefs about their children's best interests, and a somewhat structural and intersectional critique of gender inequality, Innovators work at avoiding the gender trap with and for their children. They tend to be optimistic about redefining and reducing gendered boundaries in childhood. These are promising signs for those who share Risman's goal of a greater range of play in the lives of children and adults, and her emphasis not only on individual-level gendering but also on interactional and institutional forces. Innovators' dismissal of biological explanations avoids the legitimizing of gender inequality, and these parents' resistant actions reduce interactional accountability pressures. Not content simply to follow their children's interests, Innovators feel responsible to expose their sons and daughters to a wider array of options and opportunities, cultivate myriad attributes and capacities, and question whether children's individual preferences are truly free. They try to resist some of the routine gendering traps they recognize as tempting, such as Anthony's decision to wait before surrounding Molly with dolls, or a comment Ed made about buying his daughter her own train set to make sure his son was not "hoarding them, which would have been so easy to not even notice." Innovators generally advocate adult practices similar to those suggested by gender scholars: avoiding language that constructs gender difference and disempowers girls and women; trying to steer clear of excessive gender marking in clothing; encouraging integration rather than gender-segregated activities; and exposing both boys and girls to a range of life's pleasures. Also consistent with the consensus among many gender scholars is their interest not only in teaching the skills and interests necessary for girls to compete in various occupations within the world of paid employment but also in encouraging a similar focus on teaching the skills and interests necessary for boys to be capable, loving caregivers. This combination shows significant potential for matching women's occupational opportunities with men capable of sharing the burdens of carework, especially given that Innovators weave it together with recognition of gendered power.[25] As noted previously, revising gendered expectations not only for women but also for men is important for individual heterosexual couples but also for removing the interactional and institutional constraints that perpetuate gender inequalities at home, at work, and in political power. Innovators were also the group most likely to report that they view the child who was the focus of our interview as "a kid" rather than as a boy or girl. Yet another force resisting gendering and favoring social change is the ability of parents in this group to see gender as a source not only of difference but of power, and to make connections between gender and other forms of inequality such as race and sexual orientation.

Even Innovator parents, however, have adapted their resistance based on positive feelings about both gender atypicality and gender typicality, allowing and sometimes encouraging them to let their children follow the path of least resistance, possibly a more gendered path than the parents prefer. As Thomas remarked, for example, he followed Jasmine's lead when shopping for her first bicycle: "We allowed her to pick out her own, and it just so happened that she went to the pretty bike with the pink colors and the little flags hanging off, with a little girl book bag in the front." Similarly, many of these parents casually accept the inevitability of some degree of socially constructed gendering, as in Miriam's comment about Rachel's interest in pink and ballet and princess costumes ("How could I avoid it even if I tried, and how could they?"), or Walt's belief that, inevitably, he would be more protective of a daughter than a son ("I don't know why, I think it's just society"), or Kevin's casual comment that "some things are hard to resist, they are into some things where we can't say no."

Although they recognize social determinants of gendered outcomes, Innovators seem to dismiss daily accountability as one of those determinants, except in dramatic circumstances such as Miriam's hospital experience. That ability to downplay accountability is part of what allows them to confidently sidestep the gender trap. But it may also limit their recognition of what other parents and children are facing in terms of interactional forces. They are particularly notable for the absence of attention to pressures toward hegemonic masculinity, such as Miriam ignoring those "double takes" as Seth clutches a stuffed animal or Anthony's lack of concern about his grandmother's "hissy fit" over the doll he bought for Nathaniel. Although Innovators' willingness to disregard accountability to hegemonic masculinity frees them individually, it may also restrict their otherwise broad recognition of the complex social forces that need to be modified to realize the change they seek. For some of them, their almost casual emphasis on tradition in their articulation of social determinism may also curtail their vigilance, as they see the reproduction of gender as something rooted in the past, through individually held beliefs that will change slowly over time and not as something also rooted in contemporary institutional power structures and reproduced now in everyday interactions.

These limitations and adaptations are important, but the potential evident among Innovators is equally important. Their optimistic and upbeat demeanor, their preference for less gendered childhoods and attention to power and intersecting inequalities, their acceptance of social determinism and recognition of the need for effort by a variety of social actors and institutions, and their actions oriented to undoing gender for both girls *and* boys are all resources that can and do contribute to resisting the gender trap.

6

"Surviving in a Gendered Culture"

Resisters

Resisters, numbering only five parents among all those interviewed, resembled Innovators in some ways but differed markedly in others. Like Innovators, Resisters reported resistant actions and also endorsed less gendered childhoods. They also shared a tendency to report relatively little action that reproduces gendered childhoods. Resisters focused nearly as much attention as Innovators on social forces over biological ones. And, to an even greater extent, they emphasized the importance of power, societal structure, and intersectionality. They differ, however, in voicing a preference for avoiding the gender trap, not only by accepting what might be considered unusual behavior, but also by actively rejecting what they view as gender-typical behavior. They also strongly differed from Innovators in the fear and anxiety they expressed, their invocation of hegemonic masculinity as a constraint, their deeply felt sense of accountability to others, and their less optimistic reading of the possibilities for significant change. In these ways, their resistance is more wary and guarded than that of Innovators.

Stefan: "Just Because It's Natural Doesn't Mean It Should Be Encouraged"

A typical Resister is Stefan, a forty-four-year-old, white, middle-class, school guidance counselor in a gay partnership. He and his partner, Todd, live with their three-year-old son, Henry, who was adopted as an infant. From the living room of his two-story brick house in a charming urban

172

neighborhood of closely packed homes, Stefan spoke about buying Henry a doll, because he feels that learning to be nurturing will benefit his son in the future. "We've ordered a doll for him because he loves little babies and I think he can practice, it's so good for caring and everything." Describing Henry as very boyish in his interests, he said that he and Todd support what their son likes but also expose him to other interests.

> I think as dads, we've softened his natural tendencies by requiring politeness, by doing puppet shows, by watching *Sound of Music,* by doing stuff that somebody who is very caught up in the macho side of things wouldn't do perhaps. . . . We value reading, we value culture, we value sophistication and treating people with kindness and respect, . . . so we emphasize these things, things I kind of think a lot of people might consider almost anti-male.

Henry had not requested any toys or activities that Stefan considered more typical for a girl, but his parents had provided some on their own initiative. When I asked Stefan how he might feel if Henry actively requested such toys or activities, he promptly offered a hypothetical example.

> Well, let's say like a Barbie, what if that was what he wanted to play with? I'd feel perfectly fine with that and want to make sure that he was protected. I can remember a few times my father made fun of me because I wanted to do girl type things, so I'd want to make sure I didn't give him those messages.

Evident throughout Stefan's interview was this desire to protect his son from restrictive notions of gender and to craft a range of capacities within Henry. Stefan reflected on his experience working in a public high school environment, which sometimes "does not tolerate" sensitive boys. But he also sees negative repercussions for boys who fit the hegemonic masculine mold.

> Even the typical boy, I think so much of society is geared kind of towards excessive competition, excessive rules like boys don't cry, you

can't have emotions. That is not at all great for a kid. . . . I don't think it's a huge surprise that most of the school violence is from boys, not just because they're more programmed by media and such to be violent but I think there is a fair amount of inner turmoil that they haven't been really taught to deal with.

The possibilities that Stefan hopes to create for his son have been shaped by his experience as a gay man, along with high school training programs for teachers and counselors on gender identity, as distinct from sexual orientation.[1]

So much relates to gender, and this is kind of new to me, too, but in addition to who they're attracted to, people are talking more now in schools about how do you define yourself. I know a lot of kids have anguish around that and I guess I'd like him [Henry] to feel comfortable with his gender and gender identity whatever it is. I assume it's traditional boy identity from what I've seen, but I want him to feel comfortable whatever it is. . . . I think you should have some consciousness about gender and kind of how you want to play that out for your kid, how to do it so it's healthy and comfortable for the child.

Stefan is unusual among Resisters in the degree to which he sees a biological foundation as underlying some gender differentiation, but he views social pressures as playing a larger part by amplifying those differences. "I do think to some degree there is something natural about boys being a certain way and girls being a certain way. And then society, I think, steps in and reinforces it . . . what could be a natural instinct gets reinforced to some bizarre extreme." Even if some of the foundation for gender differentiation is rooted in nature, that does not necessarily mean we should accept it, according to Stefan. He thinks that males may have a tendency to be more competitive and females more nurturing but that all people need both capacities.

Just because it's natural doesn't mean it should be encouraged. . . . So much of society just reinforces all that, like the media, the magazines, it gets reinforced way too much. . . . If our world is even going to survive, then I think somehow we have to ride both kinds of the human instincts, and encourage them in everyone.

Stefan sees socially constructed gender expectations and accountability as obstacles that lead back to the gender trap. "The American attitude is very male, very macho for boys, so if you want to raise a kid who doesn't end up like that, it's hard because it's against almost everything our society enforces." Later Stefan talked more about how difficult it is to avoid viewing gender as rigidly defined. "I personally think that without society's pressure, a lot of us would be more flexible, I think, in gender, sexuality, whatever, . . . we're all kind of forced to be very concrete." Stefan particularly stresses institutional rather than only interactional articulations of social determinism. Although Resisters and Innovators tend to stress social origins, they differ in the ratio of interactional versus institutional sources that they identify: Innovators are weighted toward interactional sources, Resisters toward institutional sources. Along with the general acknowledgment of accountability, Stefan also notes the particular pressure he feels as a gay parent: "We have to be a little bit conscious of going too far, you know, as gay men the last thing we want to do is put him in anything that's remotely girly." He argued that some of Henry's boyish interests must be "innate," because he and Todd "certainly didn't put those ideas in his head," "we're more gender-neutral people; we're not caught up in being guys." But then he goes on to imply that they may steer their son at least somewhat in that direction, noting, "Well, we've made some accommodations to his being a boy, because I think we have to be particularly sensitive around that as two gay parents."

Stefan resisted various gender-typical expectations, while also encouraging those he considered helpful to Henry's ability to thrive under "society's pressures." He wants to build a more open, expansive range of possibilities for Henry, a "healthy" and "comfortable" range that allows him to "ride both kinds" of human tendencies. But like other Resisters, Stefan does so with an eye toward accountability and a belief that at least some typical gendering is inevitable.

I'm thinking some of it's unavoidable. I mean, even acting out a harmless Disney video, there are so many troubling issues in those. . . . If you consciously decided to totally avoid it, you couldn't really, because even just being exposed to other kids brings all that in. So I think putting it in perspective and minimizing it is probably the direction I would like to go, that's about the most you can hope for.

Sena: "You Just Give In, You Just Get Tired"

Sena struck the chords of inevitability and accountability even more loudly than Stefan did. A professional artist, thirty-seven years old, and a heterosexually partnered Asian American mother of two daughters, Sena identifies as middle class. Once we settled down on the futon in her small, sunny condominium, she spoke quietly, with self-assurance, and had clearly given gender issues considerable thought. She had always hoped for a daughter, assuming she could share her passion for talking and shopping, even though, as she noted, Asian Americans place "a lot of emphasis on having a boy." Peers, grandparents, aunts, and uncles all came up in our conversation as interactional sources that Sena believes contributed to her daughters' typically girlish interests. But she also highlighted institutional sources such as media, advertising, and societal norms in general. Explaining the origins of three-year-old Lily's focus on looking pretty, Sena told me:

> She's picked up on the response she gets when she's dressed in girly clothes, with her hair full of cute ribbons or barrettes, she's picked up on the rewards that it brings. But if we were living in a culture that valued her for being physically strong, because she is physically strong, I think she would be focused on that instead. . . . Parents play a part, but parents don't create the gender stereotypes under which they have to operate. You know, I would point my finger at the businesses who sell all this stuff, and I would point my finger at advertising, and I would point my finger at other elements of our popular culture.

176

By highlighting the role of "businesses who sell this stuff," Sena suggests the power media and corporations derive from gendered patterns. Later in the interview she spoke even more pointedly about the vested institutional interests she sees behind the marketing of gendered products for children: "with our daughters, I think we're just sort of falling into the pattern of consuming girly stuff. I mean, it's capitalism, you know? I guess I'm a conspiracy theorist. We're getting sucked in and buying it."

Interactional sources of gendering were also on Sena's mind as she explained her sense of inevitability, citing gifts from relatives. For the first year of Lily's life, Sena asked relatives to "please [not] send us anything pink," and she dressed Lily in less gender-typed colors. But it took too much effort to enforce that request and eventually she yielded: "that moratorium lasted until about my oldest daughter's first birthday, and then all the pink frilly stuff started coming in droves." Sena also reported that she had never intended to adorn Lily's hair with accessories, but that, too, just began to happen.

> People would give me barrettes, barrettes would appear out of nowhere, from lots of people. . . . Lily was so excited, so I just sort of started using them. . . . It came to me one morning when I was putting barrettes in her hair, and I thought, "Hmmm, okay, well, I've given in on so many levels I'm sure, but here's a really tangible example of how I've given in to this particular notion of femininity."

Daily reinforcement when she dresses in typically girlish attire strikes Sena as an important interactional source that also shapes her daughter's preferences: "Lily's now at the point where she's picking up on all those cues, and I mean, sometimes it is somewhat inevitable, because you know we live in such a gender-focused society." In an intersectional outlook typical of Resisters, Sena considers the gendered attention Lily receives as shaped by the way that strangers who are not Asian American take notice of the "sort of, to them, exotic beauty" of her children.[2] And she worries that these everyday interactions will cultivate a distinctly gendered identity for Lily and her younger sister, Marissa.

People will come up to me in the supermarket and say, "Your daughters are just so beautiful," as though I couldn't possibly know that myself. Literally taking the time to grab my hand, as though it's something very serious that they have to make sure that I understand. . . . As they get older [my daughters] will pick up on it.

Sena sees these situations as having a direct effect particularly on Lily, who is old enough to interact more fully with peers as well as adults. She is concerned that all this emphasis on beauty, appearance, and fashion will limit Lily's self-image to one based only on looks.

We go places, and people will say, "Oh, you look so pretty," so there are some real tangible rewards for her. There are ways to keep those comments coming, and I think she's figured that out. And I think she's also figured out that it's important for girls to be considered pretty. She talks about being beautiful all the time, I mean, I have a heart attack every time she says, "I'm not smart, I'm beautiful." And I keep saying, "Well, you can be smart *and* beautiful." And she says, "No, I'm just beautiful." So, clearly, she's receiving that message.

This example conveys a distinguishing aspect of what motivates Resisters. They are not only open to, even encouraging of, gender atypical outcomes, but they also sometimes react negatively toward gender typicality. For an Innovator, Lily's interest in fashion and appearance would likely feel comfortable and positive, as long as it was combined with broader interests. For Sena, on the other hand, being smart and beautiful are culturally constructed as mutually exclusive, an analysis echoed by feminist social critic Naomi Wolf in her influential book *The Beauty Myth*. In her exploration of historical beliefs about female beauty, she writes, "Culture stereotypes women . . . by flattening the feminine into beauty-without-intelligence or intelligence-without-beauty; women are allowed a mind or a body, but not both."[3] Sena's critique, which reminded me of Wolf's observation, was the reason why she wishes Lily would avoid emphasizing beauty and appearance. Sena offers a somewhat "zero sum" approach to traditional femininity and broader opportunities, worrying that, given the power of gendered structures, traditional femininity is a trap that cannot be woven together easily with other elements of human experience.[4] This is in contrast to Refiners, such as Belinda who sees compatibility between traditional femininity and success in male-dominated careers, or Innovators such as Marcus who said of his daughter "If she wants to be the stereotypical little girl, she can be." These parents are optimistic about crafting a mixture of gender typical and atypical patterns that allows their children "the best of both worlds." Sena is more skeptical of traditionally feminine pursuits, believing that entrenched social messages construct them as incompatible with less traditional ones.

Despite Sena's detailed examples of interactional social construction, she emphasized institutional factors even more, imbuing her analysis of those factors with attention to the role of gendered power. She "pointed her finger at" businesses, advertising, and popular culture to explain the forces she grew tired of resisting, and spoke about institutional constraints that girls and women face in the educational system, workforce, and families. She believes that parents can resist these structural pressures but only with limited success.

> I don't think it's realistic for parents to do it on an individual basis. . . . You need to think about advertising, the images of women and men in popular culture, appropriate notions of masculinity and femininity that we learn through various aspects of society. . . . It's really sick and saddening.

Sena acts to widen the range of her daughters' activities and interests: avoiding gender-typical clothing and an overemphasis on appearance, encouraging Lily to participate in age-appropriate martial arts, and promoting the passion that she and her spouse, Doug, share for sports. Watching professional baseball on television is a major pastime in her household, and Sena was alarmed to discover that Lily saw it as a "boy's sport," as she only watched men playing it. As Sena put it, "We jumped all over that one, and in fact we had a babysitter who played on her high school softball team, so we called and asked her to talk to Lily about that right away." At the same time Sena is cautious about overly defying gendered constraints.

I would like to see parents allow their children to explore, encompass a broader range in terms of gender rules. But, on the other hand, I think so much blame is put on parents for everything that ever goes wrong that I don't really want to put yet another burden on parents. . . . It's very hard for all of us as parents who have expectations and dreams and hopes and ideas about who our children should be, it's hard to deal with any aspect of our children not meeting those expectations and being treated badly because of it.

Later on, Sena stated even more directly the balance she feels compelled to strike: "For me, part of the giving in has been providing my girls with survival techniques for getting through a gendered culture."

Tanya: "Stuck in That Building and You Can't Get Out"

Facing a similar onslaught by a "gendered culture" is Tanya, a thirty-four-year-old, white, woman in a gay partnership. She said that she and her partner, Lucy, have "had no luck yet" in slowing the flow of gendered toys grandparents give to their sons, two-year-old Riley and four-year-old Graham, and during our interview I noted that the spacious, open first story of their contemporary home was filled to capacity with toys. Tanya, who identified as upper-middle class, had worked as a writer before taking time off to be at home full-time with Riley and Graham, and Lucy continues to work as a business consultant. Like all the gay and lesbian parents I interviewed, Tanya is white.[5]

Tanya reported that she had always hoped to have a son, one of the three women who preferred a son because of their own "tomboy" interests during childhood. She made some limited reference to biology, talking about Graham's strong interest in how mechanical things work, even though she and Lucy are "not at all mechanically inclined," and noted both her sons' fascination with vehicles. "Under a year, both of them—it sounds goofy—they both started making like car noises and truck noises, like these noises that they are really good at. . . . We did nothing, they just did that on their own." More commonly she points to the influences of peers, relatives, media, school, and society in general to explain her sons' interests. She used terms such as "rules being stamped on" and "kids getting programmed" to characterize how gendered patterns develop. Tanya described Graham, the focal child of our interview, as typically boyish in some ways and not at all in others. Despite the accountability concerns captured in how "furious" she felt with Lucy over the pink sleeper incident I recounted in the introduction to the book, she works hard to support, even encourage, Graham's engagement with atypical interests. She purposely designed his nursery to be "loosey-goosey, very gender-neutral," and promotes play that fosters domestic competence. "They have a whole kitchen set, and when they do the kitchen set thing, I mean, he's the cook and we have a toy washing machine thing set up, too, so he does laundry." Though Graham has not asked for a Barbie, Tanya told me, "I'd be fine with that if he wanted something like a Barbie, that's totally cool as far as I'm concerned." She mentioned that purple is one of his favorite colors, as is lime green, both of which she considers more typical for girls. Yet, with her mother's help, she searches out clothes in his preferred colors.

> Boys' clothes get into this black and blue color category at like two, which is so unfair because what if they like the bright colors? Before purple, Graham's favorite color was lime green. And it's very difficult to find boys' clothes, like everything purple or lime green will have a doll embroidered on it or there's a lacey neck or something like that. You can't find a shirt that's just a purple shirt. My mom is really good [at it], she goes into the girl's section and sorts through until she finds clothes that are the right color yet don't have the styles that are super-lacey.

Tanya also circumvents the gender trap by avoiding heteronormativity. Resisters were the only group in which heteronormativity was nearly absent, whereas, in every other group, half to three-quarters of the parents assumed that their children would identify as heterosexual. The only comment I might have coded as heteronormative among Resisters came from Tanya, but in the end she spontaneously acknowledges the possibility that her sons might develop a same-sex orientation.

I want them to grow up to be kind to their girlfriends. I mean that in a lot of different ways, but including in regard to sex. . . . And even if they end up having sex with men, whatever, I don't want them to be that sort of stereotypical rouge male, just looking for a place and an opportunity kind of a thing, not showing respect for their partner.

This is the closest any of the Resisters came to normalizing, and thus reproducing, presumed heterosexuality. Perhaps because three of the five parents in this group are gay or lesbian, is not surprising that they are less likely to make this assumption. But neither of the two heterosexual parents in this category made that assumption, and Tanya, the only parent who nearly did so, is one of the gay parents. For that reason I believe that the absence of heteronormativity in this group represents more than just the sexual orientation of the parents but also a reflection of their outlook regarding gender structures. Sociologist Karin Martin's research on what she calls "sexual socialization" documents how commonly heteronormativity appears in advice books for parents and in the everyday talk of mothers and popular children's films.[6] She argues that heteronormativity presents the same kind of "stalled revolution" challenge that Hochschild articulated in her work on the division of labor in dual-earner heterosexual households; that is, those who seek to deconstruct gendered childhoods are frustrated by the invisible force of heteronormativity as well as parental fears concerning links between gender nonconformity and non-heterosexual orientation.[7] The notable absence of heteronormativity among Resisters suggests they are neither stalled at this juncture nor caught in this particular gender trap.

Viewing gendered expectations not as vestiges of some outdated tradition but as a "way to manipulate and control," Tanya used the metaphor of a building to describe her intersectional analysis. She talked about "straight white males" as "having a lot of privilege," but she argues that these males are also harmed in the process. She casts gender as a matter of power and gendered paths as troubling structures from which she wishes to escape.

It's one thing to be locked out of a building and looking in, wanting like anything to get inside, and it's another thing to be stuck in that building and you can't get out. I don't know, but I really think I'd choose the green pastures outside. . . . Those of us on the outside, we can struggle, and we get in here and there. But if you are the ones locked in, it's really hard to break out.

Noting that her white, upper-middle-class sons will likely inhabit that imaginary building, especially if they identify as heterosexual, Tanya detailed their ensuing obligations.

I would want my sons to understand and to appreciate that there are people who are locked out, and to be aware of that. And that by being locked in, yes they are somewhat restricted but they also have the keys if they can find them, and they can open those doors for other people and they can get things going. They have a responsibility, in fact, to do that. And they'll make their lives better by making the outsiders' lives better also, . . . opening up to let themselves out and other people in.

This comment is similar to Walt's desire that his sons avoid any kind of prejudice against other people. When Walt says, "There's just too much prejudice around, we're not going to do that," he, too, is implying that his sons have a responsibility to others. Tanya also observed that her efforts to loosen gendered constraints for Riley and Graham might multiply over time, which resembles Anthony's comment about "a small ripple" effect down the generational chain. According to Tanya, her own efforts will not suffice to create broad-scale social change around gender expectations.

Will I see it in my lifetime? Probably not. But my sons might see more, and if they have children, they'll see even more. Like what I do for my children is not just for my children, but it's for their children and what kind of fathers they would turn out to be. And for their kids, their kids might see it, a really different world.

These examples, from Innovators and Resisters, suggest a dimension of undoing gender somewhat unique to these groups: the desire that their children become agents of social change. These parents seek to free their own children from the gender trap, hoping that their efforts will spread across their immediate social networks and down through their family lines.

Like all other Resisters, however, Tanya remains wary of the risks, concerned about accountability to others and the cost of ignoring it. She told me, for example, that Graham has asked to wear dresses and tights, because his female peers at preschool have them and it looks like fun. She bought him "running tights," hoping to strike a compromise between his desire for tights and the boundaries of mainstream behavior. And she was pleased when she found a slip he could dress up in rather than an actual dress because she worried that he would want to wear the dress to preschool. That worry was rooted in her anxiety and fear about accountability to others rather than her own individual preferences.

> Theoretically, why shouldn't a boy be able to wear a dress whenever he wants? I'm totally okay with that. Yet, practically speaking, I'd be awfully uncomfortable if Graham really wanted to wear the dress to school. I'd have to let him do it, so I wouldn't scar him forever. But then I don't know what would be worse, me scarring him or the kids scarring him, because truly I might scar him and oppress him but for goodness sake, you're not going to make it out of there alive.

Though perhaps casually chosen, the phrase, "You're not going to make it out of there alive," similar to Sena's use of the term "surviving," indicates the Resister perception of the high stakes involved in defying conventions. Sena saw those gendered stakes as complicated by racialized notions of female beauty and by her having felt as a teenager that she was perceived by peers as "that ugly, chinky, smart girl." The memory added racial and gendered nuances to her daughter's casual claim that "I'm not smart, I'm beautiful." For Tanya, and almost all the gay and lesbian parents I interviewed, the gendered stakes were raised much higher by homophobia.[8] Tanya went further in expressing the accountability that Stefan raised when he said, "The last thing we'd want to do is put him in anything remotely girly," thus suggesting that Tanya's outlook might be more akin to Innovator Miriam's if, like Miriam, she were heterosexual.

> If I were straight, I would be totally fine with it and could care less and I'd probably let him wear pink and dresses and tights whenever he wanted. . . . I do feel very sensitive in certain respects because of the whole lesbian thing. . . . I feel like I'm under more of a microscope. . . . I feel as if I, I don't know, that I've loaded the dice for my children to a certain extent, in terms of prejudice and issues that they will face for sure because of who their parents are, that I can't compound it.

Tanya certainly would feel less vulnerable to this assessment if she did not have to face structured homophobia. She may, however, be understating the accountability pressure that she would still feel, given her previous observation that Graham "might not make it out of there alive" if he went to school in a dress.

Adrienne: "I'm More Vigilant That There's Nothing Too Feminine"

Another lesbian mother of two sons, Adrienne made remarkably similar comments concerning her sons, four-year-old Cody and one-year-old Luke. With a no-nonsense professional demeanor, she spoke in long, confident bursts that required little prompting throughout a three-hour interview. Adrienne, forty-four years old, is white, is employed as a higher-education administrator, and identifies as upper-middle class.

> Given my family, I'm more vigilant that there's nothing too feminine. . . . You know how we're all policed as mothers, like, "Are you a good enough mother?" There's this like abstract social voice always watching you, and as a gay mom I feel that about my son all the more so. If it could be assumed that he was effeminate at all, that would be a problem. . . . Society would hold me responsible. . . . Like, "Aha, here's this guy in a same-gender household, two moms, see what's happening?" . . . I feel the burden of being policed.

185

Adrienne and other Resisters prefer and believe that children benefit from less gendered upbringings, and she resists offering Cody gender-typical opportunities. She seeks to broaden his range of experiences and encourages nurturance, caring for others, and domestic abilities.

> To some extent I leave the gender game open, you know, my son is picking out flowers last night out of the garden to put on his castle for knights, and I didn't worry, he ought to love flowers. He's beginning to learn how to cook, he loves fabric, he has a good eye for color. On the other hand, he's got a great eye for pitching, he ought to be able to do a lot of things.

She went on to elaborate these goals into Cody's future life course, noting more choices that "leave the gender game open."

> He ought to be able to be a hairdresser or a baseball player or an artist, a dancer, it's completely open in that way. . . . It's very important to me that he feels he can do any occupation, that he can befriend anybody, that he can partner with anybody over time, that gender not constrain him in those ways. And my goal is to raise a sensible man, a very sensitive man, who has a good sense of himself, is very caring toward others, who has been able to actualize his potential.

Adrienne reported with pleasure that her sons' babysitter had bought them baby dolls. The babysitter also asked Adrienne if she could buy Cody a Barbie doll, after he enjoyed playing with one belonging to the sitter's daughter. Adrienne said, "Absolutely, yes." Cody loves his play set of knights and castles, considering some knights male and others female, although Adrienne noted that they are actually all male. She is glad he has this impression and encourages it. "Someone came over to visit the other day," she told me, "and they asked, 'Where's the damsel that you rescue?' And I said, 'Hey, the damsels are knights, they don't need any rescuing.'" Though she offered more social than biological explanations for gendered outcomes in childhood, Adrienne views boys and men as naturally more able to "zone in" and "compartmentalize," and she considers Cody's interest in construction

186

equipment a naturally boyish interest. "He has always loved construction, and he did not get that from us. Even as a baby, one of his first words was backhoe." All the gay and lesbian parents in the Resister category—Stefan, Tanya, and Adrienne—offered some biologically determinist explanations for their children's behavior, and each fit the contours of the "fallback" articulation. Though focused more on social determinants, and highly critical of those, each of these white, middle- or upper-middle-class gay parents felt that, absent gendering on their part, some of the gender-typical outcomes they have seen in their child must be natural. The most highly educated and privileged parents appear to be the most inclined to underestimate the effect of social forces on their own child despite their strong belief in the power of those forces more generally, even, or perhaps especially (as among the gay and lesbian parents, all of whom offered this kind of response), when they themselves are leading unconventionally gendered lives as adults. With racial and class privilege bolstering their confidence in their own agency in the world, these parents may imagine that they can craft the childhood outcomes they desire. When they are unsuccessful, they may be the quickest to assume that only something immutable—biological determinism—could intervene between their gender-neutral efforts and the gendered outcomes they witness.[9]

Describing gender as a matter of power and inequality and invoking an intersectional perspective are other tendencies Adrienne shares with the rest of the Resisters. She compared gender to both race and class as social markers shaping people's lives in ways she considers unfair. Gender inequality, in her view, both benefits and constrains Cody.

> Boys get more affirmation, much more affirmation. . . . I think he's already benefiting from that social preference for boys. The downside of early masculinity though would be dealing with how violent the world of boys is. . . . But I believe sexism will always make the deal sweeter. No matter how violent the world is, how mean men can be to other men, their privilege will still outweigh that.

Adrienne was critical of male privilege that flows from conventional masculinity, arguing that it gives men unfair advantages. But she also believes that men who adhere to conventional expectations are limited by violence and restricted emotional expression. Despite these criticisms, she still feels compelled by accountability to gendered assessment that is magnified by heterosexist structures, which prompts her to guide her son toward, at least, an approximation of that conventionally defined masculinity. Along with comments about policing and vigilance, Adrienne referred to press scrutiny of lesbian parents as a factor in her own approach to raising Cody.

> The *New York Times* last week had yet another article surveying all the recent trends in gay families, and that seemed like the big question, how is it possible to raise sons if you don't have a man in the house? . . . That's why I have all these thoughts about his masculinity, all this attention to masculinity, does he have an identity, is it going well? Because I know other people are out there wondering that about my family. . . . I know I have to shore up his masculine identity.

In this excerpt, Adrienne focuses more on masculine identity than on the performance of masculinity in everyday life, implying a concern for how Cody thinks of himself rather than how he acts in the world. But her previous comment that, if "he was effeminate at all that would be a problem," indicates that she apparently links gender performance to gender identity. Though Risman would think of "gender identity" as an internalized and thus individual-level phenomenon, what she refers to as "gendered selves," and gender performance as interactional, she argues that these levels are inextricably linked.[10] Adrienne implies something similar with her parallel references to "shoring up" Cody's masculine identity and her caution about any effeminate behavior. Risman, of course, also emphasizes institutional forces, and Adrienne is probably referring to these forces when she speaks about "sexism" as "mak[ing] the deal sweeter" for boys and men.

Joanna: "It's Very Difficult to Admit You're Not Raising Your Family like That"

Joanna had the largest household of any of my interviewees, living with her five home-schooled children plus her heterosexual partner, Larry, and

188

six months pregnant with her sixth child at the time of our conversation. Perhaps it was that full house that prompted her to request an interview at my office. A twenty-seven-year-old white woman who identified as low income, Joanna's three daughters and two sons range in age from two to nine but three-year-old Jeremy was the primary focus of our interview. I had imagined that Joanna, a pregnant, home-schooling mother of five might be short on sleep, but she appeared energetic as she talked about her children and rarely required any prompting throughout an interview that lasted over two and a half hours.

Like Tanya, Joanna cited her own "tomboy" childhood to explain why she always preferred to have a son. She sees gendered rules as created by parents and media, and rippling out through peer interactions even to children whose parents have, like Joanna, tried to avoid these constraints.

> It starts with the parents, like dads may roughhouse more with their boys and they get them involved in aggressive contact sport activities, and they let them be exposed to more television that's oriented to boys and has aggressive behavior, and all of that can lead to more aggressive, even violent, behavior. And then when one boy is like that, the other boys see it and it does seem to be a domino. Even if my child may not have experienced that at home, it still can domino onto him.

Joanna never brought up a biological explanation for gender differentiation and believes she is working to relax gendered constraints on her sons and daughters. She prefers a "blending of the genders," so that all her children know how to cook, sew, maintain cars, act nurturing, and compete. Joanna's four-year-old daughter, Samantha, loves pink and frilly dresses, contrary to Joanna's tastes. But Joanna tries to meet Samantha's desire to a limited extent, encouraging in her a broader array of colors, styles, and interests. "I'd like her to be more flexible." She wants both her sons and daughters to consider careers more typically associated with the other gender, and tries to watch out for media or school influences that promote gender typing in that regard. Although Larry is not as concerned about these issues as Joanna, she asks him not to discourage Jeremy's tendency to cry, noting that her husband has "made a comment to him about, you know, crying like a girl, but I say, 'Whoa, wait a minute, he has a right to express his frustration, his sadness.'" Joanna has also appealed to Larry to teach both their sons and daughters about car repair (a hobby of his) and not to comment negatively if the boys want to play with dolls. In her words: "I've made a strong point of telling my husband, I don't want this gender separation." Upon her request, an uncle bought Jeremy a doll as a gift, and she encourages Jeremy to take care of it. Joanna was especially bothered by restrictions on boys' emotional expression.

> In some ways, I think girls almost have it easier just because they're able to cry, boys aren't allowed to cry. "Be tough," you know, that's what everyone tells boys. If boys cry, that's off limits to a lot of people. But of course they should cry, they're human, they're just being human. It's so tough, they have to hold all of that in, and girls can more or less let it out.

Like Adrienne, however, Joanna is critical not only of this kind of constraint on boys and men but also critical of male power that constrains women. In describing barriers to women's access to predominantly male occupations, she focuses not on tradition but on power: "with women coming into their workplace, men feel threatened by that and they rebel against it, they make it really hard for women to succeed in those jobs."[11] She also noted structural obstacles that face men who want to take on domestic responsibilities.[12]

> In men's bathrooms at the malls, they don't have changing tables for babies. So if a dad is out with his baby, hello, how can he change that diaper except on the bench in the hallway or something, you know what I mean? And that's one good example of how society has deemed that dad isn't supposed to change diapers. . . . It's not fair to the women, it's not fair to the children, it's not fair to anyone.

In response to whether she is trying to teach her children anything particular about boys and girls or men and women, Joanna provided one of the longest answers of any participant. Even an excerpt offers a clear sense of the range of lessons she hopes to convey and some of the concrete steps she takes.

> I try to expose them to enough that they realize that not all doctors are men, not all nurses are women. . . . I want them to be aware that there's opportunity, or there should be, to do anything. . . . When I read a book and it says something about a nurse, if the picture is female nurses I'll be sure to say, "You know, boys can be nurses too." . . . I even had a thing with this local historical site (a nineteenth-century farm) where we went with a group of home-schooled children. They take the boys out and do the farm chores and the girls stay in and do the cooking work. And I said, "Wait a minute. I want my son to come in and do this and I want my daughter to go see what that is, even though that's the way life was back then." I wanted the kids to experience both, and the people up there had a hard time accepting that because they're trying to represent what it was like in that time. I understand that, but I don't think you have to perpetuate that in order to explain it to the kids. . . . And then I think it's up to me to explain it to my children and say look, you know, some women are as muscular as a lot of men, they can handle even the most physical job just fine, plus a lot of those jobs don't really take muscle or anything anyway. And many men are very nurturing to their children and make excellent stay-at-home dads. If by talking about all of that I can help my children realize it, and help society accept it more, that's what I want to do.

Nevertheless, Joanna appeared more anxious than any other Resister about accountability. This may result, in part, from her persistent efforts to resist the gender trap, which places her children at greater risk of performing gender differently. Another factor may be that she is the only parent in the group not privileged by a relatively high socioeconomic status, and so she may feel uncertain of her own agency and at greater risk of assessment concerning the class-based gender standards Pyke describes.[13] Fear and anxiety seemed to accompany her comments about gender accountability, sometimes in brief phrases, such as "I don't want my kids to feel like the odd balls out," and sometimes at greater length.

> I don't meet many people that are so open as far as all of this. I've met some, but generally people like to stick to boy-girl things. I think society feels more comfortable like that. And again, if you are the one who is different, if you are the woman who works pumping gas, "Oh, she must be gay," some people would say. Same thing, if he's a nurse or something he must be gay, you know, [people] label you instantly that there must be something wrong with you if you're doing this 'cause men should be like construction workers and women should be nurses. . . . It's very difficult to admit that you're not raising your family like that. . . . I really care what people think to a certain point. To some point I really don't, but I don't want people to think something of me that I'm not. I don't want them to think that [of] my children either, I don't want my children to be hurt by that in the future.

Despite her strong feelings about resisting gendered childhoods and her efforts to put those feelings into action, as well as her lack of heteronormative assumptions, Joanna implies the fear that her children might be viewed as gay if they cross certain gender divides. She refers negatively at one point to homophobic people, but I did not follow up on her responses enough to know the extent to which she is comfortable with her children identifying as non-heterosexual. My impression, however, is that she is not homophobic herself; rather, enough homophobia permeates her immediate social world for that fear to be significant. She went on later to tell me a story about a friend whose five-year-old son was teased by older children for having a poster depicting a female character from a popular children's television show, leaving Joanna worried about responses to some of Jeremy's interests.

> I don't want somebody making fun of him because he might cook, you know, or because he might have dolls. That's the thing, if he plays with Barbie dolls it's almost like you want to tell him, "Well, don't tell anybody else," just because I get so afraid of the way they'd react.

Joanna had not yet offered such advice to her son and hoped to avoid do-ing so. But her temptation—the fact that she would "almost" want to tell him, "Well, don't tell anybody else"—combined with other comments she made, suggests that Joanna is cautious as she resists gendering her children. She told me that she does not "want them to feel like they have to hide their interests and curiosities because somebody's going to think something bad of them," but she is clearly worried that is exactly how they may feel.

"That's Something I Always Feel Up Against"

Resisters stand out in the degree to which their reproductive actions are indirect. They are more likely to allow rather than actively encourage gen-der typicality, and are also the group by far the most likely to harbor nega-tive feelings about gender-typical attributes and behaviors for both boys and girls. In addition, their resistant actions are more direct compared to those of their Innovator peers, and they express the most positive feelings about atypical outcomes of any group. Their actions and preferences are the most pointedly resistant and least pointedly reproductive of any of the five groups. They are also the only group for whom heteronormativity is not a common background feature. They respond more specifically to my query about whether they are trying to teach their children anything spe-cific about boys and girls, or about men and women, and their responses are often lengthy, focused not only on resistance but on criticism of gen-dered power. Along with their Innovator peers, they highlight social deter-minants over biological ones, but they focus more on institutional sources of social pressure than on interpersonal sources. Resisters are the group most likely to bring up power, structure, and intersectionality as they talk about gender. Tanya's intersectional emphasis on structural power includes criticism of the social privilege enjoyed by heterosexual, white men, but she remains optimistic about the potential for social change through structures such as public policy. Reflecting on her own experiences as a school athlete in the 1980s, she noted:

I don't think that the world is going to change anytime soon, but over time I think it will. I mean, think about thirty years of Title IX, and

look at the difference there. I played sports in high school, and it prepared me for good opportunities in college. . . . But it ended there,
there was no professional anything for women. Now there's some
professional stuff. I mean, the world changes but it changes in incre-
ments and it takes a real push like Title IX to help make that happen.[14]

Tanya, with her emphasis on incremental change, expressed the most
optimism among Resisters, though her hopefulness about the possibility
for dismantling the gender trap was perhaps muted. Stefan views social attitudes toward gender as linked with attitudes toward sexual orientation,
and gave reasons for both hope and worry as he assessed the prospects for
what he considers progress.

You get kind of a new guard out front, pushing for more openness,
whether it's for kids or for occupations or for gay parenting, all of
those kinds of changes. That threatens a lot of people, and so the
people at the other end dig in deeper. I think there's that kind of process that goes on, people are changing but there are many people who
don't want that to happen. . . . The undercurrent is change, but there
is that throw-back element out there that could do just the opposite.

Among the five parents in this group, responses about the potential
for change encompassed references to other obstacles including men's
tendency to fight women's entry into traditionally male occupations, the
pervasive influence of stereotypical images of gender in advertising and
media, homophobia, right-leaning political ideologies, and conservative
religious groups. These parents are not invoking the obstacle of outdated
tradition but of structured power. They work at resisting the gender trap,
and several commented on their children's obligation to do the same. They
believe that gendered patterns can be shifted in part by the interactional
forces of everyday actions of parents, peers, and community members. But
they also believe that broader structural forces need to be addressed at the
institutional level. Though serious about her analysis of the role of media
and marketing, Sena captured some of this overarching sentiment when

she joked that real change in gender expectations for children would not happen "until Nike tells us to 'Just Do It!'"

Their beliefs and experiences also make Resisters considerably more fearful than Innovators of the costs of straying from gendered paths. For Sena, the only parent without sons in this group, accountability led to a sense of frustrated inevitability, conveyed in the language of "giving up" and "getting sucked in." She uses the term "survival" in describing her efforts to teach her daughters how to navigate the gendered terrain around them, but Sena considers the stakes even higher for boys. "For boys who maybe don't fall straight down the middle, they have to be much more closeted about it, and I think maybe 'closeted' is a good word." Some variation on this theme was evident across the Resister parents. As Adrienne summed it up, "There's a double standard. . . . For a boy to cross the divide of what's considered appropriate, that is such a huge step, and I think it raises a lot of thoughts for people."

These comments resonate with the contours of hegemonic masculinity outlined by scholars such as Connell, Messner, and Kimmel.[15] The Resisters were not arguing that gender inequality is without costs to girls and women, or even that it is more costly to boys and men; but they believe that straying off the gendered path provokes more accountability pressure for boys and men, because that path is a source of power for them. As a group composed primarily of parents of sons, this may help to explain their level of anxiety. The accountability factor is further intensified for gay and lesbian parents, who were particularly concerned about how their sons would be judged. Adrienne echoed what I heard from other gay and lesbian parents: "That's something I always feel up against." This sentiment also captured the general sense of gendered accountability reported by the heterosexual parents in this group, Sena and Joanna. They, too, "feel up against" something, forced to navigate interactional social expectations and institutional structures that pose risks for themselves and their children that are especially acute because of their efforts to do childhood gender differently.

Although it is not generally prudent to generalize about such a small number of parents as Resisters, my commitment to an intersectional approach, as well as the context provided by the scholarly literature, allows some speculation about and sensitivity to certain patterns here. Resisters comprise the most common category for the gay and lesbian parents interviewed for this book, suggesting both their dedication to resisting gendered constraints and the extra vigilance they feel compelled to adopt. Judith Stacey and Timothy Biblarz, writing in the *American Sociological Review*, offer a convincing case that gay and lesbian parents tend to allow their children more freedom in gendered expectations.[16] Psychologists Erin Sutfin and her colleagues report the same conclusion that the children of lesbian mothers tend to have less gender-stereotypical environments and less traditional ideas about gender.[17] In her analysis of lesbian families sociologist Maureen Sullivan argues that, through their partnerships, the co-parents she interviewed provide "potential for the undoing of gender: the delinking of gender from power and forms of inequality within nuclear families."[18] In their daily interactions in their households and with heterosexual friends and strangers, Sullivan believes these parents are chipping away at gendered structures. Tanya, too, saw her family as a potential agent of change, describing how the heterosexual members in her church react positively to her family, a reaction she hopes signals that they have developed a more positive view of gay families in general. Stefan similarly commented on his family's daily interactions in their community. Sullivan also notes the importance of the pressure that the class-privileged women in her study often exert on medical and legal institutions as they seek family rights. Sociologists Susan Dalton and Sarah Fenstermaker, who have studied institutional change, raise the same notions of related interactional and institutional challenges posed by class-privileged lesbian co-parents as they navigate state adoption bureaucracies.[19] The clustering of gay and lesbian parents in the Resister category examined in this book is consistent with the work of these scholars, indicating the tendency of such parents to resist the gender trap not only in their adult partnerships but also in their approach to raising their children. Meanwhile, however, their concerns about accountability in relation to their children's gender performance indicate that they pay an additional social price in a homophobic society, a cost that arises more for sons than for daughters. All the gay and lesbian parents with sons spontaneously mentioned this sense of additional accountability, what Tanya referred to as "loaded dice," regarding their sons' masculinity.

Besides the gay and lesbian parents in the Resister group, the two heterosexual mothers also are taking an approach reminiscent of what political scientist Colleen Mack-Canty and sociologist Sue Wright term "third wave feminist parenting."[20] In interviewing twenty families where the parent(s) self-identified as feminist, they found that most of these couples "go beyond nonsexist parenting," a trend the authors consider typical of second wave feminism's emphasis on equality of treatment and opportunity. Instead, they seek to craft a kind of parenting that encourages their children to "become conscious of and to challenge hierarchy and oppression generally." Mack-Canty and Wright consider an emphasis on intersectionality and a critique of power and hierarchy the particular contributions of third wave feminism, and they see the families they studied as embodying that contribution. In the context of their emphasis on intersectionality and opposition to hierarchy, it becomes all the more intriguing that the Resisters interviewed for this book—the group most likely to focus on structure, power, and intersectionality—is comprised of parents who all experience at least one subordinated social location on the basis of sexual orientation (Tanya, Stefan, and Adrienne), race (Sena), social class (Joanna), and/or gender (four of the five parents in this group are mothers).[21]

The configuration of beliefs and practices among Resisters represents the deepest challenge to gendered parenting, and even gendered childhoods, of any approach taken by parents I interviewed. This configuration also highlights the themes I considered in the introduction: the multiple levels of the social construction of gender, gendered power, and intersecting inequalities. Far from reproducing gendered outcomes by rote or viewing these outcomes as essentially dictated by nature, these parents engage in an especially complex and ambivalent balancing act, where they view gendered childhoods as socially constructed and problematic. They actively seek to disrupt gender binaries and traditional masculinity and femininity, preparing both their daughters and sons to pursue a wider range of human experiences. Combined with their recognition of structural obstacles, their approach potentially can avoid some of the traps and stalled revolutions I have discussed, including the division of labor in heterosexual households and gendered carework, occupational gender segregation, pressures toward heteronormativity, essentialized male aggression, and essentialized preoccupation with appearance among girls and women. At the same time these parents' efforts to do gender differently are complicated by their strong sense of accountability to others, the anxiety provoked by the hegemonic status of a particular form of masculinity they fear will constrain their sons, and their belief in deeply structured power as underlying both gender and other intersecting forms of inequality. The latter factors limit these parents' willingness to resist, leaving them cautious and wary as they navigate what feels to them less a gendered path and more a gendered minefield. Their recognition of structure and accountability is a resource in their efforts to undo gendered constraints on their children, as it helps them orient their actions toward the interactional and institutional levels rather than only the individual-level of their child's gendered identity. But it also mutes the optimism that Innovators expressed, perhaps discouraging Resister parents from pushing even harder against the boundaries of gendered expectation for their children. In their wariness about the social costs of resistance, they offer an important reminder that social change cannot originate only within individual families but, as Risman summarizes, "must occur simultaneously at the level of identities, interactions, and institutions."[22]

CONCLUSION

"A Better World"

Dismantling the Gender Trap

"Is that kid's meal for a boy or a girl?" a cashier asked me at a fast-food restaurant. Why, I wondered, were chicken nuggets different for boys and girls? Of course, it was not the food but the free toy that came with the meal that was intended for a boy or girl. Instead of asking if I preferred, for example, race cars or dolls, Spiderman or My Little Pony, the cashier assumed that my children's gender determined which toy they would want. Though I had hoped to sidestep that trap as I raised my twins, it was much more difficult than anticipated. As with all the parents' stories in this book, my efforts required juggling a complicated set of beliefs, actions, and responses from other people, as well as from my own children. The hard work of trying to navigate around the gender trap is, as I have argued throughout, well worth the effort. Gender as a social structure continues to limit opportunities and lead to an inequitable distribution of social resources; the groundwork for those limitations and inequalities begins in childhood, even in our pre-parenthood anticipation of the children we may someday have.

The literature based on quantified observation and experimental manipulation documents some of the unconscious ways in which parents accomplish gender for their children.[1] My interviews capture these subtle gendering activities exhibited by some parents who, while claiming to follow natural gender differences, also report actions likely to construct exactly these differences. More notable across all groups of parents, however, was a dynamic and often conscious process of weighing the costs and benefits of

199

conventional gendering. That process involves a range of social actors with whom parents are in dialogue, from relatives and friends to their children's peers and even strangers, as well as social institutions such as schools, hospitals, media, commercial interests, and community groups. Parents draw on their beliefs about the acceptability of gendered divisions, their analysis of power and inequality, their assumptions about essential gendered tendencies, and their assessment of the social risks and rewards of traditionally gendered outcomes. Within the framework of those various beliefs, the participants balanced the tensions between biological and social determinism, between reproductive and resistive action, to forge a range of gendered paths through childhood.

In her interview Tanya was pessimistic about rapid social change but thought that gendered constraints would loosen in the long run.

> Someday, eventually, I do think there's a good chance of things being different, I think most people would want it to be. Most people love their children, and want a better world for them. What kind of a better world would that be? One where people don't hate people and restrict people. And part of that is society's gender rules, I mean, it's always about a way to manipulate and control. So I think people try to do the best they can for their kids most of the time, and they will see that letting up on those rules is a good way to do that.

The parents who participated in this study certainly expressed love for their children and a strong desire to offer them opportunities and the freedom to pursue their interests. Some parents seek to maintain gendered childhoods, because they see gendered divisions of labor and interests in adulthood as positive outcomes. Those parents' desire to create a better world for their children is unlikely to motivate significant resistance to gender expectations. Yet even they sought a somewhat greater range for their children, particularly their daughters. And whereas some were strongly opposed, most parents expressed at least some objections to gendered constraints, though many worried about the costs of straying from the conventional path, especially regarding their sons. Thus opposition to gendered constraints, and even the more limited desire for greater range, is a resource for social change. Parents' hopes and fears, their aspirations and anxieties, offer a foundation from which to question existing gender structures that are inseparable from intersecting structures of race, class, and sexuality. By documenting the degree to which many parents are consciously crafting their children's gender—motivated by personal preference, perceptions of their child's welfare, accountability to others, or a sense of inevitability— my analysis suggests that parents could be encouraged to shift these conscious efforts toward less gendered directions, prompting new approaches. But individual parents cannot do it alone. A sociological perspective reveals a need for the collective effort of multiple social actors and social institutions, focusing not only on individual preferences but also social interactions and institutional forces. This concluding chapter revisits the literature on gender and family, and reviews the main patterns emerging in my interviews and their implications for avoiding the gender trap.

Tensions and Practices

My goal has been to investigate gender as it is socially constructed at the individual, interactional, and institutional levels, and to examine both gendered power and the intersections of gender with inequalities of race, class, and sexuality. Chapter 1 documents parents' preferences for sons and daughters, arguing that the highly gendered anticipation in which my participants engaged is a form of doing gender with the potential for self-fulfilling prophecy among their own children and a tendency to reinforce frameworks of accountability which eventually constrain both their children and those of others. The gender trap is baited before children even arrive. I also explore parental beliefs about the origins of gendered childhoods. Although biological determinism and social constructionism advance conflicting explanations for gender variations, most parents drew on both perspectives as they attempted to understand the gendered patterns in their own children and in children more generally. Just as parents combined nature and nurture in their explanations for the origins of gendered childhoods, most reported a range of actions both reproducing and resisting conventional gendered outcomes. For daughters, much of the reported gender reproduction involved "indirect gendering," which focused on following whatever interests the child expressed and emphasized the acceptance of gender-typical outcomes more so than the rejection of atypical ones. In contrast, direct gendering was more common for sons than daughters and involved not only accepting gender typicality but also rejecting, or avoiding, atypical outcomes. The resistant actions that parents talked about most frequently for daughters centered on occupational aspirations, toy vehicles, and sports/outdoor activities; for sons, the most frequent topics were domestic skills, nurturance, and empathy. Indirect action was more common for sons than daughters with regard to resistance, and direct action more often included caveats for sons. Motivated by factors such as personal preference, the interests or welfare of children, a feeling of inevitability, and accountability to gendered assessment, parents sought to refine gendered expectations more for daughters than for sons, while also in many ways reproducing the gender trap.

After outlining gendered anticipation and the tensions between biological and social explanations, and between reproductive and resistant actions, I classify parental gendering practices into five different groups. In chapter 2 we meet the Naturalizers, who view gendered outcomes as primarily biological in origin but also report actions that reproduce those outcomes. Across the interviewees, greater biological determinism was associated with a greater tendency to reproduce gendered patterns at the level of action, but Cultivators, introduced in chapter 3, reveal that a focus on biology is not always the backdrop to reproduction. Cultivators are similar to Naturalizers in their reproduction-oriented action, but they combine this action with a more socially deterministic outlook that readily acknowledges the role of parents in gendering their children in relatively traditional ways. The Refiners in chapter 4 believe that both biology and society shape gendered childhoods, and they combine reproduction and resistance about equally in their actions. They tend to view gender as a matter of difference, not power, but also tend to regard gender constraints as unhealthy limitations on their children's individual freedom. Chapter 5 discusses the Innovators, whose actions tend to disrupt traditionally gendered outcomes and who believe that society is the chief source of childhood gender patterns. These parents are also more inclined to criticize gendered power. In chapter 6 the Resisters are shown to share the Innovators' emphasis on society, criticism of gendered power, and resistant action, but with a more wary and anxious outlook incorporating strong concerns about accountability to others. Each group's approach to parenting offers benefits and drawbacks in terms of sidestepping the gender trap, a topic discussed previously and revisited in the present chapter.

Parents Doing Gender

In comparing the five groups of parents as they plot a course through the tensions I identify, a number of themes emerge. Similarities and differences in the specific articulation of these themes highlight the ways in which parents in the United States do gender with and for their children.

Girly Girls? Refined Femininity

Much of what parents expressed concerning hopes and plans for their daughters would win the approval of supporters of less gendered childhoods and greater gender equality. Most parents, for instance, favored an expanded range of opportunities for girls, with many emphasizing access to the skill-development potential of competitive sports, the positive sense of agency that is fostered by outdoor pursuits, and the benefits of aspiring toward more wide-open occupational arenas. Some also sought to expose their daughters to the kinds of toys, puzzles, and activities they see as promoting spatial, mechanical, and scientific aptitudes. Many of the same parents exhibited gender typing in that they anticipated daughters to be more emotionally connected and more interested in shopping and talking; and they viewed female nurturance, emotionality, and aesthetic appreciation for fashion, color, and style as either biologically determined or positive social outcomes to be encouraged. They combined traditional femininity with at least some interest, or in many cases a great deal of interest, in a refined, expanded set of skills and opportunities for girls.

Internal contradictions and external constraints, however, complicate the refined femininity sought by many parents, paving the way back to the gender trap. Refined femininity implicitly devalues femininity in fundamentally the same way as hegemonic masculinity does more explicitly, rendering those traits or activities traditionally defined to be feminine as appropriate only to a fixed extent and only for girls, not potentially valuable for all persons. Few parents said they would not want their son to be "too boyish," but many commented negatively on too much pink or too much princess culture. Regarding his daughters, Lou, a Cultivator, observed, "Too girly or feminine, I don't like that, I want them to be feminine but I don't want them to be overly girly girl." Most parents either allowed or supported and encouraged their daughters to have dolls, take dance lessons, wear cute clothing and accessories, be interested in arts and crafts, or associate with other icons of femininity. They often acknowledged the positive feedback those daughters received from peers, relatives, and more distant social actors for being pretty, quiet, nice, and nurturing. And, like Belinda, a Refiner, many hoped that their daughters could choose freely between a high-powered or technical career more often associated with men and the world of intensive motherhood or, better yet, shift smoothly from one world to the other and back again. But the language of choice masks important structural constraints, including occupational gender segregation, the glass ceiling and gendered wage gap, the imbalance of political power based on gender, the second shift, and the class-based hegemony of the male career. Unless boys are prepared with the skills and capacities to contribute to both the economic and political arenas and to the carework so often assigned socially to women, most girls will not have the free range of options these parents are hoping for. If heterosexually partnered, these girls may face the second shift and the hegemony of the male career, and occupational gender segregation may lead them toward careers that do not allow them financial independence. If raising children without a partner, these girls eventually may discover the link between the feminization of poverty and gendered structures, such as occupational gender segregation and privatized family responsibility, structures that concentrate women in lower-wage jobs and provide little social support for the carework demands they simultaneously face.[2] These structures, as I have argued throughout, are infused with intersecting patterns of inequality, as illustrated by Maurice's assumption that the world will be his daughters' oyster, ignoring inequalities of race, class, and nation that are often reinforced by class-advantaged women's efforts to combine paid employment and carework.

In addition, the focus on fashion and appearance that many parents celebrate for their daughters but not their sons has potential consequences for girls, including what Wolf refers to as the "third shift" (the beauty work that women add to their shifts in the paid economy and in unpaid family carework), the risk of self-esteem and body-image issues linked to objectification, and eating disorders.[3] The appearance expectations and princess culture that many parents accepted tend to buttress gendered inequalities, as well as racial and class privilege and heteronormativity, through the ideal of white, affluent beauty and the construction of women as the objects of the male gaze. The chivalry and protectiveness that some parents felt their daughters deserve, along with parents' assumption that their daughters are passive compared to boys, may have possibly adverse implications, too. By reproducing the normative conception of female weakness, this protective attitude contributes to the risk of domestic violence and sexual assault. It also generates dependence on and subordination to men by reinforcing an image of women as less suitable for leadership, authority, or initiative in families, organizations, politics, and other social arenas.

Along with these complications associated with the refined femininity that many parents were trying to craft, it is important to note that the broader range encouraged for young girls might be narrower by adolescence. In her analysis of elementary and middle school students, Thorne argues that girls are given more gender leeway than boys during early childhood, "but the leeway begins to tighten as girls approach adolescence and move into the heterosexualized gender system of teens and adults." [4] Although I believe that the parents I interviewed would still welcome the chance to broaden their daughters' gendered options beyond their preschool and elementary school years, perhaps they will experience greater anxiety and accountability pressure during the teenage years, a question that clearly merits future inquiry.

Rough and Tumble Boys: Hegemonic Masculinity

Beginning with the gendered anticipation that reproduces stereotypically masculine interest in sports and outdoor activities, as well as men's structural role as carrier of the family name, parents of boys laid the foundation for a more traditional construction of gender. The interests and attributes reportedly encouraged by parents, which some view as having a biological origin, adhere closely to what scholars of gender call "hegemonic masculinity,"[5] a form of masculinity characterized by aggression, limited emotionality, and heterosexuality, together with scrupulous avoidance of so-called feminine attributes such as passivity, excessive emotionality, and feminine icons. The work of parents to maintain boundaries that approximate hegemonic masculinity may discourage boys from developing a full emotional range, exploring aesthetic pleasures, and learning to resolve conflicts peacefully. It also limits their ability to pursue interests, occupations, and identities socially defined as feminine. All this has implications for boys' and men's physical and mental health, as they are encouraged to handle stress with toughness and independence.[6] It also has important consequences for their approach to conflict with family and peers, which often play out differently depending on the class- and race-based resources available to the individual.[7] Many parents carve out some space within this hegemonic ideal for encouraging nurturance, empathy, and basic domestic skills, but their attempts to broaden the range of play for boys are carefully policed in a manner that tends to reinforce both gender and heteronormativity, assuming as it does that the nurturance and domestic skills their sons need would supplement the more primary ones offered by a female partner. To some extent, the outlines of hegemonic masculinity prepare men to assume social power under conditions of gender inequality, particularly those men also advantaged by hierarchies of race, class, and sexuality. Schrock and Schwalbe address this important point in a recent, comprehensive review of the social science literature on masculinity. As they argue convincingly, boys and men who enact masculinity are allowed "to claim membership in the dominant gender group, to affirm the social reality of [that] group, to elicit deference from others, and to maintain privileges vis-à-vis women."[8] Although they recognize intersectionality and thus the ways in which some groups of men dominate others, Schrock and Schwalbe advocate careful attention to the effects of enacting masculinity in "reproducing an unequal gender order."[9] It is crucial, meanwhile, to recognize the costs that trying to approximate hegemonic masculinity has for boys, as the narrow trap of this particular normative conception limits boys' options, poses risks to their health and well-being, separates them from girls, and devalues femininity. The enforcement of hegemonic masculinity produces and reproduces the same gendered status quo that many parents prefer not to see constrain their sons and daughters.

Some parents did go beyond the circumscribed terrain of nurturance, empathy, and domestic skills, further encouraging their sons to appreciate color, texture, and style, to widen their emotional and expressive range, and to develop sensitivity and an ethic of caring and connection. But these parents were generally Innovators and Resisters, with the latter especially highlighting social risks to their sons if their gender performances were not at least somewhat typical. Most parents stopped short of deviating significantly from hegemonic masculinity, tweaking it to incorporate the limited amount of compassion and care Messner notes but not enough to prepare their sons to fully share the second shift with the heterosexual partners they assume will eventually join them.[10] And though many parents encouraged their daughters to aspire to traditional male occupations, few encouraged their sons to consider traditional female ones. Reproducing a framework of accountability to the expectation that they will be primary breadwinners and secondary caregivers, this version of masculinity contributes to what Hochschild calls the "stalled revolution." If changes to women's lives are not accompanied by corresponding changes to men's lives, then efforts to chip away at the gender trap will meet with only limited success. Channeling boys toward high activity levels, chivalry, toughness, and emotional restraint also reproduces the assumption of male strength, power, and authority, just as the corresponding expectations of girls noted previously reproduce their potential subordination.[11]

Heterosexual fathers seem to play a central role in the enforcement of hegemonic masculinity. This is evident in the direct endorsement of this type of masculinity that many heterosexual fathers expressed, in the accountability to their male partners that many heterosexual mothers expressed, and in the accountability to the heterosexual world that all the gay and lesbian parents of sons expressed. Efforts to understand the routine production of gender in childhood need to pay careful attention to the role of heterosexual fathers as guardians of gender boundaries, especially for their sons; practical efforts to loosen gendered constraints on young children by expanding their parents' normative conceptions of gender need to be aimed at parents in general and especially at heterosexual fathers. Tanya's argument that "most people love their children and want a better world for them" applies to the heterosexual fathers I interviewed, just as it applies to the heterosexual mothers and gay and lesbian parents. If more of these fathers, particularly the white, middle-, and upper-middle-class fathers in my study, could be convinced of the limits that hegemonic masculinity imposes upon their sons, and of how it contributes to the stalled revolution that also traps their daughters, that desire for a better world might lead them to try different ways of doing gender with and for their boys.

Straight and Narrow: Heteronormativity and Homophobia

The vast majority of parents of both sons and daughters not only assumed that their children would grow up to identify as heterosexual, but they steered them in that direction through routine invocations of heterosexuality. Resisters were the only exception, with both gay and straight parents in that group diverging from the general tendency to assume and reinforce children's heterosexuality. Sexuality also came up in connection with implied or expressed links between gender nonconformity and non-heterosexual orientation. A number of parents, primarily Cultivators, raised this connection as a matter of concern. Some even talked about heterosexuality as an outcome they work to produce by encouraging normative gender performance. This line of thought is captured in examples such as Jerome's comment that he is raising his son "to be a boy, a man," and therefore would be disappointed if Jack identifies as gay, and Cameron's explanation that he considers it "bad" for his son to have "things that are meant for girls," perhaps because "his sexual orientation might get screwed up." Brianna, a lesbian mother of a daughter, did not hold homophobic attitudes herself but believes that many heterosexual parents of sons do. In her words: "I think it's much more uncomfortable for parents of boys to tolerate their sort of sissy behavior than it is to tolerate tomboy behavior for girls." When I asked her why she thought that was so, she replied, "Homosexuality, the homosexuality issue. There's real fear there. You can be a tomboy, but there's not the fear you are going to be a lesbian, but if you're a boy and you tend to be a sissy, there's the fear that he's going to be a homosexual."

Her assessment was supported by the parents I interviewed: when participants spontaneously linked sexual orientation to gender nonconformity, it was almost always in relation to boys, consistent with the perspective offered by scholars of hegemonic masculinity, and with Brianna's analysis as well. Brianna's perceived fear also comes up in Martin's scholarship on parenting advice. Martin argues that the presumption of heterosexuality, and the implied links between gender nonconformity and sexual orientation, lead to a stalled revolution, just as I have argued that the prospect of a stalled revolution for men and women in heterosexual families is raised by parental efforts to offer greater opportunities for daughters without similar broadening efforts for sons. In her analysis of best-selling parental advice books, Martin notes that heteronormativity "limits the discourse and advocacy of gender-neutral child rearing among popular child care advisors."[12] She goes on to claim that "the success of a gender revolution may require a sexual revolution, which is still missing."[13]

The fears among some parents, as well as the negatively evaluated links between gender nonconformity and sexual orientation, are troubling in their implications for children and for the prospects for a less gendered world. These beliefs impose constraints on boys who do not conform to traditional expectations, whether they grow up to identify as gay or not. They also constrain boys who conform to those expectations based on their fear, or their parents' fear, of associating themselves with anything outside the dominant definition of masculinity. These fears and perceived links between gender and sexuality support dichotomous conceptions of gender and heteronormativity, marginalizing and silencing those who do not identify as heterosexual and exclusively one gender or the other. A related fear is the homophobia that is evident in this pattern of beliefs, which imposes serious costs on those who identify as gay or bisexual, including stigma, discrimination, violence against lesbian, gay, bisexual, transgender, or questioning individuals, and queer youth suicide.[14] The powerful synergies among dichotomous conceptions of gender, heteronormativity, and homophobia also limit the freedom of people of all sexual orientations to explore gender as a continuum rather than a strict binary, and thus limit the possibilities for a world in which power and opportunity are less restricted by gender.

Biology and Society

Though the balance between biological and social explanations for gendered childhoods was struck differently in each of the five types of parenting practice explored in this book, most parents expressed at least some endorsement of both. All but two participants recognized at least one social source of gendered outcomes, and most discussed multiple sources. Some parents offered emphatic critiques of socially enforced gender expectations they consider problematic, and others offered more narrowly construed and casual comments about limited social influences. But all the many references to gendered childhoods as socially shaped highlight an opportunity to encourage parents to resist and reconstruct gendered patterns. Far from thoughtlessly accepting gender differentiation as a biological mandate in the way some previous literature suggests, most participants believed that at least some gendered outcomes originate in social forces, especially interactional forces including peers, parents, relatives, teachers, and strangers. To the degree that parents view gender as socially constructed, they can be encouraged to reconstruct it in new ways, drawing on their desire to free their children from gendered constraints and their recognition that social forces, including everyday interactions, help to reinforce and maintain those constraints. Particularly promising in this regard is the articulation of social determinism that incorporates attention to institutions, structure, and power, rather than only to interactions and traditions, as the former highlights the complexity of achieving change.

At the same time, the persistence of biological determinism among about three-fourths of the participants also reveals a likely obstacle to disrupting the gender trap. References to nature, like those to society, ranged from broad and sweeping to narrow and tangential, but their various forms suggest the potential of biologically determinist discourse to render inevitable and even legitimate gender differentiation and the gendered power it supports. The long history of ideologies that rely on biology to justify gender inequality demonstrates the risk they pose, casting gendered structures as benign reflections of nature. These ideologies are echoed in the way some parents invoked Darwinian or divine intent in their references to biology, viewing gendered divisions of labor as beneficial or even necessary to social life. This "just-so story," as Kimmel refers to it, masks the power and inequality that are central to gendered social structures.[15] It reflects an absence of what sociologist C. Wright Mills famously called the "sociological imagination," an ability to analyze the connections between individual outcomes and broader social forces.[16] An especially interesting variant of this limited sociological imagination is evident among the parents who offered the "fallback" articulation of biological determinism. Puzzled by the uneven results of their own efforts to resist gendered outcomes for their children, these parents resorted to biology. This articulation was more common among middle- and upper-middle-class white parents, which probably indicates their socially advantaged sense of agency in the world. These parents expect that the efforts they make will tend to succeed, and thus they may fail to notice the myriad other social forces shaping their children's preferences and choices.

The same risk comes up in many parents' desire to let their children lead the way in terms of gendered interests. When viewed as biologically determined by gender or as individually chosen, socially enforced gender traps can appear more harmless or inevitable than they look when viewed through a sociological lens. Children's agency is crucial to keep in mind when analyzing childhood gendering processes, and children do manage to resist and refine gendered messages in creative ways.[17] My focus here, however, is how parents guide their children along gendered pathways, and from that perspective it is important to keep in mind the risk of parents mistaking an interactionally or institutionally structured path for an individual preference or a natural dictate. Many of the gendering actions that parents report were indirect, a willingness to follow where a child was perceived to be leading. When a child steps off the structured path, there is good reason to suspect that this may be an individual choice. But when the child leads the parent down that path, it is more difficult to discern the extent to which the itinerary is an individual choice or a socially structured one. In these cases, the sociological imagination comes in particularly handy in sorting through the possibilities. Even parents critical of the heavy-handed gender rules more common in the past may be unaware of the subtle gendering processes surrounding their children, which have parents themselves playing an important part. Broader discussion of scholarship that documents these processes and critically examines the assumption of biological differences would help parents more accurately identify and support their children's individual interests, something almost all the parents I spoke with hoped to achieve.[18]

Beliefs about Gender

Laced through the main tensions that organize the present analysis, the tensions between biological and social explanations and between reproductive and resistive actions, parents also reported various beliefs about gendered childhoods that have implications for their approaches to gendering their children. Three domains of belief help differentiate the parenting practices originally classified into types on the basis of how parents explained the origins of gender variations and acted in relation to gender expectations. Beliefs about the value of gender differentiation, the possibilities for change, and power, structure, and intersectionality varied in relation to the five types of parenting practice. Naturalizers and Cultivators tended to have positive views of gender differentiation, considering it good for society and for their children. Innovators and Resisters rejected that view, consistent with their tendency to identify power, structure, and intersectionality in their analysis of gender. Between these two extremes, Refiners conceptualized gender as a source of difference rather than power but were worried that gender differentiation limits their children's individual development. In terms of the possibilities for change, Naturalizers and Cultivators tended to be either pessimistic or simply find the question irrelevant, whereas Refiners were almost casually optimistic. Innovators and Resisters were motivated to seek change but conscious of the hard work required and the structural hindrances entailed. Since recognizing structure and power was often associated with identifying social, especially institutional, sources of gendering, that many parents discussed social determination without addressing power or structure suggests that other goals for advocates of less gendered childhoods, in addition to increasing an awareness of how gender is socially constructed, should include encouraging a recognition of the roles of power, structure and intersectionality, and greater attention to the costs of gender differentiation. Beliefs about whether change is possible represent both a resource and an obstacle. Strong pessimism may discourage action but casual optimism underestimates the work involved in making change, leaving parents and other interested parties ill-prepared to make a significant dent in the deeply entrenched gender order.

Parental Motivations

Parents expressed an assortment of motivations for doing and undoing gender, all of which help explain how the gender trap is reproduced and resisted. Personal preferences are one such motivation, closely linked to beliefs about the costs and benefits of gender differentiation but also analytically distinct. Though shaped by social structures and experiences, these parental preferences are individual-level phenomena. Some decisions parents made, explicitly and implicitly, were based on their comfort with both gender-typical and -atypical outcomes, as well as their desire to share particular activities with their children. Gender reproduction motivated by personal preference was particularly common for same-gender parent-child pairs but was reported by parents in every possible combination of parent and child gender. Gender resistance spurred by personal preference was conveyed by both mothers and fathers more enthusiastically for daughters than for sons. Children's interests and welfare were also frequently cited as reasons for parental gendering actions. Regarding the reproduction of traditionally gendered outcomes, this motivation was usually expressed in terms of respecting the child's individual rights and interests, though it was sometimes described in terms of how the child might benefit from adopting particular gendered interests or attributes. For resistance-oriented action, children's interests and welfare were emphasized, with healthy development and welfare especially common in maternal explanations as well as in the context of widening gendered options for daughters.

Like personal preferences, beliefs about children's welfare and catering to children's interests, though socially shaped, are beliefs that parents hold as individuals. Sometimes beliefs about children's welfare were linked to

213

the desire to develop skills that parents believe will help their child navigate the social world, but even more typical were invocations of the child's personal satisfaction and individual rights. Inevitability and accountability, by contrast, are more explicitly interactional motivations little addressed in the existing literature, with parents consciously weighing social risks and the likelihood of success as they craft their actions. Inevitability, whether expressed cheerfully or with frustration, came up only in relation to reproduction, generally as an explanation for indirect gendering actions. It is, in a sense, the opposite of the limited sociological imagination infusing the fallback articulation of biological determinism and the tendency to view children's preferences as freely chosen. Rather than underestimating social forces, parents who referred to certain gendered outcomes as inevitable were viewing social pressures as overly determining their children's paths. Like the related belief that it is impossible to reduce gender typing in childhood, this is an important motivation to consider in terms of social change and may reflect a somewhat realistic assessment of the structural barriers that make change difficult, but its denial of individual and collective agency may discourage even some parents critical of the gender trap from trying to resist it.

Accountability is a pivotal element in West and Zimmerman's original approach to doing gender and one that was strikingly evident in many of my interviews.[19] In a more recent commentary on doing gender as a theoretical framework, Fenstermaker and West argue that accountability is "the most neglected aspect of our formulation. . . . Few of those who have used our approach have recognized the essential contribution that accountability makes to it."[20] That aspect of Fenstermaker, West, and Zimmerman's approach is of pointed relevance to my analysis, highlighting a key motivator for parental gender accomplishment. Often quite consciously, parents weigh accountability pressures, responding to them as they arise and anticipating them, managing their children's gender performance in accordance with this interactional-level process. Parents report some relatively direct translation of their personal preferences and individually held beliefs into actions that gender their children, whether in accordance with traditional expectations or otherwise. But many parents also report an interactional terrain teeming with everyday accountability to friends, family, their children's peers, and even strangers, some casual and others more intensely felt. This accountability is crucially important to the theoretical understanding of parental gendering and to practical efforts to loosen gendered constraints on children. Even for those parents whose personal preferences and beliefs about their children's welfare lead them to prefer resistance, and for parents who might be convinced to adopt those preferences and beliefs, accountability to gendered assessment is a separate barrier that pushes toward a gender-typical path. West and Zimmerman highlight how interactional and institutional levels work together in the accomplishment of gender and thus, by extension, the accountability dilemma parents face if they attempt to do gender differently with and for their children: "If we do gender appropriately, we simultaneously sustain, reproduce, and render legitimate institutional arrangements. . . . If we fail to do gender appropriately, we as individuals—not the institutional arrangements—may be called to account."[21] Accountability pressures often came up in relation to daughters. As Miriam recounted, a stranger in a bakery line mistook her daughter, a toddler at the time, for a boy, and upon being told her error, demanded an explanation for the child's unfeminine attire: "A girl? Well then why are you putting her in black? That's why the sexes are all mixed up today!" But such pressures were more striking with regard to sons. In phrases such as "loaded dice," fears ranging from "picked on" to "ostracized" to "beaten up," and even Miriam's reference to homophobic murder, it is for their boys, and those boys' approximation of hegemonic masculinity, that the interviewed parents experience and fear the call to account for both themselves and their children.

Implications for Social Change

Childhoods that are less constrained by gender require parents to critically reflect and change; that kind of reflection and change can be encouraged by sociological analysis of the role parents play in reproducing the gender trap. Many parents already prefer less gendering and actively pursue at least some degree of resistance. Others might be more likely to resist if they better understood how what they accept as routine gendering helps reproduce the gender traps they are trying to avoid, such as the second shift, the objectification of girls, occupational gender segregation and the gendered wage gap, and hegemonic masculinity. In addition, some parents who see themselves as simply following their child's lead might take a new approach if they were more fully informed about the potential of their own subtle gendering actions, and both the subtle and explicit gendering actions of others, to shape their child's apparently "freely chosen" interests. Parental fear and anxiety are themselves resources for advocates of less gendered childhoods; this fear and anxiety can motivate parents to stay on the gendered path, but they also may motivate efforts to chip away at the social rules parents fear will penalize their children. Loosening gender restrictions, however, requires more than just a new mind-set. It also requires interventions in the everyday dynamics of accountability, as well as organized efforts, at the level of social movements, community action, and legislative/policy agendas, to relax the rigid contours of hegemonic masculinity and the more malleable but still salient contours of refined femininity to which many parents feel accountable. As Connell's analysis documents, such loosening threatens the very structures of heterosexual male privilege and the racial and class privilege from which they are inseparable.[22] Although these are deeply entrenched structures, Deutsch reminds us in her call for increased attention to the way social actors undo gender, "even when structural conditions produce gender difference and gender inequality, these are mediated through social interactions that always contain the potential for resistance," resistance that can, in Risman's terms, "reverberate throughout the structure."[23]

Miriam intervenes with her daughter's teacher over appearance pressures in the peer culture of preschool girls. Joanna requests that the curriculum at the historical site not separate boys and girls. Kevin "applaud[s] the other stuff that might be considered girlish" with his sons. Many parents search for books that offer their children a broad range of gender-related images. In these examples and many more, parental resistance can and does promote change. Gender expectations are shifted at the individual level and frameworks of accountability are shifted at the interactional level when Walt sends his sons out in the world with instructions not to judge others on the basis of their gender performance or sexuality, when Anthony envisions his children as part of a "ripple effect" of intergenerational change, when Lisa encourages her son's interest in nursing as a potential career, and when Olivia encourages her daughter's interest in firefighting. When Brianna invokes gendered power, noting her plans to talk to her daughter about the ways in which women are "somewhat oppressed," and Thomas deploys an intersectional analysis, intending to warn his daughter of constraints she may encounter as an African American woman, parents' perspectives can help prepare children to confront gendered structures. But parents cannot do it alone. These individual efforts, and the many other acts of agency reported by the parents interviewed in this book, require interactional- and institutional-level support, including greater awareness and commitment on the part of educators and educational institutions, the availability of a wider selection of media images, and collective action aimed at infusing the interactional arena with multiple sources of acceptance and, better yet, applause for less constrained gender performance. Public policy must address gender differentiation and gender inequality in educational systems, occupations, and political power, discourage gendered distortion of body image, reduce gendered and homophobic violence, and support the carework of families and communities. In all these interactional and institutional domains, gendered processes must be understood in the context of their interconnections with class-, race-, and sexuality-based inequalities.

The parents who shared their time, experiences, and understandings of gendered childhoods identified obstacles that stand in the way of undoing gender. For some, the obstacles were rooted in nature and thus were unchangeable; others thought that loosening gender restrictions was unnecessary or even counterproductive. For many parents, change was an appealing notion, and the obstacles to it seemed socially constructed; they cited factors including media, marketing, bureaucratic institutions, peer pressure, deeply rooted traditions, homophobia, lack of information, and men's interests. Parents, of course, are among the social actors with a pivotal contribution to make in avoiding the gender trap, from the moment they contemplate having children through the entire process of raising them. But they are constrained by gendered accountability and gendered structures, their vulnerability to which is further shaped by their own locations in the intersecting dimensions of inequality by race, class, gender, and sexuality. Much has changed in the last few decades; there are new possibilities for gendered patterns at the individual, interactional, and institutional levels. But that change has only gone so far, stalled by a deeply entrenched gender binary, by the internal contradictions and external constraints of refined femininity, hegemonic masculinity, and heteronormativity. Parental agency can be fully effective in helping to avoid these traps only if framed by a well-informed, intersectional analysis of the social construction of gender and its consequences for gendered power and buttressed by the kind of "concerted effort in lots of places at once" to which Anthony referred.

The "better world" Tanya believes most parents want for their children often includes the hope for a less narrow gendered path, and through their beliefs and actions parents can help achieve that. And not only parents but everyone—whether we have young children or not, whether we have ever parented or not—can contribute to that effort. Resistant analyses and acts, both small and large, can make a real difference, redefining gendered identities, shifting frameworks of accountability, and pressuring institutions from inside and out. Embracing those resistant analyses and acts, in ourselves and in our responses to those around us, offers a critical opportunity. Gendered childhoods are not fixed in nature or inevitable in society. With concerted effort, we can reduce the force of the gender trap and open up the possibility of a better, less constrained, and more equitable world for our children and for ourselves.

APPENDIX

Research Methods

In-depth interviews were used in this book to achieve a deeper understanding of the subject than could be gained through surveys or experiments. Although surveys and experiments can include a larger number of parents, and therefore be more easily generalized to a broader group, I wanted parents to speak at length rather than in response to the check-box options of a survey or the confined counting of behaviors in an experiment or observation. Carefully controlled experiments and quantitative observational studies have documented the gendering actions that parents take, often unconsciously, and large surveys have documented some parental beliefs and actions as well, but I wanted to add to that valuable foundation a nuanced, in-depth understanding of how parents think about their children's gender and how they report acting in relation to it, as well as the motivations for their actions.

I planned to conduct about forty open-ended interviews, a typical number for a qualitative interview study, with a diverse sample of parents. I intended to interview until I had reached "saturation" (the concept many qualitative researchers use to refer to the point at which each additional unit of data collection yields little new information) and achieved a reasonable range of social backgrounds across the interviewees. I focused on parents who had at least one child between three and five years of age, as this is the period when most children begin to develop a clear understanding of society's gender expectations and thus when they develop gender identity and begin to engage in more gender-typed behavioral patterns (Maccoby 1998).

The Participants

Participants were recruited through postings in local child care centers, parents' resource organizations, community colleges, libraries, local businesses, and public-housing projects in central and southern Maine. I also recruited through personal networks, primarily by asking members of my college community to forward information about this book to eligible parents whom they knew outside the college. I did not interview anyone I knew personally or who was affiliated with the college. Once interested volunteers came forward, each one who completed an interview received a postcard which they could pass along to other parents who might be interested in participating. Given these methods of recruitment, and typical of qualitative interview projects in general, my eventual participants come largely from my local area, central and southern Maine. I conducted a small number of interviews elsewhere in New England, however, as four of the forty-two interviews were completed in Massachusetts. I took several breaks along the way, analyzing what I was hearing so far, presenting papers at academic conferences on emerging patterns, and refining my approach to developing an adequately diverse sample.

Recruiting materials included a general reference to "parents' experiences raising sons and daughters" and did not emphasize gender conformity or nonconformity. Thus recruitment was not focused on trying to find parents struggling with gender-related issues but rather a cross-section of parents. The materials also noted that participants would receive a modest honorarium of $25 for their time, which was funded by an internal research grant from the college.

I was especially concerned about having a diverse sample in terms of race, social class, sexual orientation, and family type, as well as having both mothers and fathers. At first the volunteers were white mothers from a variety of economic and family backgrounds. Once I completed the first fifteen interviews, all of which involved white, heterosexual parents, mostly mothers, I began more targeted recruitment. I continued to interview mothers, but I especially sought fathers, parents of color, and gay and lesbian parents in order to broaden the diversity of my sample.

By the end of data collection, I had interviewed forty-two parents: twenty-four mothers and eighteen fathers. Interviewees represent diverse family types: single-parent and two-parent families, including some blended families. The children include biological children, adopted children, stepchildren, and foster children. The final sample of parents represented a variety of class locations, racial/ethnic groups (including white, Asian American and African American), and sexual orientations. Seven interviewees are people of color, and twelve are from families of color or multiracial families (including white parents with adopted children of color and parents whose biological children are biracial). Sixteen interviewees identified themselves as poor/low income or working class (four and twelve, respectively), seventeen as middle class, and nine as upper-middle class. Interviewees' educational backgrounds range from less than high school to holding a doctoral degree. Five interviewees are gay (two fathers and three mothers), and all these are white and identified as middle or upper-middle class. This is typical of gay and lesbian participants in this kind of study, as discussed in chapter 6. As with any qualitative interview project, the number of people in any given subgroup is especially small, so it is important not to generalize beyond the sample, and I treat patterns in parental approaches by race, class, and sexual orientation as speculative at best. My main objective in developing a diverse sample of participants was to include a broad range of backgrounds in my sketch of how parents think about children's gender, rather than to focus on making comparisons across subgroups.

All participants are from New England, and nine of every ten participants are from Maine. Those from Maine come from rural, suburban, or small urban areas, as even the largest urban area in Maine has only around 250,000 residents. In addition, although most of the areas within Maine from which I drew participants are not unusually liberal in any way, Maine as a whole is probably an easier place to push some gender boundaries compared to more pointedly conservative areas of the United States. But given the considerable concern about accountability to others exhibited by the parents interviewed, I expect that, had I interviewed in a more conservative region, I would only find more evidence for my argument that parents are constrained by interactional-level forces as they work to manage their children's gender.

Interviewees range from twenty-three to forty-nine years of age. All the fathers interviewed were engaged in paid employment outside the home; among those in heterosexual partnerships, their female partners were roughly equally split among full-time homemakers, those employed part-time in the paid labor force, and those employed full-time. Among the mothers interviewed, about one in three is a full-time homemaker, with the remainder employed part-time or full-time in the paid labor force. Interviewees average 2.5 children, with a mode of 2 and a range of 1 to 6. The parents are split among those having only daughters (eleven), only sons (twelve), or at least one of each (nineteen). The focal children who were the object of the largest number of questions include twenty-two sons and twenty daughters.

The Interview Process

The interview process began with a brief written questionnaire. Volunteers were provided with a stamped, self-addressed envelope and asked to return the completed questionnaire if they wished to participate. This allowed me to customize the interview schedule, select a focal child for those with more than one child in the targeted age range, and gather basic background information before the interview. As the book progressed, I also used this questionnaire to broaden diversity in the sample. The brief questionnaire included a grid in which the parent was asked to fill in the gender and age of each child, and indicate whether he or she was the parent's biological child, their partner's biological child, or an adopted or foster child; additionally, an "other" option was made available but never selected. Short check-box questions addressed the parent's age, educational attainment, current occupation, work status, and partnership status (and, if partnered, the partner's age, sex, education, occupation, and work status). Further questions addressed child care arrangements, the division of household labor and child care (if partnered), and beliefs about whether it is best for heterosexual couples to divide housework and child care by gender. The final questions addressed the parent's racial/ethnic and class self-identification.

Parents who returned the written questionnaire and had the required background were interviewed using an interview guide listing the topics I wanted to cover. The questions were based on a review of the scholarly literature on gender and parenting. The guide was loosely structured, primarily to ensure that all the intended topics would be raised. Questions were broad, and parents were encouraged to carry the conversation where they thought it should go, expand and explain their responses, offer detailed examples, and raise issues they considered important. The interviews focused around a single child between the ages of three and five, chosen randomly when more than one of an interviewee's children were in that age range. Questions about other children were also raised, if that child was living with the participant and under the age of eighteen. The responses that form the basis for my analysis are, therefore, weighted toward preschool age children but do include parental reflections about children from early infancy to the teenage years.

The interviews began with a question asking interviewees to recall a time before they had any specific plans to have children and remember whether they had any preference for sons versus daughters. I then asked a parallel question about the time when they were awaiting the birth, adoption, or foster placement of the focal child; I asked if the interviewees knew, at the time of the pregnancy or adoption of the focal child, whether they would be having a son or a daughter, and if they did know, whether this affected how they prepared for the child's arrival in terms of decorating the child's room or buying toys. Whether they learned the child's sex before or after birth, we also discussed how the interviewees felt upon learning the child's sex. I asked how parents thought about dressing the focal child when he or she was a baby, in terms of whether they were concerned with having others recognize the baby as a boy or girl. Next I asked whether parents had noticed any tendencies during infancy that struck them as related to their baby's gender.

The remainder of the interview focused on the current activities, toys, clothes, behaviors, and gender awareness of the focal child, the parents' perceptions of the origins of these outcomes, and their feelings about their child's behaviors and characteristics in relation to gendered expectations. I also asked much shorter versions of the same questions about any other children the interviewee had. Though not strictly read from a script, the general form of these questions tended to be as follows: "Tell me about (the focal child), in terms of how gender-typical you think he or she currently tends to be in terms of interests and ways of acting; in other words, do you think he or she tends to act 'like a boy' or 'like a girl?'" Whether they responded that their child is typical, atypical, or some combination, I probed for how they thought those tendencies developed and how they felt about them. I included specific follow-up questions related to clothing, toys, activities, books, television, and other media. In response to these questions, three-quarters of the parents reported that the focal child seemed to them typical of the social expectations of a boy or girl. About one-quarter described the focal child as a mix of gender-typical and gender-atypical, with only one interviewee describing the child as gender-atypical overall (and even in that case, not dramatically so). I was careful not to define the terms "gender typical" or "gender atypical" but let parents talk about it in their own terms.

For interviewees with at least one son and daughter, I asked what was "similar and different about dealing with sons and daughters"; for those with only one child, or only sons or only daughters, parents were prompted to compare their experience to that of other parents they know and talk about what strikes them as similar or different. To make more general assessments of gendered childhoods, I questioned the similarities and differences in the children themselves: "Regardless of the way your own kid(s) act, some people consider little boys and little girls to be quite different; do you think that's generally so?" Depending on parents' responses, I asked where they thought the differences originated, or, if they thought there were few differences, why they imagined that other people might think there were such differences. Regarding the focal child, I asked whether the interviewee thought that the child was aware of the different expectations that sometimes surrounded boys and girls, and about the child's awareness of different expectations for men versus women. Another pair of questions focused on any direct instruction the interviewee might be offering the focal child in terms of gender.

"What kinds of questions does (the focal child) ask about boys and girls, or men and women, and how do you try to answer?" and "Are there any particular things that you're trying to teach your kids about boys and girls or men and women?"

Next, I asked whether the parents thought that they treated their sons and daughters differently. If they had only one child, or only sons or daughters, I asked them to speculate about whether they thought their treatment would vary if they had both sons and daughters. A specific question addressed whether the focal child had ever asked for a toy or activity that the parents would more commonly associate with the other gender, and, if yes, what the parents did and how they felt about it. Those who did not have this experience were asked what they thought they would do and how they would feel.

Interviews ended with general questions about the desirability and feasibility of less gendered childhoods, with the basic wording, "Some parents try to encourage their kids to avoid tendencies that might be considered typical for their gender, like encouraging daughters to be more assertive and sons more nurturing, and avoiding clothes with gendered associations such as pink for girls and blue for boys, whereas other parents don't think there's any need to do that. What do you think about whether parents should do that or not?" A follow-up question expanded this in the direction of how children are affected: "Do you think kids today would be better off without as many gender-related expectations, or do you think these kinds of expectations fit pretty well with what kids like anyway?" Regarding feasibility, I asked "Do you think it's possible to reduce the amount of gender typing kids engage in?" This final section of the interview included the brief question of whether the interviewee tended to think of the focal child as a boy, as a girl, or simply as a "kid." To ensure that parents got the last word, my final exchange with parents was to invite them to add any comment they wished to make and to indicate whether I had omitted something they wished to speak about. Each interview was tape-recorded, with the interviewee's consent. Most were conducted in the interviewees' homes, but seven of the forty-two participants preferred their place of employment or some other site. I conducted three-fourths of the interviews myself, with the remainder conducted by three research assistants who worked with me at different times over the three-year study period. All three were experienced qualitative researchers with sociology backgrounds, and I called on their assistance when my schedule prevented me from completing an interview. The assistants used the same interview schedule and were trained to engage in the same kind of conversational interview approach.

Reflections on the Interview Experience and Validity of Participant Responses

Though a few of the interviewees were nervous or gave brief responses, most interviews became relaxed, extended conversations. The vast majority lasted between one and two hours; the shortest was about forty-five minutes (with a father who elaborated little in his responses even with considerable prompting), and the longest was well over three hours (with a mother who told long, detailed, and amusing stories about her children's daily lives). All but a few of the interviews were completed by a parent (either myself, at the time the parent of two elementary school age sons, or one of the research assistants who happened to be the parent of an elementary school age daughter and a high school age son). For the two of us, the conversation about parenting and children often continued after the official questioning had ended. My approach to qualitative interviewing is influenced by Herb and Irene Rubin's advice from their 2005 book, *Qualitative Interviewing: The Art of Hearing Data*, which includes framing the interview as a "conversational partnership." Although the interviewee and his or her children were the focus, I did not hesitate to answer questions or make brief comments about my own life, and I instructed the research assistants to feel free to do the same. Like many qualitative researchers, I believe this sort of openness and reciprocity sets interviewees at ease and improves the quality of the interview data. When interviewees asked us questions along the way, they were always brief, so it was easy to keep the focus on them while still participating as a conversational partner.

Parents expressed a range of views in a manner that left me confident that they were relatively open and honest. In my own interviews, and in my reading of the transcripts completed by a research assistant, I had no sense of a limited socially approved line of responses that might have been shaped by what interviewees thought a college professor would want to hear. Some interviewees did ask if their responses were helpful and if they were on the right track; we always assured them that there were no right or wrong answers, that we only wanted to hear their honest thoughts and reflections. Surely the interview content was shaped by the interaction between interviewer and interviewee in a variety of ways, as is all social science data collection. But the range of views expressed, the relaxed atmosphere of the interviews, and the high level of engagement on the part of the volunteer participants all suggest a rich and open conversation that represents the parents' beliefs and experiences. All the parents seemed to enjoy talking about their children and thinking through their own approach to parenting, commenting not only on positive aspects of their experiences with their children but often on challenging aspects as well.

At the end of each interview, the interviewer prepared notes describing the setting, the interviewee, and the interview itself. The notes also reveal warm and open interaction, even in cases where the interviewers indicated they had little in common with the interviewee or disagreed with some of their opinions about parenting and gender.

Coding and Analysis

The taped interviews were transcribed verbatim, mostly by several research assistants. I transcribed two of the forty-two interviews myself, because audio-quality problems made it helpful to have the benefit of being a participant. Over a period of several years, during and after interviewing, I analyzed the transcripts looking for themes, patterns, and contrasts in the interviewees' stories and their beliefs and feelings. To facilitate the process of coding, I employed a qualitative data analysis software program, NVivo. Over time, as I used insights from the existing research on gender and parenting, my own experience of the interviews, and the inductive process of rereading the transcripts, I began to develop the analysis that organizes this book. After coding for a huge array of details related to parents' beliefs, actions, and motivations, I sifted through the transcripts again to look for distinct configurations that would eventually come to represent the five types of parents discussed in the book. It is not feasible here to describe my approach to coding all the categories I assessed systematically in the transcripts, well over 150 categories. But I will provide readers with an overview of how I identified the material within the main analytic categories that drive my analysis. My overall approach to coding combined both deductive coding framed by categories within the scholarly literature and inductive coding that focused on emergent themes within the transcripts.

Coding Beliefs about the Origins of Gendered Childhoods

Given that I included specific questions about the origins of gender variations throughout the interview, responses to those questions offered a clear starting point for coding beliefs about origins. I coded as biological explanations all references to the origins of gender variation among children that in some way referenced biology, nature, or essential differences. This included mentions of biology and physiology, as some parents referred to the brain, physical strength, and reproductive capacities. I also included references to hormones, nature, God, and instincts. Some phrases such as "just born that way" and "hard-wired" are coded into this category as well, when their context was such that biological or essential differences between boys and girls were clearly implied. I base my analysis of social explanations on all references parents made to society, culture, or people in general, as well as references to specific social actors including parents, friends, peers, relatives, teachers, schools, or media. These references were easy to distinguish from biological explanations. Interpersonal sources of social influence were usually stated explicitly. Broader institutional factors sometimes came up explicitly as well, and comments about TV and commercials illustrate how direct such mentions could be. Other references, for example, to "society" and "some people," are a bit more implicit but still clearly indicate a social explanation.

Coding Parental Actions

In their responses to the kinds of questions described previously, and the variety of other avenues that opened as we followed their lead, parents made many comments clearly indicating the actions they take that encourage or tolerate gendered outcomes. As I coded parental actions, I focused only on those actions parents specifically reported doing or planning to do, as well as hypothetical actions if they were clearly expressed as actions (e.g., responses regarding what the participant would do if their child asked for something more commonly associated with the other gender). Within these clearly identifiable actions, I then focused on whether the actions reproduced outcomes which the participant considered gender typical. I distinguished between direct and indirect actions; the former were those that parents undertook on their own that encouraged gender-typical outcomes, and the latter involved actions in which participants tolerated gender-typical outcomes their child was pursuing or requesting. In keeping with my overall approach of allowing interviewees to define what was typical and atypical, my focus was on outcomes the interviewee explicitly identified as typical. Once I had identified those excerpts, I combed through them for the additional themes and patterns presented throughout the book. To identify interview text that captured resistant parental actions, I followed the same process. Given that many of my interview questions dealt with what parents considered gender typical and atypical about their children, and what they might be trying to teach those children in relation to gender, they offered many responses that marked what they consider atypical and explored their own role in shaping such outcomes. Again I focused only on what was clearly specified as action, not thoughts or feelings, and on indirect actions that either tolerated or allowed outcomes the child wanted and that the parent considered atypical, or direct actions that actively encouraged such atypical outcomes. Here, too, once I had coded such resistant actions, I sifted through the coded text to see what additional patterns emerged.

Although beliefs about the origins of gendered childhoods and actions that reproduce or resist gendered patterns are the main analytic distinctions that differentiate my five types of parenting practice, parental motivations are also an important part of my analysis. The set of categories under this heading mark text in which parents explained why they engaged in their actions. First I coded all instances of motivations for action, and then within those I coded further for variations. These distinctions are described in chapter 1 and expanded upon in chapters 2 through 6; motivations ranged from personal preferences to a desire to follow the child's lead to beliefs about what is in the child's best interests to a sense of inevitability and accountability, whether actual judgment or the perceived risk of judgment by others. I focused on clearly marked expressions of motivation, considering a motivation to be only what parents told me rather than trying to mine their responses for unconscious motivations.

Coding Interviewees

With these major analytic categories coded within each transcript, I might have gone on to focus primarily on those categories rather than also coding the parents themselves into distinct types. But throughout the interviews, and especially later when rereading the transcripts, coding, and further refining those codes, it was apparent that a more holistic approach better captured the tensions parents were balancing. Thus I decided to focus on the combinations of beliefs, actions, and motivations parents crafted. I also drew on the number and character of responses coded into each of the types of beliefs and actions detailed here, classifying Naturalizers as those whose beliefs about origins were more often biological than social and whose actions were more often reproductive than resistant. Cultivators had the same balance of coded actions but more often held socially determinist beliefs. Among those whose actions were more resistant than reproductive, all tended to lean toward social explanations; no interviewees combined primarily biological beliefs with primarily resistant actions. This might have left me with just one category of Resisters, but reviewing the transcripts of the parents within that group highlighted the gulf separating what I eventually called Resisters from Innovators, and it was that inductively evident gulf that led me to differentiate the two. Similarly, the Refiner category was necessary as I tried to assess where each parent fit. Although most tended toward one side or the other on each of the tensions, the Refiners were clearly "in the middle." Even with that category added, determining which category best captured a given parent's approach required careful judgment. Like all qualitative researchers, I focused on the meaning within the transcripts rather than the quantity of information to determine, for example, whether a given parent was more focused on biology or society in explaining gendered outcomes, or more oriented toward reproduction or resistance in their actions. As I describe in chapters 2 through 6, even within categories there was some range as well.

Ethics and Confidentiality in Reporting

Before I began recruiting or interviewing individuals to participate in this book, I submitted a proposal to the Bates College Institutional Review Board, which approved my procedures and recruiting materials. All participation was completely voluntary, and interviewees filled out an informed consent form prior to the beginning of the interview. They were told that they were welcome to skip any question and to end the interview at any time, although no interviewee chose to do either. The names and addresses of the interviewees were stored separately from their questionnaires and interview transcripts, with the latter documents identified only by a code number.

To ensure confidentiality in the reporting of quotes and observations drawn from the interviews, I use pseudonyms for all participants. Accurate references are made, however, for background characteristics such as race, social class, gender, sexual orientation, or partnership status, or facts such as the number, age, or gender of the children. I made small changes if there was the slightest possibility of identifying a participant, such as a reference to where they live or some fact about their background. Similarly, regarding occupations, small changes have been made to protect the participants' confidentiality while retaining the level and type of work in which they are engaged. The sufficient number of stay-at-home parents allowed me to report that occupation without risking confidentiality.

NOTE: In the *sexual orientation* column, an asterisk (*) denotes that interviewees were not asked about sexual orientation but had previously been heterosexually partnered.

In the *status / age* column, P stands for Partenered and S stands for Single.

NATURALIZERS	CHILDREN (AND AGES)	GENDER	RACE/ ETHNICITY	SEXUAL ORIENTATION	CLASS IDENTITY	STATUS AGE
Anna (Stay-at-home parent)	Two daughters (5 and 2)	Mother	White	Heterosexual	Middle class	P, 34
Bruce (Accountant)	One daughter, one son (6 and 4)	Father	Asian American	Heterosexual	Middle class	P, 41
Carole (Elementary school teacher)	One son, one daughter (5 and 1)	Mother	White	Heterosexual	Middle class	P, 32
Christine (Stay-at-home parent)	One son, two daughters (7 to 3)	Mother	White	Heterosexual	Working class	P, 31
Jamie (Part-time house cleaner)	One son (3)	Mother	White	*	Low income	S, 25
Jerome (Lawyer)	One son, one daughter (6 and 4)	Father	White	Heterosexual	Upper- middle class	P, 32
Maurice (Hospital administrator)	Two daughters, one son (8 to 4)	Father	White	Gay	Upper- middle class	P, 38
Maya (Clerical worker)	Two daughters, one son (5 to 3)	Mother	African American	*	Low income	S, 29
Pamela (Paralegal)	Two sons (4 and 1)	Mother	White	Heterosexual	Middle class	P, 36

NOTE: In the *sexual orientation* column, an asterisk (*) denotes that interviewees were not asked about sexual orientation but had previously been heterosexually partnered.

In the *status / age* column, P stands for Partenered and S stands for Single.

CULTIVATORS	CHILDREN (AND AGES)	GENDER	RACE/ ETHNICITY	SEXUAL ORIENTATION	CLASS IDENTITY	STATUS AGE
Bob (Insurance agency manager)	Two daughters (5 and 2)	Father	White	Heterosexual	Middle class	P, 34
Cameron (Industrial manager)	Two sons (4 and 1)	Father	White	Heterosexual	Middle class	P, 37
Charles (Small business consultant)	Two sons, two daughters (5 to newborn)	Father	White	Heterosexual	Middle class	P, 30
Derek (Computer programmer)	Two sons (5 and 3)	Father	Asian American	Heterosexual	Middle class	P, 31
Elaine (School administrator)	One son, one daughter (4 and 2)	Mother	White	Heterosexual	Middle class	P, 38
Gwen (Business executive)	One daughter (5)	Mother	White	Heterosexual	Upper- middle class	P, 42
Jennifer (Electrical engineer)	Three daughters (12 to 4)	Mother	Asian American	Heterosexual	Upper- middle class	P, 41
Karen (Medical transcriptionist)	One son, one daughter (5 and infant)	Mother	White	Heterosexual	Working class	P, 38
Lou (Small business owner)	Two daughters (5 and 2)	Father	White	Heterosexual	Middle class	P, 35
Olivia (Stay-at-home parent)	Three daughters (5 to 1)	Mother	White	Heterosexual	Working class	P, 30

NOTE: In the *sexual orientation* column, an asterisk (*) denotes that interviewees were not asked about sexual orientation but had previously been heterosexually partnered.
In the *status / age* column, P stands for Partenered and S stands for Single.

REFINERS	CHILDREN (AND AGES)	GENDER	RACE/ ETHNICITY	SEXUAL ORIENTATION	CLASS IDENTITY	STATUS AGE
Belinda (Stay-at-home parent)	One daughter, one son (7 and 3)	Mother	White	Heterosexual	Middle class	P, 38
Ben (Entrepreneur)	Two daughters, two sons (5 to infant)	Father	White	Heterosexual	Upper- middle class	P, 35
Brianna (Surgeon)	One daughter (3)	Mother	White	Gay	Upper- middle class	P, 49
Celine (Part-time restaurant hostess)	Two daughters, two sons (10 to 3)	Mother	White	Heterosexual	Working class	P, 32
Grace (Part-time custodian)	Three sons, one daughter (18 to infant)	Mother	White	*	Low income	S, 41
Lisa (Child care worker)	Two sons (both 5)	Mother	White	*	Working class	S, 32
Lori (Stay-at-home parent)	One daughter, one son (3 and infant)	Mother	White	Heterosexual	Middle class	P, 29
Marie (Stay-at-home parent)	Two daughters (5 and 2)	Mother	White	Heterosexual	Middle class	P, 34
Teresa (Teacher's aide)	Two sons (4 and 1)	Mother	White	Heterosexual	Working class	P, 31
William (Banker)	Four sons, one daughter (14 to 1; 2 live elsewhere)	Father	White	Heterosexual	Middle class	P, 43

NOTE: In the *sexual orientation* column, an asterisk (*) denotes that interviewees were not asked about sexual orientation but had previously been heterosexually partnered.

In the *status / age* column, P stands for Partenered and S stands for Single.

INNOVATORS	CHILDREN (AND AGES)	GENDER	RACE/ ETHNICITY	SEXUAL ORIENTATION	CLASS IDENTITY	STATUS AGE
Anthony (Sales representative)	Two sons, one daughter (5 to 1)	Father	White	Heterosexual	Working class	P, 29
Ed (Customer service representative)	One son, two daughters (7 to 3)	Father	White	Heterosexual	Working class	P, 36
Eric (Construction worker)	One son, one daughter (5 and infant)	Father	White	Heterosexual	Working class	P, 39
Kevin (Construction manager)	Three sons (10 to 3)	Father	White	Heterosexual	Middle class	P, 39
Marcus (Appliance repairperson)	One daughter (3)	Father	White	Heterosexual	Working class	P, 38
Miriam (Stay-at-home parent)	Two daughters, two sons (5 to 1)	Mother	White	Heterosexual	Upper- middle class	P, 34
Thomas (Office worker and part-time college student)	One daughter (3)	Father	African American	Heterosexual	Working class	P, 23
Walt (Shop floor supervisor)	Two sons (both 4)	Father	African American	Heterosexual	Working class	P, 33

RESISTERS	CHILDREN (AND AGES)	GENDER		SEXUAL ORIENTATION	CLASS IDENTITY	STATUS AGE
Adrienne (Higher education administrator)	Two sons (4 and 1)	Mother	White	Gay	Upper- middle class	P, 44
Joanna (Stay-at-home parent)	Three daughters, two sons (9 to 2)	Mother	White	Heterosexual	Low income	P, 27
Sena (Professional artist)	Two daughters (3 and 1)	Mother	Asian American	Heterosexual	Middle class	P, 37
Stefan (Guidance counselor)	One son (3)	Father	White	Gay	Middle class	P, 44
Tanya (Stay-at-home parent)	Two sons (4 and 1)	Mother	White	Gay	Upper- middle class	P, 34

NOTES

NOTES TO THE INTRODUCTION

1. For a recent account of the importance of consumer goods to children's sense of belonging within peer cultures, and parental actions and motivations in relation to their children's requests for those goods, see Pugh (2009). Pugh's fascinating book does not focus on gender, but rather class, as Pugh unpacks the complex process through which parents of varying economic means negotiate their children's consumer desires.
2. Mattingly and Bianchi (2003).
3. Institute for Women's Policy Research (2010).
4. Budig and England (2001); Budig and Hodges (2010).
5. Correll, Benard, and Paik (2007). These scholars also find the same pattern in an audit study of actual employers.
6. McLanahan and Percheski (2008).
7. Andersen and Witham (2011: 129).
8. On workplace authority, see R. Smith (2002); on formal politics, see Paxton, Kunovich, and Hughes (2007); and on leadership perceptions, see Eagly (2007).
9. On domestic violence, see Umberson et al. (2003); on sexual harassment, see Uggen and Blackstone (2004); and on sexual assault, see Catalano et al. (2009).
10. See, e.g., Mahalik et al. (2005); and Moradi and Huang (2008).
11. Examples include Black et al. (2009); Davis (2003); Larson (2001); and Martin and Kazyak (2009).
12. Sabo (2005, 2008); Schrock and Schwalbe (2009).
13. Jackson and Dempster (2009).
14. Pyke (1996); Moen and Roehling (2005).
15. Baird and Grieve (2006).
16. Aveline (2006: 797).
17. See, for example, Almeida et al. (2009); Birkett, Espelage, and Koenig (2009); and Kosciw, Greytak, and Diaz (2009).
18. Lorber (2005: 7).
19. Ibid., 16–17.
20. Ibid., 24. For decades, feminist scholars offered a relatively simple differentiation of the terms "sex" and "gender," using the former to refer to biologi-

NOTES TO THE INTRODUCTION

cal differences and the latter to refer to the social understandings layered upon them. More current scholarship has refined this conceptualization to better recognize how even biological sex categories are social constructs. As Lorber puts it, "Female and male physiology are produced and maintained by both testosterone and estrogen, so sex is more of a continuum than a sharp dichotomy. The changing physiological characteristics of children and adults at different stages of the life cycle and according to physical abilities multiply the two sexes" (ibid., 22).

21. Kimmel (2008a: 28).
22. Fuchs Epstein (1988: 71).
23. Ibid., 98.
24. MacKinnon (1987).
25. Schrock and Schwalbe (2009).
26. Ibid., 280 and 278, respectively.
27. Risman (1998: 151).
28. Ibid., 29.
29. West and Zimmerman (1987: 126).
30. Fenstermaker, West, and Zimmerman (2002 [1991]: 29).
31. Fenstermaker and West (2002 [1991]: 219). West and Zimmerman (2009) have recently reemphasized the importance of accountability in their approach.
32. Hill Collins (2005: 11).
33. McIntosh (2004 [1988]).
34. For an excellent, recent edited collection addressing the influence of the concept of intersectionality on contemporary scholarship, see Berger and Guidroz (2009).
35. Rubin, Provenzano, and Zella (1974).
36. See, for example, overviews of this literature offered by Coltrane and Adams (1997); Maccoby (1998); and McHale, Crouter, and Whiteman (2003).
37. Risman and Myers (1997) and Mack-Canty and Wright (2004), for example, address feminist parents; Stacey and Biblarz (2001) summarize existing scholarship on gay and lesbian parents; and Blakemore and Hill (2008) compare feminist parents to what they call "traditional" parents.
38. See extensive reviews of the literature by Coltrane and Adams (2008) and Maccoby (1998).
39. Data on toys and activities are available in Wood, Desmarais, and Gugula (2002) and Beets et al. (2007); Cherney and London (2006) analyze the implications of differential toy and activity selection, which often reinforces visual-spatial skills and independent initiative for males. For clothing, a good example is Cahill (1989); for room décor, see Pomerleau et al. (1990).

238

40. Vocalization differences are documented in Clearfield and Nelson (2006); a more speculative analysis of how pregnant mothers talk to their unborn children documents a similar pattern (see K. Smith 2005). Emotions and autonomy in family stories are the subject of Fiese and Skillman (2000) and Reese, Haden, and Fivush (1996).

41. Play styles are explored by Lindsey and Mize (2001). Neuroscientist Lise Eliot's (2009) review of experimental literature indicates that parents unconsciously challenge their infant sons to take on more adventurous pursuits, including, for example, choosing a steeper incline on a climbing ramp during an experimental activity. Through various similar examples, Eliot (2009) argues that some of the brain differences commonly viewed as predictive of boys' and girls' differential interests are, in fact, created by the differential activities encouraged for them from the earliest ages by parents and other adults. Focusing on the developing brain as responsive to the environment, Eliot concludes that small physiological differences in boys' and girls' brains are magnified greatly by their interactions with gendered environments.

42. Chores are included within a comprehensive analysis by Raley and Bianchi (2006).

43. See Krafchick et al. (2005); Martin (2005); and Riggs (2008).

44. Scholarship on many of these factors is reviewed throughout the book.

45. For elaboration on this approach, see Coltrane and Adams (1997); Maccoby (1998); and Thorne (1993).

46. Cahill (1986: 177).

47. I balance this attention to children's agency by recognizing how it is shaped by interactional and institutional forces, including adult cues that may be unconscious. One study, for example, reports that children younger than one register cues from their mothers in terms of which toys elicit a particularly positive facial expression or tone of voice (Hornik, Risenhoover, and Gunnar 1987); a similar process likely occurs with other adult caregivers.

NOTES TO CHAPTER 1

1. See Gallup News Service (2007); and Leonhardt (2003). More than three decades ago Williamson (1976) documented parents' preference for a son in the United States, which is considerably weaker than in less developed nations. More recent studies have pointed in the same direction (e.g., Arnold and Kuo 1984; Arnold 1997). For gender differentiation in son preference, see Steinbacher and Gilroy (1990); Pooler (1991); Hammer and McFerran (1988); and Marleau and Saucier (2002). Surveys have documented that gender balance

(at least one boy and one girl) is the preference of many in the United States if not asked for a single preference (see, e.g., Sensibaugh and Yarab 1997; and Van Balen and Inhorn 2003).

2. Some scholars have argued that another indication of men's son preference is their greater investment in marriage and child rearing if they have sons (Raley and Bianchi 2006), their greater likelihood to marry if a child born outside marriage is a son (Lundberg and Rose 2003), and the lesser likelihood of divorce if they have sons (Katrev, Warner, and Acock 1994; Dahl and Moretti 2008).

3. Although only a small number of previous studies directly assess parents' reasons for preferring a son or daughter, the studies I found are consistent with the patterns that arose among my interviewees. See Gallup News Service (2007); and Goldberg (2009).

4. West and Zimmerman (1987: 140).

5. Fenstermaker, West, and Zimmerman (2002 [1991]: 38).

6. Scant scholarly literature explores pre-birth gendered anticipation, as opposed to gender preference. But some support for anticipatory gendering appears in a study of pregnant women and their male partners conducted by Sweeney and Bradbard (1988). The authors found some differences between expectant parents' perceptions of male and female fetuses, from among parents who knew the sex of their child, and these were generally consistent with gendered expectations.

7. For a detailed overview of these theories, see Fuchs Epstein (1988). Briefer and more basic, but still excellent, overviews are available in selected chapters of Rhode (1999) and Kimmel (2008a).

8. See Antill (1987).

9. Rhode (1999: 43).

10. Antill (1987) also found that biological factors were mentioned more often in relation to boys than girls.

11. Messner (2000).

12. Ibid., 770.

13. Antill (1987).

14. Messner (2000: 770).

15. The role of peers in childhood gendering is increasingly recognized; see the introduction to this book. Thorne's (1993) book *Gender Play* has become a classic in this literature. In a recent review on family life and children's gendered identity and interests, McHale, Crouter, and Whiteman (2003) encourage researchers to acknowledge siblings as a source of peer influence, as many of my participants did.

16. Almost half the interviewees knew in advance the sex of the preschooler who was the focus of our interview, whether through routine or medically necessary ultrasound and amniocentesis, or through information they received from an adoption or foster agency.

17. This argument was central to feminist critiques of the invisibility of women in enlightenment thought (e.g., Wollstonecraft 1989 [1792]; Mill 1970 [1869]) and early second-wave feminism (see, e.g., de Beauvoir 1970 [1949]). This continues in various forms, including critiques of the use of male terms to apply to all people. A large literature addresses this kind of sexist language; for an accessible essay arguing for its continued relevance as a form of gendered power, see Kleinman (2002). Experimental literature documents the continuing tendency to assume a generic, unspecified person to be white and male in the contemporary United States (Merritt and Harrison 2006).

18. None of the parents I interviewed was dealing with significant non-normative gender performance among their children. But literature exploring how parents and human services professionals navigate transgendered or highly gender-variant childhoods indicates the complexity of the issues such children face (see, e.g., Rottnek 1999; Cohen-Kettenis and Pfafflin 2003; and Raj 2008).

19. Kitzinger (2005: 477).

20. See Rubin (1975); also Rubin (1993 [1984]), in which she argued that the social construction of sexuality/heterosexuality, though interconnected with the social construction of gender categories and gendered power, is also analytically separable.

21. See Rich (1980).

22. For a valuable synthesis of recent scholarship, see Ward and Schneider (2009), the introductory essay to a special issue of *Gender & Society* focused on heteronormativity.

23. See, e.g., Martin (2009).

24. See Connell (1987: 248); also Connell (1995).

25. Martin (2005) concludes that authors of child-rearing books are increasingly supportive of gender-neutral child rearing, but, especially for sons, that support is limited by invocations of homosexuality as a risk to be managed. Riggs (2008) draws a similar conclusion in his analysis of advice books on fathering. Also see Aveline (2006); Antill (1987); Kite and Deaux (1987); McCreary (1994); Sandnabba and Ahlberg (1999); and Thorne (1993).

26. Connell (1995: 77).

27. As Messner (2007: 467–468) sums it up, "Many professional-class white men in the 1980s and 1990s began to symbolically distance themselves from . . .

traditional masculinity and forged new, more sensitive forms. . . . Toughness, decisiveness, and hardness are still central to hegemonic masculinity, but it is now normally linked with situationally appropriate moments of compassion . . . most often displayed as protective care—often for children."

28. West and Zimmerman (1987).

29. Connell (1987, 1995)

30. See Messner (2007).

31. See Connell (1995: 68).

32. Kimmel (1994: 119).

33. Connell (1987: 186).

34. West and Zimmerman (1987: 127).

35. This concept, and the scholarship surrounding it, is introduced more fully in the next chapter.

36. An excellent overview of scholarship on the devaluation of traditionally feminine pursuits and its implications for gendered social change is available in England (2010).

37. See, e.g., Wolf (1991). A large literature in social psychology centers on objectification theory. For a summary, see Moradi and Huang (2008); for an early treatment of the topic, see Goffman (1979); and for analyses aimed at popular audiences, see Lamb and Brown (2006) and Kilbourne (2000). Appearance focus and objectification are also relevant in connection to the literature on gender and consumption, which argues that, historically and currently, shopping as an activity and consumer objects have been important to the social construction of femininity. See, e.g., Lury (1995); de Grazia and Furlough (1996); and Zukin (2003). This connection has been established and explored in childhood as well; see Cook and Kaiser (2004); Martens, Southerton, and Scott (2004); and Russell and Tyler (2005).

38. Connell (1995).

39. Deutsch (2007: 114).

40. Risman (2009: 83). For the earlier work, see Risman (1998, 2004). Whereas both Deutsch (2007) and Risman (2009) argue for increased emphasis not only on how gender is "done" but also how it is "undone," West and Zimmerman (2009) prefer to describe this process using the term "redone" to indicate that "doing" is still at issue, just a different kind of doing.

41. I return to this strategy in chapter 4. As I discuss there, this kind of "gender blind" approach has the potential to challenge gendered structures but also to reproduce them.

42. Messner (2007).

43. The literature on gender and work documents occupational gender segregation and an accompanying wage gap favoring traditionally male occupations, so

it is not surprising that parents encourage their daughters to cross gendered lines in potential occupations. For an introduction to that literature, I recommend Padavic and Reskin (2002).

44. Previous literature also reports that fathers with no sons are less likely to promote gendered expectations for girls/women (Kane 1997; Warner and Steel 1999).

45. Deutsch (2007: 113).

NOTES TO CHAPTER 2

1. Freeman (2007) reports that children as young as three often assume that their parents would prefer they engage in gender-typical play, even when those parents claim otherwise. This suggests that the behavior Naturalizers view as biological may not only be shaped by social forces beyond parents but may also be shaped, unknowingly, by parents as well, as children pick up on their subtle cues.

2. Naturalizers are no more likely to consider their children gender-atypical, and so this pattern cannot be explained by greater exposure to atypicality. Rather, their greater aversion to atypicality seems to prompt them to discourage it more often.

3. This links well to Martin's (1998) analysis of how similarly aged children's bodies are also gendered through the instructions they receive in preschool settings, with girls directed toward quieter and calmer bodily comportment, and boys allowed greater levels of activity and volume. As Martin concludes, "In preschool, bodies become gendered in ways that are so subtle and taken-for-granted that they come to feel and appear natural" (510).

4. For a thoughtful and relevant analysis of how some kindergarten teachers and schools respond to fighting among young boys, see Jordan and Cowan (1995).

5. For a more detailed discussion of these ideals, see Maccoby's (1998) excellent synthesis of the literature on gender in childhood and adolescence. In terms of appearance, see McKinley (2006) for an application of the concept of objectified body consciousness, which she argues develops from the way that girls are encouraged to view their appearance and attractiveness as objects to be managed and judged. For a discussion of psychological theories of sexual objectification, see Moradi and Huang (2008).

6. For literature on heteronormativity, see the notes to chapter 1.

7. Naturalizers tend to see the actions they report not as gendering actions but rather as unremarkable or merely responsive to the child's preferences. As noted in the introduction, the literature on parental gendering documents parents' unwitting actions that may shape gendered outcomes in children.

8. Rhode (1999: 43) offers a comprehensive overview of previous research across a broad range of topics related to gender inequality. See Coltrane and Adams (1997: 243); also Coltrane and Adams (2008), in which the authors offer a review of the literature on this topic.

9. See chapter 1 for more information.

10. Messner (2009) also argues that parents essentialize outcomes in boys more often than in girls, a pattern he refers to as "soft essentialism."

11. Rhode (1999: 44).

12. Thorne's (1993) participant observation study of how elementary school children and teachers construct gender in their daily interactions has become a classic in the sociologies of gender and childhood, with its compelling focus on children as active social agents. Although my focus here is on parents, Thorne's work was important in sparking my interest in gendered childhoods. Another study of how children navigate their gendered worlds that was influential in my early thinking is Davies (1989), who addressed the linguistic construction of gender and argued that the verbal marking represented by the gendered terms "girls" and "boys" helps bolster the dichotomous views of gender I referred to in the introduction.

13. See the introduction for more on the centrality of gendered power to feminist scholarship, including the work of MacKinnon (1987).

14. See chapter 1 for more on this argument.

15. Hochschild (2003 [1989]).

16. Hochschild (2003 [1989]) analyzed interviews and in-home observation with dual-earner heterosexual couples from various race and class backgrounds. Her book attracted wide readership within and beyond the academy, influencing much subsequent thought about gender issues.

17. For a thorough review of the literature on this concept, see England (2005).

18. A few recent examples that encompass a range of class and race locations include Stone (2007); Moen and Roehling (2005); Hays (2003); and Hondagneu-Sotelo (2001). Each presents extensive evidence from the author's own research, as well as a review of the broad scholarly literature on gender, work, and family.

19. See Gerson (2010) for an excellent extension of this literature; she argues that heterosexual couples who exhibit what she terms "gender inflexibility" have more difficultly coping with economic and personal constraints when these arise.

20. Hondagneu-Sotelo (2001) argues that affluent women who hire immigrant domestic workers "purchase release from their gender subordination in the home, effectively transferring their domestic responsibilities to other women who are distinct and subordinate by race and class, and now also made subor-

dinate through language, nationality, and citizenship status" (23). Ehrenreich and Hochschild (2002: 12) also address the globalized connections that are reinforced when affluent U.S. families resolve domestic needs by drawing on low-wage labor from poor countries. "The First World takes on a role like that of the old-fashioned male in the family—pampered, entitled, unable to cook, clean, or find his socks. Poor countries take on a role like that of the traditional female within the family—patient, nurturing, and self-denying." For earlier influential analyses of intersectionality and domestic service, see Rollins (1987) and Romero (1992).

21. Walzer (1998) documents that mental labor associated with child rearing, "worrying, processing information, and managing the division of labor" (32), falls disproportionately on mothers, constraining their ability to combine paid employment and parenthood, and straining their relationships with their husbands.

22. Messner (2007: 464).

NOTES TO CHAPTER 3

1. These expectations resonate well with Connell (1987, 1995), Kimmel (1994), and Messner's (2007) previously cited academic work on hegemonic masculinity. Also see Pollack's (1998) analysis aimed at a general readership, in which he argues that boys in the contemporary United States are expected to live up to a highly constraining "boy code," requiring strength, independence, toughness, aggression, power, and rejection of any "sissy stuff" (23–24); see, too, Kindlon and Thompson (2000).

2. Schwalbe et al. (2000).

3. For a discussion of the class basis of chivalrous protection historically, see Cohen (2005: 329), who documents that chivalry "cast women as delicate and requiring protection, positioning men not just as superior but as protectors and governors because of their physical and mental strengths." In a classic feminist argument, Griffin (1971: 11) argued that chivalry is "an age-old protection racket," in which the violent behavior of some men allows others to trade their protection for women's subordination while constructing women as weak and dependent. Some aspects of her argument have been criticized, but her analysis remains a classic early statement of the influential argument that male violence against women is deeply intertwined with routine gendered power, rather than being a matter of individual aberration. Her approach also highlights the role of fear and vulnerability in how girls and women are taught to think of themselves. For a more recent consideration, see Hollander (2001).

4. See Messner (2009: 159–160).

5. Ibid., 170.

6. The literature documents that even young children associate occupations with gender in notably traditional ways; see, for example, Liben, Bigler, and Krogh (2001, 2002).

7. For reviews of scholarly literature on the effects of parental modeling of gendered divisions of labor on children, see Cunningham (2001a, 2001b).

8. As noted previously, even children under one year of age pick up facial cues from caregivers regarding different toys (Hornik, Risenhoover, and Gunnar 1987), and preschoolers often assume that their parents would not want them to play with gender atypical toys (Freeman 2007). Thus it seems likely that some of these children's preferences—the things their parents view them as "really into"—are shaped by messages received from those parents, both directly and indirectly.

9. A significant body of scholarship in social psychology documents this individual-level tendency toward nurturance, while also acknowledging within-sex variation. For a summary, see Maccoby (1998). The orientation toward others expected of girls and women drew the critical attention of early second-wave feminists such as de Beauvoir (1970 [1949]) and Friedan (1963), and was explored in more psychologically oriented classics such as Gilligan (1982) and Chodorow (1978). On interactional-level pressure, see Walzer (1998), discussed in chapter 2. Also see Hays (1996) for an analysis of middle- and upper-middle-class "intensive motherhood," which she argues shapes the individual beliefs of, and the interactional pressures surrounding, contemporary mothers in the United States.

10. See Stone (2007).

11. See chapter 2 for a discussion of this concept.

12. Stone (2007: 213–214). Moen and Roehling (2005: 10) discuss what they term the "career mystique," which "perpetuat[es] a regime of roles, rules and regulations reifying imaginary divides—between home and workplace, between men and women, between paid work and unpaid carework." Gerson (2009: 735) argues that these kinds of structural constraints limit men's and women's options: "We are poised at a moment when changing lives are colliding with resistant institutions."

13. See Pyke (1996); Stone (2007); and Connell (1987, 1995).

14. See Pollack (1998); Kimmel (2008b); and Sabo (2008) for overviews documenting the costs of masculinity aimed at a general readership. Both Kimmel and Sabo are particularly attentive to the intersections of race, class, and sexuality with the social construction of masculinity, and to masculinity as a source of both power and constraint. In a review aimed at scholars, Schrock and Schwalbe (2009: 289) draw similar conclusions, again with attention to intersectionality. Regarding physical and emotional health, they argue that the "effort to signify a masculine self . . . can be toxic."

15. Cherney and London (2006: 722).
16. Russell and Tyler (2005: 227). See notes to chapter 1 for more on gender and consumption in childhood.
17. As indicated in the notes to previous chapters, psychologists have studied the individual-level effects of interactional and institutional pressures on young women, documenting that young women, more than young men, objectify their own bodies and focus on their appearance as influential for self-esteem and achievement.
18. For thoughtful analyses of media images, see Martin and Kazyak (2009) on how Disney movies represent "heterosexiness" in a racialized manner; Gotz et al. (2005) on how young girls' make-believe worlds are influenced by media images emphasizing harmony, beauty, and appearance; and Gilbert (1998) on the fashion industry. Another excellent resource is Cole and Sabik's (2009) work on how race, sexuality, and being able-bodied intersect with gendered ideals of beauty. For work aimed at a popular audience, see Lamb and Brown's (2006) account of how marketers construct girlhood; and Levin and Kilbourne's (2009) exploration of the sexualization of childhood.
19. Examples of the long-standing literature documenting this pattern are Black et al.'s (2009) discussion of product packaging; Davis's (2003) analysis of commercials; Hamilton et al.'s (2006) exploration of books; Leaper et al.'s (2002) study of television; and Sheldon's (2004) analysis of computer software.
20. Pyke (1996).
21. Ibid., 530. This analysis is also consistent with much of Stone's (2007) argument, developed from her interviews with women from a more limited range of class locations.
22. Regardless of parents' sexual orientation, Fulcher, Sutfin, and Patterson (2008: 330) find that "parents who divide paid and unpaid labor more unequally had children whose occupational aspirations were also more (gender) traditional."
23. Ibid., 533.
24. See references above regarding care work and objectification.

NOTES TO CHAPTER 4

1. See chapter 1 for a discussion of biological determinism and gender inequality.
2. The currently typical association of pink with girls and blue with boys is a relatively recent phenomenon, according to Paoletti and Kregloh (1989): in the early twentieth century, pink was considered a more suitable color for boys and blue for girls.
3. See Bonilla-Silva (2009); and MacKinnon (1987, 1991, 2007).
4. Lorber (2005: 176).

5. For an intriguing study of how preschool teachers sometimes reproduce gendered childhoods by relying on "gender neutral" approaches, see Mac-Naughton (1998). She argues that when teachers attempt to channel girls into play areas traditionally occupied by boys by recasting them as gender-neutral spaces, their efforts often fail because they underestimate children's agency and the powerful social influences to which children respond.

6. For an intriguing analysis of the construction of masculinity in Star Wars, see Bettis and Sternod (2009). No single brand-name product was mentioned for boys as often as Barbie and Disney Princesses were for girls, but Star Wars was referred to with some frequency.

7. See chapter 3 for a more detailed discussion of sports and gendered childhoods.

8. As Wohlwend (2009: 58) notes, the Disney princess line of consumer items has been remarkably successful, with "$4 billion in global retail sales for 2007."

9. Baker-Sperry and Grauerholz (2003: 711) argue that the classic fairy tales most likely to be retold in contemporary books and movies are those involving a beautiful and passive princess, "gendered scripts" that "serve to legitimatize and support the dominant gender system" (see also Baker-Sperry 2007 on Cinderella). Heteronormativity in popular G-rated movies, including princess-themed films, is addressed by Martin and Kazyak (2009), who also consider how gendered discourses intersect with discourses of race, class and nation. Hurley (2005) highlights how Disney princess imagery reinscribes white privilege, and Lacroix (2004) criticizes limiting images of Asian women among Disney heroines. Also see Lamb and Brown (2006: 66–71) for a lay audience analysis of the Disney princess narrative.

10. Connell (1987: 183) identifies "emphasized femininity" as less singularly defined than hegemonic masculinity but still culturally powerful. Its features include "compliance with (gender) subordination," orientation toward "accommodating the interests and desires of men," as well as celebration of "sociability over technical competence," fragility and dependence on men, and "sexual receptivity in relation to younger women and motherhood in relation to older women" (187).

11. Some scholars have focused on the role of humor in policing gender boundaries, negotiating gender politics, and forging bonds among men. Lyman (2010) explores the role of gender-based humor in reinforcing male bonds across other dimensions of inequality. Pascoe (2007) argues that homophobic humor forges bonds among teenage boys and young men, reproducing hegemonic masculinity by policing deviations from it. For other analyses of humor as reinforcing and potentially disrupting gender inequalities, see Schafer (2001), and Case and Lippard (2009).

12. Messner (2007: 467–468). Messner argues that white, professional men increasingly reject "hypermasculinity," crafting a more "compassionate" and "sensitive" but still "tough, decisive and hard" masculinity.

13. Pyke (1996: 531–532).

14. Ibid., 532.

15. See Hochschild (2003 [1989]) and Stone (2007), as well as the following selected examples from the intervening twenty years: Hays (1996); Walzer (1998); Deutsch (1999); Garey (1999); Blair-Loy (2003); Jacobs and Gerson (2004); and Moen and Roehling (2005).

16. Carework professions earn less on average (England, Budig, and Folbre 2002). In addition, parenthood has a negative effect on women's lifetime earnings but not on men's because of women's greater likelihood of shifting to part-time or interrupted employment (see Budig and England 2001; Padavic and Reskin 2002; Moen and Roehling 2005), particularly among white women (Glauber 2007; Greenman and Xie 2008).

NOTES TO CHAPTER 5

1. Anthony's analysis is supported by the literature on children's advertising (e.g., Davis 2003; Larson 2001).

2. For an influential analysis of unexpected opportunities and constraints at work shaping gendered parenting decisions, see sociologist Kathleen Gerson's (1986) study of women and her subsequent (1993) study of men.

3. Risman (1998); Deutsch (1999); Craig (2006); Doucet and Merla (2007); Coltrane and Adams (2008).

4. Risman (1998: 48).

5. Also see Risman (2004) for an update on how she has refined some aspects of her understanding of men's "mothering" by emphasizing even more the interconnections between individual, interactional, and institutional levels in shaping gendered parenting.

6. Walzer (1998).

7. For an introduction to issues related to transgender youth, see Grossman and D'Augelli (2006); and Diamond and Butterworth (2008); on transgender adults, see Fausto-Sterling (2000); Halberstam (2005); Girschick (2008); and on intersexuality, see Preves (2003).

8. For a review of the literature conceptualizing this gendered pattern as "relational aggression" and a critique that focuses on girls' agency, see Currie, Kelly, and Pomeranz (2007).

9. Risman (1998: 161).

10. See chapter 3 for literature on the detrimental effects of hegemonic masculinity on boys' and men's physical and emotional health. Miriam also introduces

a related but distinct aspect of what hegemonic masculinity requires, namely, the rejection of aesthetic pleasures that are socially defined as feminine.

11. Hays (1996).

12. Ibid., 4.

13. Miriam's view is reminiscent of another sociologist's class-focused analysis of parenting styles, fitting neatly into what Annette Lareau (2003) refers to as the "concerted cultivation" approach, through which middle- and upper-middle-class parents cultivate within their children a set of abilities and tendencies that are valued among elites, and thus reproduce class inequality.

14. See, for example, Jerome among the Naturalizers and Charles among the Cultivators.

15. See chapters 2 and 3 for a discussion of chivalry.

16. Hill Collins (1990, 2005).

17. An excellent overview of intersectional theorists, including sociologist Hill Collins and a range of others from various academic disciplines and activist/artistic arenas, is available in McCall (2005).

18. Public opinion research also suggests that people of color are more likely than whites to adopt an intersectional analysis and that experience with racial inequality heightens awareness of some aspects of gender inequality (Kane 2000; Kane and Kyyro 2001; Foster 2008; Kane and Whipkey 2009). Simien and Clawson (2004) focus only on African American respondents, but their exploration of black feminist consciousness is also relevant.

19. Hill Collins is also known for developing a standpoint theory of black feminist consciousness (1990): black women's unique standpoint in relation to intersecting inequalities lends them a particularly deep understanding of those structures. I see a similar process of experiences of racial inequality shaping Walt's and Thomas's perspectives as well.

20. Pyke (1996: 531); see also Connell (1995); Pyke's use of the term "compensatory masculinity" is discussed in chapter 4.

21. Thorne (1993); see chapter 2.

22. See Coltrane and Adams (2008); and Maccoby (1998); both offer reviews of the literature that document a greater tendency for fathers to enforce gender boundaries.

23. Pyke (1996). For another relevant analysis of middle-, and especially upper-middle-class, high-tech workers, see Cooper (2000), who concludes that heterosexual men consider themselves less gender-traditional than working-class men though they routinely invoke the demands of their high-pressure jobs to defend doing less than they might at home. Also see Messner (2007) on middle- and upper-middle-class masculinity, discussed in chapter 4.

24. Pyke (1996) notes that despite some more traditional *attitudes* about gender expressed within compensatory masculinity, working-class men were more likely to share household responsibilities with their heterosexual partners. She sees this as partly the result of their lack of adherence to the hegemony of the male career. Shows and Gerstel (2009) draw a related conclusion in a comparison of heterosexually partnered fathers who are physicians and emergency medical technicians (EMTs). Other scholars who suggest greater child care responsibility among working-class men include Deutsch (1999); Coltrane (2004); and O. Sullivan (2006).

25. See chapter 2 for a discussion of carework.

NOTES TO CHAPTER 6

1. See chapter 5 for references to the literature on transgender youth in particular. For examples of scholarly literature addressing school-based experiences for gender nonconforming students more generally, see Lamb et al. (2009); and Meyer (2008).

2. The constraint imposed by racial "othering" has been noted by some scholars of race, gender, and beauty; see, for example, Lacroix (2004) on the "orientalization" of Disney heroines; and McCabe (2009) on how Latina college students experience exoticized views of their sexuality. Others address how dominant standards of female beauty privilege whiteness, defining racial "others" not as exotic but as less beautiful: see Sengupta (2006) on representations of beauty in adolescent girls' magazines; Hunter (1998) on hair straightening and skin bleaching among African American women; Nakano Glenn (2008) on skin lightening in international perspective; and Gimlin (2000) on cosmetic surgery demand as motivated by racialized ideals of female beauty. For an overview, see Cole and Sabik (2009).

3. Wolf (1991: 59). Like many foundational statements in social thought, Wolf's sweeping claims have been met with both praise and extensive criticism. Her book sparked significant thought, consolidating past work and stimulating new debates about the role of beauty, appearance, and body work in the politics of gender.

4. Wolf (1991) argues that excessive time spent on beauty and appearance work distracts girls and women from other pursuits, another way in which this focus can be viewed in zero-sum terms.

5. Given that all the gay and lesbian parents in my study were white, and middle or upper-middle class, I cannot disentangle racial and class privilege from sexual orientation. As Ryan and Berkowitz (2009: 167) note in explaining the lack of racial and class variation in their sample of forty gay and lesbian parents, "leading lives beyond the closet is more possible for white and middle-

class people." There is racial and class heterogeneity among gay and lesbian families, but middle- and upper-middle-class whites among such families are overrepresented for systematic reasons.

6. For the analysis of parenting-advice books, see Martin (2005); for how heterosexual mothers talk about sexuality, see Martin (2009); and on children's movies, see Martin and Kazyak (2009).

7. Hochschild (2003 [1989]).

8. For additional consideration of gay parents' experiences of homophobia for themselves and their children, see Clarke, Kitzinger, and Potter (2004); and Ryan and Berkowitz (2009).

9. Though all the gay and lesbian parents I interviewed offered this "fallback" articulation at least once, I suspect that race and class privilege have more to do with this pattern than does sexual orientation, given the overall association between race, class, and fallback articulations across sexual orientation in my sample.

10. Risman (1998).

11. Scholars have documented resistance from men as a factor limiting women's entry into traditionally male occupations. See Cockburn (1991); Prokos and Padavic (2002); and Reskin (1988); for analyses particularly attentive to intersectionality, see Paap (2006); and Yoder and Anaikudo (1997).

12. Here, too, Joanna is in good company in relation to feminist scholars: see studies of institutional barriers men face accessing parental leave or flexible scheduling, such as Fried (1998) and Levine and Pittinsky (1997), or interactional pressures for men who focus on care giving, such as Doucet and Merla (2007).

13. Pyke (1996).

14. For a thoughtful recent analysis of the impact of Title IX, see feminist legal scholar Deborah Brake's *Getting in the Game* (2010). In her words: "Title IX stands out as a law that has had a transformative impact on the lives of girls and women and on society in general" (8).

15. See chapter 1.

16. Some earlier research emphasized the lack of variation in gender typing by parents' sexual orientation (Golombock and Tasker 1994; Gottman 1990; Patterson 1992), but I consider the more recent meta-analysis by Stacey and Biblarz (2001) particularly thorough.

17. Sutfin et al. (2008). Also see Fulcher, Sutfin, and Patterson (2008) for an analysis in which they document the importance of parental division of labor and parental gender attitudes in shaping children's gendered outcomes.

18. M. Sullivan (2004: 212).

19. Dalton and Fenstermaker (2002).

20. Mack-Canty and Wright (2004: 876).
21. This is consistent with public opinion literature documenting the greater tendency for respondents from subordinate social locations to criticize social inequality and adopt more intersectional outlooks; see notes to chapter 5.
22. Risman (1998: 150).

1. For specific references, see the introduction and various chapters.
2. See Hartmann (2005); and Schaffner Goldberg (2009).
3. See Wolf (1991), including her discussion of eating disorders as linked to appearance standards; also see Mahalik et al. (2005) on "conformity to feminine norms" and eating disorders. On objectification, I have noted various references to girls' and women's objectification throughout; also see Bartky (1990) for a particularly influential exploration.
4. Thorne (1993: 170).
5. See chapter 1.
6. A host of negative consequences that stem from hegemonic conceptions of masculinity have been documented. For example, O'Brien, Hunt, and Hart (2005) reveal how masculinity expectations sometimes discourage men from seeking needed health-related assistance; Jackson and Dempster (2009) address how hegemonic masculinity can discourage strong achievement efforts in education; and McNess (2008) explores the costs to bereaved young men of emotional suppression. For broader overviews focused on health, see Courtenay (2000); and Sabo (2005).
7. For analyses of the links between hegemonic masculinity and violence, particularly domestic violence, see Schrock and Padavic (2007); Anderson and Umberson (2001); and Umberson et al. (2003).
8. Schrock and Schwalbe (2009: 289).
9. Ibid., 280.
10. Messner (2007).
11. According to Schrock and Schwalbe (2009: 281), masculinity enactment is ultimately about "claiming privilege, eliciting deference, and resisting exploitation."
12. Martin (2005: 458).
13. Ibid., 475.
14. On homophobic violence, ranging from teasing and verbal bullying to physical harassment and violent attack, two good sources are Kosciw, Greytak, and Diaz (2009); and Varjas et al. (2008). Related mental health outcomes are documented in many studies focused on distress, depression, and suicide among LGBTQ youth and adults; see, e.g., Almeida et al. (2009); Birkett, Espelage,

and Koenig (2009); Rutter (2008); Scourfield, Roen, and McDermott (2008); and Walls, Potter, and Leeuwen (2009).

15. Kimmel (2008a); see the introduction.
16. Mills (1959).
17. As noted previously, Thorne (1993) offers a classic and influential statement of this perspective in relation to gender, recognizing both structural constraint and children's agency.
18. Two recent books offering a critical review of the physical sciences literature for general audiences are Eliot (2009) and Fine (2010).
19. West and Zimmerman (1987).
20. Fenstermaker and West (2002: 212); see also West and Zimmerman (2009).
21. West and Zimmerman (1987: 146).
22. Connell (1987, 1995).
23. Deutsch (2007: 108); Risman (2004: 435).

REFERENCES

Almeida, Joanna, Renee M. Johnson, Heather L. Corliss, Beth E. Molnar, and Deborah Azrael. 2009. "Emotional Distress among LGBT Youth." *Journal of Youth & Adolescence* 38: 1001–1014.

Andersen, Margaret L., and Dana Hysock Witham. 2011. *Thinking about Women*. Boston: Allyn & Bacon.

Anderson, Kristin L., and Debra Umberson. 2001. "Gendering Violence." *Gender & Society* 15: 358–380.

Antill, John K. 1987. "Parents' Beliefs and Values about Sex Roles, Sex Differences, and Sexuality." *Review of Personality and Social Psychology* 7: 294–328.

Arnold, Fred. 1997. "Gender Preferences for Children." *Demographic and Health Surveys Comparative Studies*, no. 23.

Arnold, Fred, and Eddie Kuo. 1984. "The Value of Daughters and Sons: A Comparative Study of the Gender Preferences of Parents." *Journal of Comparative Family Studies* 15: 299–318.

Aveline, David. 2006. "'Did I Have Blinders on or What?' Retrospective Sense Making by Parents of Gay Sons Recalling Their Sons' Earlier Years." *Journal of Family Issues* 27: 777-802.

Baird, Amy L., and Frederick G. Grieve. 2006. "Exposure to Male Models in Advertisements Leads to a Decrease in Men's Body Satisfaction." *North American Journal of Psychology* 8: 115–121.

Baker-Sperry, Lori. 2007. "The Production of Meaning through Peer Interaction: Children and Walt Disney's Cinderella." *Sex Roles* 56: 717–727.

Baker-Sperry, Lori, and Liz Grauerholz. 2003. "The Pervasiveness and Persistence of the Feminine Beauty Ideal in Children's Fairy Tales." *Gender & Society* 17: 711–726.

Bartky, Sandra. 1990. *Femininity and Domination: Studies in the Phenomenology of Oppression*. New York: Routledge.

Beets, Michael W., Randy Vogel, Stanley Chapman, Kenneth H. Pitetti, and Bradley J. Cardinal. 2007. "Parent's Social Support for Children's Outdoor Physical Activity." *Sex Roles* 56: 125–131.

Berger, Michele Tracy, and Kathleen Guidroz (eds.). 2009. *The Intersectional Approach*. Chapel Hill: University of North Carolina Press.

Bettis, Pamela, and Brandon Sternod. 2009. "Anakin Skywalker, Star Wars, and the Trouble with Boys." *Thymos: Journal of Boyhood Studies* 3: 21–38.

Birkett, Michelle, Dorothy L. Espelage, and Brian Koenig. 2009. "LGB and Questioning Students in Schools." *Journal of Youth & Adolescence* 38: 989–1000.

Black, Katherine A., Jennifer A. Marola, Anne I. Littman, Joan C. Chrisler, and William P. Neace. 2009. "Gender and Form of Cereal Box Characters." *Sex Roles* 60: 882–889.

Blair-Loy, Mary. 2003. *Competing Devotions: Career and Family among Women Executives*. Cambridge, MA: Harvard University Press.

Blakemore, Judith, and Craig Hill. 2008. "The Child Gender Socialization Scale." *Sex Roles* 58: 192–207.

Bonilla-Silva, Eduardo. 2009. *Racism Without Racists: Color-Blind Racism and the Persistence of Racial Inequality in America*. Lanham, MD: Rowman and Littlefield.

Brake, Deborah L. 2010. *Getting in the Game: Title IX and the Women's Sports Revolution*. New York: New York University Press.

Budig, Michelle J., and Paula England. 2001. "The Wage Penalty for Motherhood." *American Sociological Review* 66: 204–255.

Budig, Michelle J., and Melissa J. Hodges. 2010. "Differences in Disadvantage: Variation in the Motherhood Penalty across White Women's Earnings Distribution." *American Sociological Review* 75: 705–728.

Cahill, Spencer. 1986. "Childhood Socialization as a Recruitment Process." *Sociological Studies of Child Development* 1: 163–186.

———. 1989. "Fashioning Males and Females." *Symbolic Interaction* 12: 281–298.

Case, Charles E., and Cameron D. Lippard. 2009. "Humorous Assaults on Patriarchal Ideology." *Sociological Inquiry* 79: 240–255.

Catalano, Shannan, Erica Smith, Howard Snyder, and Michael Rand. 2009. *Bureau of Justice Statistics Selected Findings: Female Victims of Violence*. Washington, DC: U.S. Department of Justice.

Cherney, Isabelle D., and Kamala London. 2006. "Gender-Linked Differences in the Toys, Television Shows, Computer Games, and Outdoor Activities of 5- to 13-Year-Old Children." *Sex Roles* 54: 717–726.

Chodorow, Nancy. 1978. *The Reproduction of Mothering*. Berkeley: University of California Press.

Clarke, Victoria, Celia Kitzinger, and Jonathan Potter. 2004. "'Kids Are Just Cruel Anyway': Lesbian and Gay Parents' Talk about Homophobic Bullying." *British Journal of Social Psychology* 43: 531–550.

Clearfield, Melissa W., and Naree M. Nelson. 2006. "Sex Differences in Mothers' Speech and Play Behavior with 6-, 9-, and 14-Month-Old Infants." *Sex Roles* 54: 127–137.

Cockburn, Cynthia. 1991. *In the Way of Women: Men's Resistance to Sex Equality in Organizations*. Ithaca, NY: Cornell University Press.

Cohen, Michele. 2005. "'Manners' Make the Man: Politeness, Chivalry, and the Construction of Masculinity, 1750–1830." *Journal of British Studies* 44: 312–329.

Cohen-Kettenis, Peggy, and Friedemann Pfafflin. 2003. *Transgenderism and Intersexuality in Childhood and Adolescence*. Thousand Oaks, CA: Sage.

Cole, Elizabeth R., and Natalie J. Sabik. 2009. "Repairing a Broken Mirror: Intersectional Approaches to Diverse Women's Perceptions of Beauty and Bodies." In *The Intersectional Approach*, edited by Michele Tracy Berger and Kathleen Guidroz, 173–192. Chapel Hill: University of North Carolina Press.

Coltrane, Scott. 2004. "Elite Careers and Family Commitment." *Annals of the American Academy of Political and Social Science* 596: 214–220.

Coltrane, Scott, and Michele Adams. 1997. "Children and Gender." In *Contemporary Parenting*, edited by Terry Arendell, 219–253. Thousand Oaks, CA: Sage.

———. 2008. *Gender and Families*. Lanham, MD: Rowman and Littlefield.

Connell, R. W. 1987. *Gender and Power*. Stanford: Stanford University Press.

———. 1995. *Masculinities*. Berkeley: University of California Press.

Cook, Dan, and S. Kaiser. 2004. "Betwixt and Be Tween: Age Ambiguity and the Sexualization of the Female Consuming Subject." *Journal of Consumer Culture* 42: 203–227.

Cooper, Marianne. 2000. "Being the 'Go-To Guy': Fatherhood, Masculinity, and the Organization of Work in Silicon Valley." *Qualitative Sociology* 23: 379–405.

Correll, Shelly, Stephen Benard, and In Paik. 2007. "Getting a Job: Is There a Motherhood Penalty?" *American Journal of Sociology* 112: 1297–1338.

Courtenay, W. H. 2000. "Constructions of Masculinity and Their Influence on Men's Well-Being." *Social Science and Medicine* 50: 1385–1401.

Craig, Lyn. 2006. "Does Father Care Mean Fathers Share? A Comparison of How Mothers and Fathers in Intact Families Spend Time with Children." *Gender & Society* 20: 259–281.

Cunningham, Mick. 2001a. "The Influence of Parental Attitudes and Behaviors on Children's Attitudes Toward Gender and Household Labor in Early Adulthood." *Journal of Marriage and the Family* 63: 111–123.

———. 2001b. "Parental Influences on the Gendered Division of Housework." *American Sociological Review* 66: 184–203.

Currie, Dawn H., Deirdre M. Kelly, and Shauna Pomeranz. 2007. "'The Power to Squash People': Understanding Girls' Relational Aggression." *British Journal of Sociology of Education* 28: 23–37.

Dahl, Gordon B., and Enrico Moretti. 2008. "The Demand for Sons." *Review of Economic Studies* 75: 1085–1120.

Dalton, Susan, and Sarah Fenstermaker. 2002. "'Doing Gender' Differently: Institutional Change in Second-Parent Adoptions." In *Doing Gender, Doing*

Difference, edited by Sarah Fenstermaker and Candace West, 169–188. New York: Routledge.

Davies, Bronwyn. 1989. *Frogs and Snails and Feminist Tales: Preschool Children and Gender*. Sydney, Australia: Allen & Unwin.

Davis, S. N. 2003. "Sex Stereotypes in Commercials Targeted toward Children." *Sociological Spectrum* 23: 407–424.

de Beauvoir, Simone. 1970 [1949]. *The Second Sex*. New York: Bantam.

de Grazia, Victoria, and Ellen Furlough. 1996. *The Sex of Things: Gender and Consumption in Historical Perspective*. Berkeley: University of California Press.

Deutsch, Francine M. 1999. *Halving It All: How Equally Shared Parenting Works*. Cambridge, MA: Harvard University Press.

———. 2007. "Undoing Gender." *Gender & Society* 21: 106–127.

Diamond, Lisa, and Molly Butterworth. 2008. "Questioning Gender and Sexual Identity." *Sex Roles* 59: 365–376.

Doucet, Andrea, and Laura Merla. 2007. "Stay-at-Home Fathering." *Community, Work & Family* 10: 455–473.

Eagly, Alice H. 2007. "Female Leadership Advantage and Disadvantage." *Psychology of Women Quarterly* 31: 1–12.

Ehrenreich, Barbara, and Arlie Hochschild. 2002. *Global Woman: Nannies, Maids, and Sex Workers in the Global Economy*. New York: Owl Books.

Eliot, Lise. 2009. *Pink Brain, Blue Brain: How Small Differences Grow into Troublesome Gaps*. Boston: Houghton Mifflin Harcourt.

England, Paula. 2005. "Emerging Theories of Carework." *Annual Review of Sociology* 31: 381–399.

———. 2010. "The Gender Revolution: Uneven and Stalled." *Gender & Society* 24: 149–166.

England, Paula, Michelle Budig, and Nancy Folbre. 2002. "Wages of Virtue: The Relative Pay of Carework." *Social Problems* 49: 455–474.

Fausto-Sterling, Anne. 2000. *Sexing the Body: Gender Politics and the Construction of Sexuality*. New York: Basic Books.

Fenstermaker, Sarah, and Candace West (eds.). 2002. *Doing Gender, Doing Difference*. New York: Routledge.

Fenstermaker, Sarah, Candace West, and Don Zimmerman. 2002 [1991]. "Gender Inequality: New Conceptual Terrain." In *Doing Gender, Doing Difference*, edited by S. Fenstermaker and C. West, 25–40. New York: Routledge.

Fiese, Barbara H., and Gemma Skillman. 2000. "Gender Differences in Family Stories." *Sex Roles* 43: 267–283.

Fine, Cordelia. 2010. *Delusions of Gender*. New York: Norton.

Foster, Carly Haden. 2008. "The Welfare Queen: Race, Gender, Class, and Public Opinion." *Race, Gender & Class* 15: 162–179.

Freeman, Nancy K. 2007. "Preschoolers' Perceptions of Gender Appropriate Toys and their Parents' Beliefs about Genderized Behaviors." *Early Childhood Education Journal* 34: 357–366.

Fried, Mindy. 1998. *Taking Time: Parental Leave Policy and Corporate Culture.* Philadelphia: Temple University Press.

Friedan, Betty. 1963. *The Feminine Mystique.* New York: Norton.

Fuchs Epstein, Cynthia. 1988. *Deceptive Distinctions.* New Haven, CT: Yale University Press.

Fulcher, Megan, Erin L. Sutfin, and Charlotte J. Patterson. 2008. "Individual Differences in Gender Development." *Sex Roles* 58: 330–341.

Gallup News Service. 2007. "Americans Continue to Express Slight Preference for Boys." http://www.gallup.com/poll/28045/americans-continue-express-slight-preference-boys.aspx (accessed August 19, 2009).

Garey, Anita. 1999. *Weaving Work and Motherhood.* Philadelphia: Temple University Press.

Gerson, Kathleen. 1986. *Hard Choices: How Women Decide about Work, Career, and Motherhood.* Berkeley: University of California Press.

———. 1993. *No Man's Land: Men's Changing Commitments to Family and Work.* New York: Basic Books.

———. 2009. "Changing Lives, Resistant Institutions." *Sociological Forum* 24: 735–753.

———. 2010. *The Unfinished Revolution.* New York: Oxford University Press.

Gilbert, Keith. 1998. "The Body, Young Children, and Popular Culture." In *Gender in Early Childhood*, edited by Nicola Yelland, 55–71. New York: Routledge.

Gilligan, Carol. 1982. *In a Different Voice.* Cambridge, MA: Harvard University Press.

Gimlin, Debra. 2000. "Cosmetic Surgery: Beauty as Commodity." *Qualitative Sociology* 23: 77–98.

Girschick, Lori. 2008. *Transgender Voices: Beyond Women and Men.* Lebanon, NH: University Press of New England.

Glauber, Rebecca. 2007. "Marriage and the Motherhood Wage Penalty among African Americans, Hispanics, and Whites." *Journal of Marriage and Family* 69: 951–961.

Goffman, Erving, 1979. *Gender Advertisements.* Cambridge, MA: Harvard University Press.

Goldberg, Abbie E. 2009. "Heterosexual, Lesbian, and Gay Preadoptive Parents' Preferences about Child Gender." *Sex Roles* 61: 55–71.

Golombock, Susan, and Fiona Tasker. 1994. "Children in Lesbian and Gay Families." *Annual Review of Sex Research* 5: 73–100.

Gottman, Julie Schwartz. 1990. "Children of Gay and Lesbian Parents." *Marriage and Family Review* 14: 177–196.

Gotz, Maya, Dafna Lemish, Amy Aidman, and Hyesung Moon. 2005. *Media and the Make-Believe Worlds of Children*. Mahwah, NJ: Erlbaum.

Greenman, Emily, and Yu Xie. 2008. "Double Jeopardy? The Interaction of Gender and Race on Earnings in the United States." *Social Forces* 86: 1217–1244.

Griffin, Susan. 1971. *Rape: The Politics of Consciousness*. New York: HarperCollins.

Grossman, Arnold H., and Anthony R. D'Augelli. 2006. "Transgender Youth." *Journal of Homosexuality* 51: 111–128.

Halberstam, Judith. 2005. *In a Queer Time and Place: Transgender Bodies, Subcultural Lives*. New York: New York University Press.

Hamilton, M. C., D. Anderson, M. Broaddus, and K. Young. 2006. "Gender Stereotyping and Under-representation of Female Characters in 200 Popular Children's Picture Books." *Sex Roles* 55: 757–765.

Hammer, Max, and James McFerran. 1988. "Preference for Sex of Child: A Research Update." *Individual Psychology* 44: 481–491.

Hartmann, Heidi. 2005. "Introduction." *Journal of Women, Politics & Policy* 27: 1–4.

Hays, Sharon. 1996. *The Cultural Contradictions of Motherhood*. New Haven, CT: Yale University Press.

———. 2003. *Flat Broke with Children: Women in the Age of Welfare Reform* Oxford: Oxford University Press.

Hill Collins, Patricia. 1990. *Black Feminist Thought*. New York: Routledge.

———. 2005. *Black Sexual Politics*. New York: Routledge.

Hochschild, Arlie. 2003 [1989]. *The Second Shift*. New York: Penguin.

Hollander, Jocelyn A. 2001 "Vulnerability and Dangerousness: The Construction of Gender through Conversation about Violence." *Gender & Society* 15: 83–109.

Hondagneu-Sotelo, Pierrette. 2001. *Domestica: Immigrant Workers Cleaning and Caring in the Shadows of Affluence*. Berkeley: University of California Press.

Hornik, Robin, Nancy Risenhoover, and Megan Gunnar. 1987. "The Effects of Maternal Positive, Neutral, and Negative Affective Communications on Infant Responses to New Toys." *Child Development* 58: 937–945.

Hunter, Margaret L. 1998. "Colorstruck: Skin Color Stratification in the Lives of African American Women." *Sociological Inquiry* 68: 517–535.

Hurley, Dorothy L. 2005. "Seeing White: Children of Color and the Disney Fairy Tale Princess." *Journal of Negro Education* 74: 221–232.

Institute for Women's Policy Research. 2010. "The Gender Wage Gap." *IWPR Fact Sheet #350*, Washington, DC.

Jackson, Carolyn, and Steven Dempster. 2009. "'I Sat Back on My Computer . . . with a Bottle of Whisky Next to Me': Constructing 'Cool' Masculinity through 'Effortless' Achievement in Secondary and Higher Education." *Journal of Gender Studies* 18: 341–356.

Jacobs, Jerry, and Kathleen Gerson. 2004. *The Time Divide*. Cambridge, MA: Harvard University Press.

Jordan, Ellen, and Angela Cowan. 1995. "Warrior Narratives in the Kindergarten Classroom." *Gender & Society* 9: 727–743.

Kane, Emily W. 1997. "Gender of Children and Parents' Attitudes toward Gender-Role Equality." Paper presented at the American Sociological Association Annual Meeting, Toronto, ON.

———. 2000. "Racial and Ethnic Variations in Gender-Related Attitudes." *Annual Review of Sociology* 26: 419–440.

Kane, Emily W., and Else K. Kyyro. 2001. "For Whom Does Education Enlighten? Race, Gender, Education and Beliefs about Social Inequality." *Gender & Society* 15: 710–733.

Kane, Emily W., and Kimberly J. Whipkey. 2009. "Predictors of Public Support for Gender-Related Affirmative Action." *Public Opinion Quarterly* 73: 233–254.

Katrev, A. R., R. L. Warner, and A. C. Acock. 1994. "Girls or Boys? Relationship of Child Gender to Marital Stability." *Journal of Marriage and the Family* 56: 89–100.

Kilbourne, Jean. 2000. *Killing Us Softly 3*. Northampton, MA: Media Education Foundation.

Kimmel, Michael S. 1994. "Masculinity as Homophobia." In *Theorizing masculinities*, edited by Harry Brod, 119–141. Thousand Oaks, CA: Sage.

———. 2008a. *The Gendered Society*. New York: Oxford University Press.

———. 2008b. *Guyland*. New York: HarperCollins.

Kindlon, Dan, and Michael Thompson. 2000. *Raising Cain*. New York: Ballantine Books.

Kite, Mary E., and Kay Deaux. 1987. "Gender Belief Systems: Homosexuality and the Implicit Inversion Theory." *Psychology of Women Quarterly* 11: 83–96.

Kitzinger, Celia. 2005. "Heteronormativity in Action." *Social Problems* 52: 477–498.

Kleinman, Sherry. 2002. "Why Sexist Language Matters." *Qualitative Sociology* 25: 299–304.

Kosciw, Joseph G., Emily A. Greytak, and Elizabeth M. Diaz. 2009. "Who, What, Where, When, and Why: Demographic and Ecological Factors Contributing to Hostile School Climate for Lesbian, Gay, Bisexual, and Transgender Youth." *Journal of Youth & Adolescence* 38: 976–988.

Krafchick, Jennifer L., Toni Schindler Zimmerman, Shelley A. Haddock, and James H. Banning. 2005. "Best-selling Books Advising Parents about Gender." *Family Relations* 54: 84–100.

Lacroix, Celeste. 2004. "Images of Animated Others: The 'Orientalization' of Disney's Cartoon Heroines from the Little Mermaid to the Hunchback of Notre Dame." *Popular Communication* 2: 213–229.

Lamb, Lindsay, Rebecca Bigler, Lynn Liben, and Vanessa Green. 2009. "Teaching Children to Confront Peers' Sexist Remarks." *Sex Roles* 61: 361–382.

Lamb, Sharon, and Lyn Mikel Brown. 2006. *Packaging Girlhood*. New York: St. Martin's.

Lareau, Annette. 2003. *Unequal Childhoods*. Berkeley: University of California Press.

Larson, Mary Strom. 2001. "Interactions, Activities, and Gender in Children's Television Commercials." *Journal of Broadcasting & Electronic Media* 45: 41–57.

Leaper, Campbell, Lisa Breed, Laurie Hoffman, and Carly Ann Perlman. 2002. "Variations in the Gender-Stereotyped Content of Children's Television Cartoons across Genres." *Journal of Applied Social Psychology* 32: 1653–1662.

Leonhardt, D. 2003. "Sugar and Spice, and Sour Dads." *New York Times*, November 16.

Levin, Diane E., and Jean Kilbourne. 2009. *So Sexy So Soon: The New Sexualized Childhood*. New York: Ballantine Books.

Levine, James A., and Todd L. Pittinsky. 1997. *Working Fathers: New Strategies for Balancing Work and Family*. New York: Addison-Wesley.

Liben, Lynn S., Rebecca S. Bigler, and Holleen R. Krogh. 2001. "Pink and Blue Collar Jobs: Children's Judgments of Job Status and Job Aspirations in Relation to Sex of Worker." *Journal of Experimental Child Psychology* 79: 346–363.

———. 2002. "Language at Work: Children's Gendered Interpretations of Occupational Titles." *Child Development* 73: 810–829.

Lindsey, E. W., and J. Mize. 2001. Contextual Differences in Parent-Child Play. *Sex Roles* 44: 155–176.

Lorber, Judith. 2005. *Breaking the Bowls*. New York: Norton.

Lundberg, Shelly, and Elaina Rose. 2003. "Child Gender and the Transition to Marriage." *Demography* 40: 333–349.

Lury, C. 1995. *Consumer Culture*. Cambridge: Polity.

Lyman, Peter. 2010. "The Fraternal Bond as a Joking Relationship." In *Men's Lives*, edited by Michael S. Kimmel and Michael A. Messner, 147–156. Boston: Allyn & Bacon.

Maccoby, Eleanor E. 1998. *The Two Sexes: Growing Up Apart, Coming Together.* Cambridge, MA: Harvard University Press.

Mack-Canty, Colleen, and Sue Wright. 2004. "Family Values as Practiced by Feminist Parents." *Journal of Family Issues* 25: 851–880.

MacKinnon, Catharine. 1987. *Feminism Unmodified.* Cambridge, MA: Harvard University Press.

———. 1991. *Toward a Feminist Theory of the State.* Cambridge, MA: Harvard University Press.

———. 2007. *Women's Lives, Men's Laws.* Cambridge, MA: Harvard University Press.

MacNaughton, Glenda. 1998. "Improving Our Gender Equity 'Tools.'" In *Gender and Early Childhood*, edited by Nicola Yelland, 149–174. New York: Routledge.

Mahalik, James R., Elisabeth B. Morray, Aimée Coonerty-Femiano, Larry H. Ludlow, Suzanne M. Slattery, and Andrew Smiler. 2005. "Development of the Conformity to Feminine Norms Inventory." *Sex Roles* 52: 417–435.

Marleau, J. D., and J. Saucier. 2002. "Preference for a First-Born Boy in Western Societies." *Journal of Biosocial Science* 34: 13–27.

Martens, L., D. Southerton, and S. Scott. 2004. "Bringing Children (and Parents) into the Sociology of Consumption." *Journal of Consumer Culture* 42: 155–182.

Martin, Karin A. 1998. "Becoming a Gendered Body: Practices of Preschools." *American Sociological Review* 63: 494–511.

———. 2005. "William Wants a Doll, Can He Have One? Feminists, Child Care Advisors, and Gender-Neutral Child Rearing." *Gender & Society* 19: 456–479.

———. 2009. "Normalizing Heterosexuality: Mothers' Assumptions, Talk, and Strategies with Young Children." *American Sociological Review* 74: 190–207.

Martin, Karin A., and Emily Kazyak. 2009. "Hetero-Romantic Love and Hetero-sexiness in Children's G-Rated Films." *Gender & Society* 23: 315–336.

Mattingly, Marybeth, and Suzanne Bianchi. 2003. "Gender Differences in the Quantity and Quality of Free Time: The U.S. Experience." *Social Forces* 81: 999–1030.

McCabe, Janice. 2009. "Racial and Gender Microaggressions on a Predominantly White Campus." *Race, Gender & Class* 16: 133–151.

McCall, Leslie. 2005. "The Complexity of Intersectionality." *Signs* 30: 1771–1800.

McCreary, Donald R. 1994. "The Male Role and Avoiding Femininity." *Sex Roles* 31: 517–531.

McHale, S. M., A. C. Crouter, and S. W. Whiteman. 2003. "The Family Context of Gender Development in Childhood and Adolescence." *Social Development* 12: 125–148.

McIntosh, Peggy. 2004 [1988]. "White Privilege: Unpacking the Invisible Knapsack." In *Race, Class and Gender in the United States*, edited by Paula S. Rothenberg, 188–192. New York: Worth.

McKinley, Nita M. 2006. "Longitudinal Gender Differences in Objectified Body Consciousness and Weight-Related Attitudes and Behaviors." *Sex Roles* 54: 159–173.

McLanahan, Sara, and Christine Percheski. 2008. "Family Structure and the Reproduction of Inequalities." *Annual Review of Sociology* 34: 257–276.

McNess, Andrew. 2008. "Happy to Talk . . . to a Point." *Youth Studies Australia* 27: 25–34.

Merritt, Rebecca Davis, and Teion Wells Harrison. 2006. "Gender and Ethnicity Attributions to a Gender- and Ethnicity-Unspecified Individual." *Sex Roles* 54: 787–797.

Messner, Michael A. 2000. "Barbie Girls versus Sea Monsters: Children Constructing Gender." *Gender & Society* 14: 765–784.

———. 2007. "The Masculinity of the Governator: Muscle and Compassion in American Politics." *Gender & Society* 21: 461–480.

———. 2009. *It's All for the Kids: Gender, Families, and Youth Sports*. Berkeley: University of California Press.

Meyer, Elizabeth J. 2008. "Gendered Harassment in Secondary Schools." *Gender & Education* 20: 555–570.

Mill, John Stuart. 1970 [1869]. "The Subjection of Women." In Alice S. Rossi (ed.), *Essays on Sex Equality*, 125–156. Chicago: University of Chicago Press.

Mills, C. Wright. 1959. *The Sociological Imagination*. Oxford: Oxford University Press.

Moen, Phyllis, and Patricia Roehling. 2005. *The Career Mystique*. Lanham, MD: Rowman and Littlefield.

Moradi, Bonnie, and Yu-Ping Huang. 2008. "Objectification Theory and Psychology of Women." *Psychology of Women Quarterly* 32: 377–398.

Nakano Glenn, Evelyn. 2008. "Yearning for Lightness: Transnational Circuits in the Marketing and Consumption of Skin Lighteners." *Gender & Society* 22: 281–302.

O'Brien, R., K. Hunt, and G. Hart. 2005. "'It's Caveman Stuff, but to a Certain Point, That's How Guys Still Operate:' Men's Accounts of Masculinity and Help Seeking." *Social Science and Medicine* 61: 503–516.

Paap, Kristen. 2006. *Working Construction*. Ithaca, NY: ILR Press.

Padavic, Irene, and Barbara Reskin. 2002. *Women and Men at Work*. 2nd ed. Thousand Oaks, CA: Pine Forge.

Paoletti, Jo B., and Carol Kregloh. 1989. "The Children's Department." In Claudia Brush Kidwell and Valerie Steele (eds.), *Men and Women: Dressing the Part*. Washington, DC: Smithsonian Institution Press.

Pascoe, C. J. 2007. *Dude, You're a Fag: Masculinity and Sexuality in High School*. Berkeley: University of California Press.

Patterson, Charlotte J. 1992. "Children of Lesbian and Gay Parents." *Child Development* 63: 1025–1042.

Paxton, Pamela, Sheri Kunovich, and Melanie M. Hughes. 2007. "Gender in Politics." *Annual Review of Sociology* 33:263–284.

Pollack, William. 1998. *Real Boys*. New York: Owl Books.

Pomerleau, Andre, Daniel Bolduc, Gerard Malcuit, and Louise Cossette. 1990. "Pink or Blue: Environmental Gender Stereotypes in the First Two Years of Life." *Sex Roles* 22: 359–368.

Pooler, W. 1991. "Sex of Child Preferences among College Students." *Sex Roles* 25: 569–576.

Preves, Sharon. 2003. *Intersex and Identity*. New Brunswick, NJ: Rutgers University Press.

Prokos, Anastasia, and Irene Padavic. 2002. "'There Oughta Be a Law against Bitches:' Masculinity Lessons in Police Academy Training." *Gender, Work and Organization* 9: 439–459.

Pugh, Allison J. 2009. *Longing and Belonging: Parents, Children, and Consumer Culture*. Berkeley: University of California Press.

Pyke, Karen D. 1996. "Class-Based Masculinities." *Gender & Society* 10: 527–549.

Raj, Rupert. 2008. "Transforming Couples and Families: A Trans-formative Therapeutic Model for Working with the Loved-Ones of Gender-Divergent Youth and Trans-Identified Adults." *Journal of GLBT Family Studies* 4: 133–163.

Raley, Sara, and Suzanne Bianchi. 2006. "Sons, Daughters, and Family Processes." *Annual Review of Sociology* 32: 401–421.

Reese, Elaine, Catherine Haden, and Robyn Fivush. 1996. "Gender Differences in Autobiographical Reminiscing." *Research on Language and Social Interaction* 29: 27–56.

Reskin, Barbara. 1988. "Bringing the Men Back In." *Gender & Society* 2: 58–81.

Rhode, Deborah L. 1999. *Speaking of Sex: The Denial of Gender Inequality*. Cambridge, MA: Harvard University Press.

Rich, Adrienne. 1980. "Compulsory Heterosexuality and Lesbian Existence." *Signs* 5: 631–660.

Riggs, Damien W. 2008. "All the Boys Are Straight: Heteronormativity in Contemporary Books on Fathering and Raising Sons." *Thymos: Journal of Boyhood Studies* 2: 186–202.

Risman, Barbara J. 1998. *Gender Vertigo*. New Haven, CT: Yale University Press.

———. 2004. "Gender as a Social Structure." *Gender & Society* 18: 429–450.

———. 2009. "From Doing to Undoing: Gender as We Know It." *Gender & Society* 23: 81–84.

Risman, Barbara J., and Kristen Myers. 1997. "As the Twig Is Bent: Children Reared in Feminist Households." *Qualitative Sociology* 20: 229–252.

Rollins, Judith. 1987. *Between Women: Domestics and Their Employers*. Philadelphia: Temple University Press.

Romero, Mary. 1992. *Maid in the USA*. New York: Routledge.

Rottnek, Matthew (ed.). 1999. *Sissies and Tomboys: Gender Nonconformity and Homosexual Childhood*. New York: New York University Press.

Rubin, Gayle. 1975. "The Traffic in Women: Notes on the Political Economy of Sex." In *Toward an Anthropology of Women*, edited by Rayna Reiter, 157–210. New York: Monthly Review Press.

———. 1993 [1984]. "Thinking Sex: Notes for a Radical Theory of the Politics of Sexuality." In *The Lesbian and Gay Studies Reader*, edited by Henry Abelove, Michele Aina Barale, and David M. Halperin, 3–44. New York: Routledge.

Rubin, Herb, and Irene Rubin. 2005. *Qualitative Interviewing: The Art of Hearing Data*. Thousand Oaks, CA: Sage.

Rubin, J. Z., F. J. Provenzano, and L. Zella. 1974. "The Eye of the Beholder: Parents' Views on Sex of Newborns." *American Journal of Orthopsychiatry* 44: 512–519.

Russell, Rachel, and Melissa Tyler. 2005. "Branding and Bricolage: Gender, Consumption, and Transition." *Childhood* 12: 221–237.

Rutter, Philip A. 2008. "Suicide Protective and Risk Factors for Sexual Minority Youth." *Journal of LGBT Issues in Counseling* 2: 81–92.

Ryan, Maura, and Dana Berkowitz. 2009. "Constructing Gay and Lesbian Parent Families 'Beyond the Closet.'" *Qualitative Sociology* 32: 153–172.

Sabo, Don. 2005. "The Study of Masculinity and Men's Health." In *Handbook of Studies on Men and Masculinities*, edited by Michael S. Kimmel, J. Hearn, and R. W. Connell, 326–352. Thousand Oaks, CA: Sage.

———. 2008. "Masculinities and Men's Health." In *Men's Lives* (8th ed.), edited by Michael S. Kimmel and Michael A. Messner, 243–260. Boston: Allyn & Bacon.

Sandnabba, N. Kenneth, and Christian Ahlberg. 1999. "Parents' Attitudes and Expectations about Children's Cross-Gender Behavior." *Sex Roles* 40: 249–263.

Schafer, Roy. 2001. "Gender Jokes/Sexual Politics." *Studies in Gender & Sexuality* 2: 277–295.

Schaffner Goldberg, Gertrude. 2009. *Poor Women in Rich Countries*. New York: Oxford University Press.

Schrock, Douglas P., and Irene Padavic. 2007. "Negotiating Hegemonic Masculinity in a Batterer Intervention Program." *Gender & Society* 21: 625–649.

Schrock, Douglas P., and Michael Schwalbe. 2009. "Men, Masculinity, and Manhood Acts." *Annual Review of Sociology* 35: 277–295.

Schwalbe, Michael, Sandra Godwin, Daphne Holden, Douglas Schrock, Shealy Thompson, and Michele Wolkomir. 2000. "Generic Processes in the Reproduction of Inequality." *Social Forces* 79: 419–452.

Scourfield, Jonathan, Katrina Roen, and Liz McDermott. 2008. "Lesbian, Gay, Bisexual and Transgender Young People's Experiences of Distress." *Health & Social Care in the Community* 16: 329–336.

Sengupta, Rhea. 2006. "Reading Representations of Black, East Asian, and White Women in Magazines for Adolescent Girls." *Sex Roles* 54: 799–808.

Sensibaugh, C. C., and P. E. Yarab. 1997. "Newlyweds' Family-Formation Preferences." *Journal of Psychology* 131: 530–540.

Sheldon, J. P. 2004. "Gender Stereotypes in Educational Software for Young Children." *Sex Roles* 51: 433–444.

Shows, Carla, and Naomi Gerstel. 2009. "Fathering, Class, and Gender." *Gender & Society* 23: 161–187.

Simien, Evelyn M., and Rosalee A. Clawson. 2004. "The Intersection of Race and Gender." *Social Science Quarterly* 85: 793–810.

Smith, Kara. 2005. "Prebirth Gender Talk: A Case Study in Prenatal Socialization." *Women & Language* 28: 49–53.

Smith, Ryan. 2002. "Race, Gender, and Authority in the Workplace." *Annual Review of Sociology* 28: 509–542.

Stacey, Judith, and Timothy J. Biblarz. 2001. "(How) Does the Sexual Orientation of Parents Matter?" *American Sociological Review* 66: 159–183.

Steinbacher, Roberta, and Faith Gilroy. 1990. "Sex Selection Technology." *Journal of Psychology* 124: 283–290.

Stone, Pamela. 2007. *Opting Out*. Berkeley: University of California Press.

Sullivan, Maureen. 2004. *The Family of Woman*. Berkeley: University of California Press.

Sullivan, Oriel. 2006. *Changing Gender Relations, Changing Families*. Lanham, MD: Rowman and Littlefield.

Sutfin, Erin, Megan Fulcher, Ryan Bowles, and Charlotte Patterson. 2008. "How Lesbian and Heterosexual Parents Convey Attitudes about Gender to Their Children." *Sex Roles* 58: 501–513.

Sweeney, J., and M. R. Bradbard. 1988. "Mothers' and Fathers' Changing Perceptions of Their Male and Female Infants over the Course of Pregnancy." *Journal of Genetic Psychology* 149: 393–404.

Thorne, Barrie. 1993. *Gender Play*. New Brunswick, NJ: Rutgers University Press.

Uggen, Christopher, and Amy Blackstone. 2004. "Sexual Harassment as a Gendered Expression of Power." *American Sociological Review* 69: 64–92.

Umberson, Debra, Kristin L. Anderson, Kristi Williams, and Meichu D. Chen. 2003. "Relationship Dynamics, Emotion State, and Domestic Violence." *Journal of Marriage & Family* 65: 233–247.

Van Balen, F., and M. C. Inhorn. 2003. "Son Preference, Sex Selection, and the 'New' New Reproductive Technologies." *International Journal of Health Services* 33: 235–252.

Varjas, Kris, Brian Dew, Megan Marshall, Emily Graybill, Anneliese Singh, Joel Meyers, and Lamar Birckbichler. 2008. "Bullying in Schools Towards Sexual Minority Youth." *Journal of School Violence* 7: 59–86.

Walls, N., Cathryn Potter, and James Leeuwen. 2009. "Where Risks and Protective Factors Operate Differently: Homeless Sexual Minority Youth and Suicide Attempts." *Child & Adolescent Social Work Journal* 26: 235–257.

Walzer, Susan. 1998. *Thinking about the Baby*. Philadelphia: Temple University Press.

Ward, Jane, and Beth Schneider. 2009. "The Reaches of Heteronormativity." *Gender & Society* 23: 433–439.

Warner, Rebecca L., and Brent S. Steel. 1999. "Childrearing as a Mechanism for Social Change." *Gender & Society* 13: 503–517.

West, Candace, and Don Zimmerman. 1987. "Doing Gender." *Gender & Society* 1: 124–151.

———. 2009. "Accounting for Doing Gender." *Gender & Society* 23: 112–122.

Williamson, Nancy. 1976. *Sons or Daughters*. Beverley Hills, CA: Sage.

Wohlwend, Karen E. 2009. "Damsels in Discourse: Girls Consuming and Producing Identity Texts through Disney Princess Play." *Reading Research Quarterly* 44: 57–83.

Wolf, Naomi. 1991. *The Beauty Myth*. New York: Morrow.

Wollstonecraft, Mary. 1989 [1792]. "A Vindication of the Rights of Woman." In *The Works of Mary Wollstonecraft* (vol. 5), edited by Janet Todd and Marilyn Butler, 2–87. New York: New York University Press.

Wood, Eileen, Serge Desmarais, and Sara Gugula. 2002. "The Impact of Parenting Experience on Gender Stereotyped Toy Play of Children." *Sex Roles* 47: 39–49.

Yoder, Janice, and Patricia Anaikudo. 1997. "Outsiders within the Firehouse: Subordination and Difference in the Social Interactions of African American Women Firefighters." *Gender & Society* 11: 324–341.

Zukin, Sharon. 2003. *Point of Purchase: How Shopping Changed American Culture.* New York: Routledge.

INDEX

271

Gendered expectations, 216; adolescence increase in, 205; for masculinity, 6, 86, 245n1; starting age in children, 219; for women, 78. *See also* Gendered anticipation

Gendered language, 76, 147, 163

Gendered power, 14–16; compulsory heterosexuality role in, 41; heteronormativity reinforcing, 46; ignoring gender as furthering, 122; Innovators' references to, 162–63, 165, 169; Naturalizers as not concerned with, 76–77, 162; Refiners' limited references to, 130, 131; Resisters' references to, 182–83, 190–91

Gendered slogans, 1

Gender identity, sexual orientation distinct from, 174

Gender inequality: compulsory heterosexuality reinforcing, 41; constraints imposed by, 5–6, 15–16; domestic, 5–6; emotional constraints on men, 15–16; intersectional, 46, 160–62, 169, 250n18; pack mentality in men, 162, 163; protection trait in context of, 86; public policy, 217; race and class intersectionality with, 169; race-specific, 160–61, 250n18; sons benefited and constrained by, 187–88; wage, 5; in workplace, 5, 139

Gendering actions. *See* Gender reproduction; Parenting practices, gender-crafting

Gender neutrality: failure of, 248n5; Innovator view of women's equality and, 147; MacKinnon on, 121–22; toys reflecting, 47

Gender recognition, infant clothing for, 39, 88, 241n17

Gender reproduction: clothing and, 179; direct, 55, 62, 71, 73, 77, 202, 229; indirect, 43–45, 55, 62, 201–2, 211, 229; as indirect for daughters, 201–2; Refiners', 130; resistance and, 47, 134–35; social class influencing men's, 250n23. *See also* Parenting practices, gender-crafting; Parenting practices, gender undoing

Gender segregation: historical site vignette, 191; lifetime earning penalties for women from, 139; occupational, 139, 204, 242n43

Gender stereotyping: Cultivator examples, 96, 102–10; Innovator concern about, 164; media images and, 1, 5, 107, 143–44, 176–77; pink and blue change in, 247n2; Resister concern over feminine beauty, 179; toys, 8, 20, 105, 164, 238n39

Gender trap: definition, 3; dismantling, 199–218; tensions facing parents, 11–12, 52, 111–12, 135, 201–3. *See also* Parenting practices, gender-crafting

Gender-typical toys, 8, 20, 164, 238n39; Cultivator encouragement of, 105; fast food vignette, 199

Gender undoing. *See* Degendering, Lorber's paradox of; Parenting practices, gender undoing

Gender Vertigo (Risman), 145, 153

Gifts, beauty messages through, 177

Hays, Sharon, intensive mothering concept, 156

Hegemonic masculinity, 42–43, 46;

Parenting practices, gender undoing,
47–51; Cultivator example of, 98;
direct and indirect, 48–49, 193;
implications of, 51–52; Innovators',
152, 155, 156; lesbian partnership
potential for, 196; race and class
influencing resources for, 156;
Refiner, 114, 121; Resisters' direct,
193; social class and, 168. *See
also* Case studies; Change, social;
Gender reproduction; Resistance
Peer culture and influence, 2,
55, 237n1, 240n15; daughters'
appearance and, 152; social
determinism role of, 240n15
Personal preference motivation, 44,
91–92, 120, 125, 213
Plaster turtle vignette, 152–53
Play styles, 239n41; comparison of
skills developed in, 105; expanded
range of, 168–69, 206
Power. *See* Gendered power
Power outage vignette, 143
Practices. *See* Parenting practices,
gender-crafting; Parenting
practices, gender undoing
Preferences, 148; children's
consumer desires, 237n1; color,
19; individual-level, 16–17, 188,
213; interactional, 188; movie,
62–63; personal, 44, 91–92, 120,
125, 213. *See also* Pre-parenthood
preferences
Pregnancy, parenting practices
during, 39
Prejudice, racial, 157–62
Pre-parenthood preferences, 27–31,
240n6; father preference for sons,
28, 82, 157, 239n1, 240n2; mother
preference for daughters, 29, 92,

148; mother preference for sons,
29, 180–81
Primary caregivers, fathers as, 144–
45, 153, 168
Princess imagery, 135, 138, 248n9
Privilege: class, 64, 155–56, 187–88,
191; male, 108, 187–88, 216
Public policy, 193, 217
Puddle of water vignette, 61–62
Pyke, Karen, 104, 108, 168;
compensatory masculinity, 136,
163; on women's limited job
involvement, 109

Qualitative interviews, 220; approach
limitations, 22–23; resources and
advice followed in, 226; saturation
concept, 219
Questions, in interviews, 109, 131,
222–26; questionnaire prior to
interview, 222–23; source of, 223

Race and class: domestic
responsibilities in light of, 80,
244n20; Hochschild's work on,
244n16; intersectionality of
gender with, 19–20, 80, 108, 157,
169, 246n14; of interviewees,
221; resources to undo gender
influenced by, 156. *See also* Social
class
Race intersectionality, 160–61,
250n18
Racial inequality: colorblind
ideologies unable to change,
121–22; gender inequality
intersectionality with, 160–61,
250n18; Hill Collins' standpoint
theory on women's, 250n19;
prejudice and, 157–62

Racial othering, beautiful daughters and, 251n2

Recruitment, of interviewees, 220

Refined femininity, 203–5

Refiners, 12, 24; accountability factor, 137; balancing act of, 111–12; beliefs overview for, 212; biological determinism belief in, 112, 113–14, 123, 127; change viewed by, 138, 140; classifying beliefs of, 231; combined approach of biology and sociology in, 112, 113–14, 124; gender blind approach of, 121–22; gender crossing allowed by, 115, 125–26; gendered expectations viewed by, 112; gendered power as limited reference for, 130, 131; gender undoing by, 114, 121; heteronormativity in, 125, 136; individualist sensibility in, 130, 132, 134; information chart on, 234; Innovators compared with, 141; middle road approach, 118, 120, 126; motivations of, 115–16, 120, 125; sixty/forty attitude on children's interests, 131–40; summary of characteristics, 202; work choice attitudes of, 29, 115

Refiners, case studies, 111–40; Belinda, 126–31; Brianna, 117–22, 208–9; Lisa, 112–17; William, 122–26

Religion, 72–73

Research: focus of typical parenting, 2–3; interview coding and analysis, 227–28; interviewee coding, 230–31; interviewee information, 220–22; interview process, 222–26; purpose of interviews as, 219;

reporting confidentiality and ethics, 231

Resistance: comparing patterns for sons and daughters, 202; Cultivators and, 90, 105; gendered power influenced by, 51; gender reproduction and, 47, 134–35; Naturalizers and, 56–57, 79, 243n2; social construction view allowing, 210–11; social costs of, 56, 99, 156, 195, 198; son-daughter variations in parents', 48–49, 202. *See also* Accountability; Case studies; Parenting practices, gender undoing

Resisters, 12, 24, 57; accountability factor, 175, 184, 188, 191–92, 195; beliefs overview for Innovators and, 212; biology fallback for gay and lesbian, 187, 252n9; change viewed by, 183–84, 193–95; classifying beliefs of Innovators and, 230–31; direct gender undoing actions of, 193; gay and lesbian predominance in, 196; gendered power referenced by, 182–83, 190–91; heteronormativity absence in, 181, 192; information chart on, 234; Innovators compared to, 193; motivations of, 178; sexual orientation of, 196, 197; summary of characteristics, 202; work choice approaches of, 186–87, 190

Resisters, case studies, 172–98; Adrienne, 185–88; Joanna, 188–93; Sena, 176–80; Stefan, 172–76; Tanya, 180–85, 194

Revolution, Hochschild's concept of stalled, 78, 182

ABOUT THE AUTHOR

Emily W. Kane is Professor of Sociology, and a member of the Program in Women and Gender Studies, at Bates College in Lewiston, Maine.